Collins

Cambridge IGCSE™

Physics

REVISION GUIDE

Carol Davenport, Mark Edwards,
Jeremy Pollard, Alom Shaha

About this Revision book

REVISE

These pages provide a recap of everything you need to know for each topic and include key points to focus on and **key terms** to be learned (full definitions are given in the Glossary). Supplementary content, for the Extended papers, is clearly marked with **S**.

You should read through all the information before taking the Quick Test at the end. This will test whether you can recall the key facts.

> **Quick Test**
>
> 1. A student pushes a box with a force of 15 N. They push it for 1.5 m. Calculate the work done moving the box.
> 2. An electric motor transfers 50 J of energy in 10 s. Calculate the power of the motor.
> **S** 3. A 0.2 kg ball is rolling down a slope with a speed of 2 m/s. Calculate the kinetic energy of the ball.
> **S** 4. A student lifts a 2 kg box from the ground and puts it on a 1.5 m high shelf. Calculate the gravitational potential energy transferred to the box.

PRACTISE

These topic-based exam-style questions appear at the end of a revision section and will test whether you have understood the topic. If you get any of the questions wrong, make sure you read the correct answer carefully.

For selected questions, Show Me features give you guidance on how to structure your answer.

> **Show me**
>
> Moment of a force = _____ + _____ from the pivot.
>
> moment = 120 Nx _____
>
> moment = _____ Nm

MIXED QUESTIONS

These pages feature a mix of exam-style questions for all the different topics, just like you would get in an exam. They will make sure you can recall the relevant information to answer a question without being told which topic it relates to.

PRACTICE PAPERS

These pages provide a full set of exam-style practice papers: Paper 1 Multiple Choice (Core)/Paper 2 Multiple Choice (Extended), Paper 3 Theory (Core)/Paper 4 Theory (Extended) and Paper 6 Alternative to Practical. Practise your exam technique in preparation for the Cambridge IGCSE™.

ebook

To access the ebook visit
collins.co.uk/ebooks
and follow the step-by-step instructions.

CONTENTS

Section 4: Electricity and magnetism

Section 5: Nuclear physics

Section 6: Space physics

Physical quantities and measurement techniques

Syllabus links:
1.1.1–1.1.3;
S 1.1.4–1.1.7

Learning aims:

- Describe how to measure length, volume and time.

- Use multiple measurements to determine very small distances or times.

- **S** Know that scalar quantities have magnitude only and that vector quantities have magnitude and direction.

- **S** Give examples of scalar and vector quantities.

- **S** Determine the resultant of two vectors at right angles.

Making measurements

Quantity measured	Instruments used
length	ruler; tape measure
volume	measuring cylinder
time	digital timer; stopwatch

> **Key Point**
>
> Human reaction time (about 0.2 s) means that digital timing methods should be used when measuring very short times.

> **Key Point**
>
> When measuring the length of small objects take several readings and calculate the average value.

> **Practical skills**
>
> To measure volume:
>
> - stand a measuring cylinder on a level surface
> - ensure your eye is at the same level as the liquid
> - read the level of the liquid at the bottom of the **meniscus**.

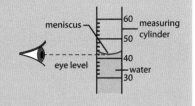

> **Key Point**
>
> Measuring cylinders often have millilitre (ml) scales. 1 ml is the same volume as 1 cm^3. 1000 ml (1 litre) is equal to 1000 cm^3.

S Scalar and vector quantities

Scalar quantities have magnitude (size) only and include: distance, speed, time, mass, energy and temperature.

Vector quantities have magnitude and direction and include: force, weight, velocity, acceleration, momentum, electric field strength and gravitational field strength.

A vector quantity can be represented by an arrow.

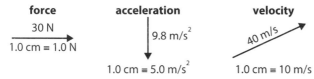

S Adding vector quantities

To add vector quantities, we calculate the **resultant** vector. When vectors such as **force** or **velocity** are in the same or opposite directions (a straight line) we can add their magnitudes.

To add vector quantities where the vectors are at an angle to each other, we use a graphical method to calculate the resultant vector.

For example, if two forces are acting at right angles to each other on an object, we can draw a scale diagram to determine the resultant force, F, acting on the object.

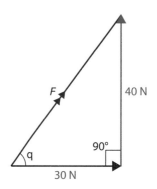

Motion and speed–time graphs

Syllabus links:
1.2.1–1.2.7

Learning aims:

- Define speed as distance travelled per unit time and calculate speed and average speed.

- Define velocity as speed in a given direction.

- Sketch, plot and interpret distance–time and speed–time graphs.

- Determine, using data or a graph, the motion of an object.

Speed

The **speed** (v) of an object is the distance (s) travelled per unit time (t). Constant speed can be calculated using the equation:

$$\text{speed } (v) = \frac{\text{distance } (s)}{\text{time } (t)}$$

When an object's speed is changing, we calculate the **average speed** using the equation:

$$\text{average speed} = \frac{\text{total distance}}{\text{total time taken}}$$

Distance–time graphs

A distance–time graph shows the distance travelled by an object plotted against time of motion. The **gradient** of the graph gives the speed of the object. Here is a distance–time graph for a bicycle journey.

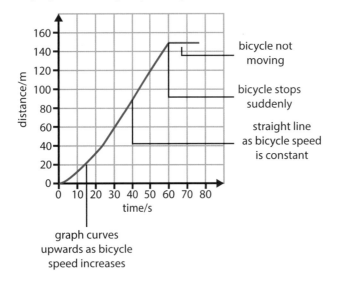

graph curves upwards as bicycle speed increases

bicycle not moving

bicycle stops suddenly

straight line as bicycle speed is constant

> **Key Point**
>
> Sometimes we need to know the direction an object is travelling in, as well as how fast it is moving. In these cases, we need to know velocity. Velocity is speed in a particular direction. Speed is always positive, but velocity can be negative.

> **Key Point**
>
> A curved line on a distance–time graph shows that the object is changing speed. If it curves upwards (increasing gradient), the object is speeding up. If it curves downwards (decreasing gradient), the object is slowing down.

Speed–time graphs

A speed–time graph shows how fast an object is moving over time. This graph shows the speed of a student running during the first 10 seconds of their run. The straight line between 0 s and 2 s shows that the student's speed is increasing. The horizontal line between 2 s and 10 s shows that the student is running with a constant speed.

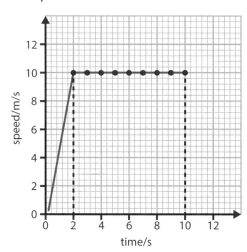

The area under the graph is the distance travelled by the student.

The table summarises the motion of an object depending on the shape of the distance–time or a speed–time graph.

Shape of graph	State of motion of object	
	Distance–time graph	Speed–time graph
horizontal straight line on *x*-axis	at rest	at rest
horizontal straight line	at rest	constant speed
curved line	changing speed	changing acceleration
straight line with positive gradient	constant speed	constant acceleration
straight line with negative gradient	constant speed	constant deceleration

Quick Test

1. A bus is driven at a constant speed along a road for 150 m. It takes 15 s to travel this distance. What is the speed of the bus?
2. A bus travels between two stops. The total distance the bus travels between the two stops is 900 m. The journey takes 180 s. Calculate the average speed of the bus.
3. On the speed–time graph above, how fast is the student running between 2 s and 10 s?
4. How far does the student run in the first 2 s of the race?

Acceleration and free fall

Syllabus links:
1.2.8; S 1.2.9–1.2.12

Learning aims:

- S Define acceleration and use the equation $a = \frac{\Delta v}{\Delta t}$.
- S Use speed–time graphs to describe the motion of an object including deceleration.
- State that the acceleration of free fall g for an object near the surface of the Earth is approximately 9.8 m/s^2.
- S Describe the motion of falling objects in a uniform gravitational field.

S Acceleration

Acceleration, a, is the change in velocity, v, over time, t. The units of acceleration are m/s^2.

$$a = \frac{\Delta v}{\Delta t}$$

Acceleration is a vector quantity and may be positive or negative. Negative acceleration, when an object's velocity is decreasing over time, is called **deceleration**.

> **Key Point**
>
> The symbol Δ means 'change in'. The change in velocity between time 1 and time 2 is (velocity at time 2 – velocity at time 1).

The graph shows the motion of a toy ship. We calculate the acceleration of the toy ship by calculating the gradient of the speed–time graph.

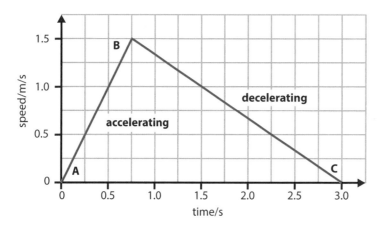

> **Key Point**
>
> The acceleration from B to C is $a = \dfrac{0 \text{ m/s} - 1.5 \text{ m/s}}{3 \text{ s} - 0.75 \text{ s}} = -0.67 \text{ m/s}^2$. The negative sign indicates that the toy ship is slowing down. It is decelerating.

Free fall motion

When an object is dropped and falls towards the ground due to the force of gravity, it will accelerate at 9.8 m/s^2. This is called the **acceleration of free fall**. When there are no frictional forces, all falling objects near the surface of the Earth will have this acceleration.

S Terminal velocity

Objects falling in a vacuum near the surface of the Earth will always have an acceleration of 9.8 m/s². Objects falling through air or liquids have lower acceleration due to frictional forces.

(1)

The diagram shows the forces acting on a skydiver when they first jump out of a plane (1) and when they are moving at **terminal velocity** (2).

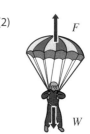
(2)

- At (1) there is only a force due to gravity, W.
- As their speed increases frictional forces, F, act in the opposite direction.
- When they open their parachute, frictional forces are very large.
- At terminal velocity (2), frictional forces are equal and opposite to weight.

> ## Practical skills

Steel ball falling through a liquid

Terminal velocity can be measured using a steel ball, which is dropped into a tube of wallpaper paste as shown.

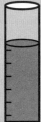

- Drop the steel ball into the tube.
- At the same time, start the stopwatch.
- Measure the time the ball passes each 10 cm mark on the tube.
- Calculate speed using 10 cm/time.
- Terminal velocity is when the speed no longer increases between marks.

> ## Quick Test

1. What is the value of acceleration of free fall when there are no frictional forces acting on an object?

S 2. Calculate the acceleration of the toy ship whose motion is shown by the graph on page 10 between points A and B.

S 3. State the value of acceleration when an object is falling at its terminal velocity.

Mass, weight and density

Learning aims:

- Explain the difference between mass and weight.
- Define and calculate gravitational field strength.
- **S** Define weight as the effect of a gravitational field on a mass.
- Define density of an object and describe how to determine density.
- Determine whether objects will float or sink, using density data.
- **S** Determine whether one liquid will float on another using density data.

Syllabus links:

1.3.1–1.3.4; **S** 1.3.5 ;
1.4.1–1.4.3;

S 1.4.4

Mass and weight

Mass (m) is the amount of matter in an object. We measure the mass of an object using a balance.

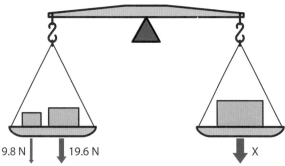

9.8 N   19.6 N   X

> **Key Point**
>
> Mass is measured in kilograms (kg), weight is a force and is measured in newtons (N).

Weight (W) is the force due to gravity acting on an object that has mass. Weight depends on the mass (m) of an object and **gravitational field strength** (g). Near the surface of the Earth g is 9.8 N/kg

S In a **gravitational field**, objects will experience a force of attraction to one another. As you get further from an object, the force of attraction reduces. An astronaut on the Moon would have the same mass as on Earth, but their weight would be less. The gravitational field strength on the Moon is lower than on Earth.

Earth

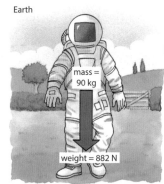

mass = 90 kg

weight = 882 N

Moon

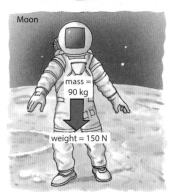

mass = 90 kg

weight = 150 N

Gravitational field strength is equivalent to acceleration of free fall.

Gravitational field strength

$$g = \frac{\text{weight } (W)}{\text{mass } (m)}$$

Weighing objects

A spring balance is used to weigh things. The gravitational force of the object causes the spring to extend.

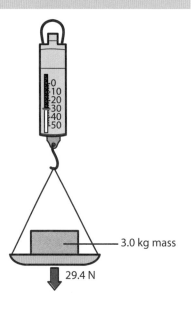

3.0 kg mass

29.4 N

Density

Density is a measure of how closely packed particles are in solids, liquids and gases.

The density (ρ) of an object depends on the mass (*m*) and the volume (*V*) of the object.

$$\text{Density } \rho = \frac{\text{mass } (m)}{\text{volume } (V)}$$

The density of a regular solid can be determined using the mass and volume of the solid.

The density of a liquid can be determined using a measuring cylinder to measure its volume and a top-pan balance to find its mass.

The density of an irregular solid can be determined using the 'displacement method' by using a top-pan balance to find the mass and a measuring cylinder with a known volume of liquid in it.

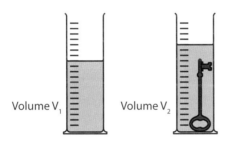

Volume V_1 Volume V_2

Floating and sinking

An object with a lower density than water will float when placed in water. An object with higher density than water will sink.

S Low density liquids will float on top of higher density liquids. This can be used to make layered drinks.

> **Quick Test**

1. Calculate the weight of an object on Earth that has a mass of 21 kg.
2. A cube-shaped block of copper has a mass of 71 g and sides of 2 cm. Calculate the density of copper.
3. A toy ball has a density of 960 kg/m^3. The ball is dropped into water with a density of 1000 kg/m^3. Explain whether the ball will float or sink in the water.

Effects of forces

Learning aims:

Syllabus links:
1.5.1.1–1.5.1.8;
S **1.5.1.11**

- Know that forces can change the size, shape or motion of an object.
- Determine the resultant of two or more forces and describe the change in velocity of an object.
- Describe different ways friction can act on an object.
- **S** Recall and use the equation $F = ma$.

Forces

Forces can change the shape, size or motion of an object.

There is often more than one force acting on an object. To know how the motion will change we need to determine the **resultant force**.

When forces are balanced there is no resultant force. The motion of the object will not change. Stationary objects stay at rest; moving objects keep moving at the same velocity.

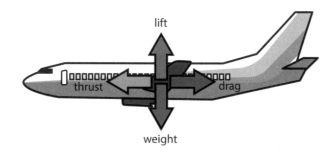

There will be a resultant force if the forces acting on an object are unbalanced. The motion of the object will change.

A resultant force can change the velocity of an object by changing its direction or by changing its speed.

Velocity is a **vector** quantity so changing either the magnitude or the direction an object is moving in will change the velocity. A ball rolling towards a wall and bouncing back in the opposite direction at the same speed will have a changed velocity because its motion has changed direction.

> **Key Point**
>
> The resultant force is the total of all the forces acting on the object. The direction the forces are acting in is important. We have to take into account the direction and the magnitude of the forces.

Friction

Friction is a force that always acts in the opposite direction to the motion of an object. Friction opposes motion and may stop things moving at all.

- Solid friction: force between two surfaces that are sliding across each other.
- Friction (drag): force acting on an object moving through a fluid (liquid or gas).

Friction forces cause heating of the surfaces, both object and fluid.

s Force and acceleration

A resultant force acting on an object will change its motion – it will accelerate. The size of the acceleration, a, depends on the mass of the object, m, and the resultant force, F, acting on it.

force = mass × acceleration

$$F = ma$$

F is force in newtons (N); m is mass in kg; a is acceleration in m/s^2.

> **Quick Test**
>
> 1. What three changes can forces make to an object?
> 2. The lift force acting on a flying jet aircraft is 810 000 N. The weight of the plane is 810 000 N. Describe what will happen to the motion of the plane.
> 3. Name the type of friction acting on a swimmer.
> 4. s A bike and rider have a combined mass of 70 kg. What force must the rider apply to make the bike accelerate at 2 m/s^2?

Turning effect of forces, centre of gravity and circular motion

Syllabus links:
1.5.2.1–1.5.2.4;
S 1.5.2.5–1.5.2.6;
1.5.3.1–1.5.3.3;
S 1.5.1.12

Learning aims:

- Determine the moment of a force and apply the principle of moments.
- Know the conditions for equilibrium.
- **S** Describe an experiment to demonstrate equilibrium.
- State what is meant by centre of gravity and describe how this affects stability.
- Describe an experiment to determine the centre of gravity of a flat shape.
- Describe factors affecting the motion of an object moving in a circle.

Turning effect of forces

The turning effect of a force is called its **moment**.

$$\text{moment} = F \times d$$

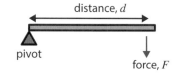

The **principle of moments**: when a system of forces is not turning the sum of the clockwise moments is equal to the sum of the anticlockwise moments.

A system is in **equilibrium** when it is not moving or rotating. In equilibrium there are no resultant forces and no resultant moment.

> **Key Point**
>
> Moment has units of newton metres (Nm) or newton centimetres (Ncm).

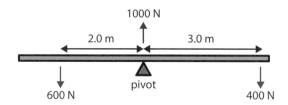

The principle of moments also applies when there is more than one force on either side of the pivot.

> **S Practical skills**

Demonstrating equilibrium

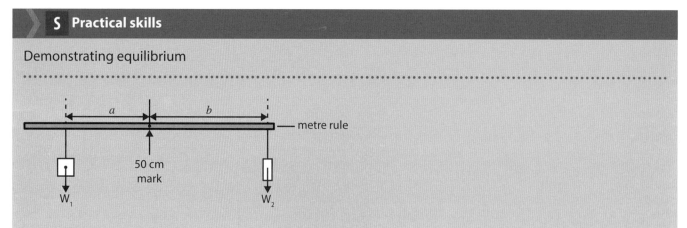

- Attach the ruler to a pivot through a hole at its 50 cm point.
- Hang a mass on one side of the ruler.
- Hang a second mass on the other side of the ruler and move it until the ruler is balanced horizontally.
- Note values for the weight of the masses, W_1 and W_2, along with the distances, a and b, of the masses from the pivot.
- Calculate $(W_1 \times a)$ and $(W_2 \times b)$ for each pair of values to verify the principle of moments.

Centre of gravity

We assume that all the weight of an object acts at one point called the **centre of gravity**. This simplifies drawing force diagrams and calculations. For regular shapes and objects the centre of gravity is at the centre of the object.

The position of the centre of gravity of an object will determine how stable the object is.

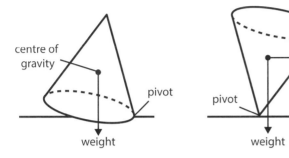

> ### Practical skills

To determine the position of the centre of gravity:

* hang the laminar object by a point close to its edge
* suspend the plumb-line from the same point and mark its position
* turn the object and repeat
* the centre of gravity is at the point where the two lines cross.

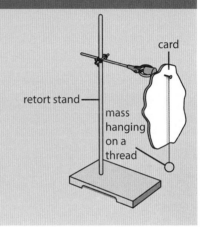

S Circular motion

A force that is perpendicular to the direction of motion of an object will cause circular motion. The **centripetal force** will act towards the centre of the circle as shown in Figure 6.1.

The centripetal force is not a new force, but describes the direction of a force already acting on the object.

The magnitude of the centripetal force on an object will increase when:

* the speed increases (for a given mass and radius)
* the radius of the circular motion decreases (for a given mass and speed)
* the mass of the object increases (for a given radius and speed).

> ### Quick Test

1. What does the moment of a force depend on?
2. Calculate the moment of a force of 10 N, which acts 0.4 m from a pivot?
3. Two children are sitting on a see-saw. The see-saw is in equilibrium. Explain what this tells you about the moment from each child.
 S 4. What happens to the centripetal force on an object undergoing circular motion if the radius of the circular motion increases?

Springs and momentum

Syllabus links:

1.5.1.6; **S** 1.5.1.9–1.5.1.10; 1.6.1–1.6.4

Learning aims:

- Sketch, plot and interpret load–extension graphs for an elastic solid.
- **S** Recall and use the equation for spring constant.
- **S** Define and identify the 'limit of proportionality' on a load–extension graph.
- **S** Define momentum and impulse, and use equations to calculate each quantity.
- **S** Apply the principle of conservation of momentum to solve simple problems.

Stretching an elastic solid

For an elastic solid, such as a wire or spring, applying a force (load) will cause the solid to extend.

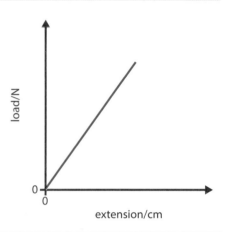

Practical skills

Observing the linear behaviour of a spring

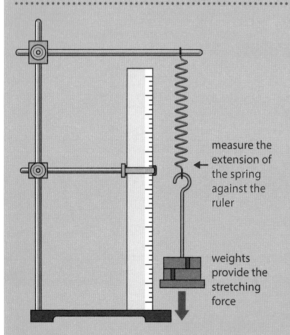

measure the extension of the spring against the ruler

weights provide the stretching force

- Hang a spring vertically and clamp a ruler parallel to it.
- Note the position of the bottom of the spring on the ruler.
- Add a mass and note the new position of the bottom of the spring. Repeat.
- Calculate the extension of the spring using (new length – unstretched length).
- Calculate the load using load = $m \times g$.
- Plot a graph of load against extension.

S For an elastic solid the spring constant is the force per unit extension.

$$k = \frac{F}{x}$$

where k is the spring constant in N/m or N/cm; F is force in N; and x is extension in m or cm.

If the load applied is too great, the extension will no longer be proportional to the load. The point at which this happens is called the **limit of proportionality**. The graph will no longer be linear.

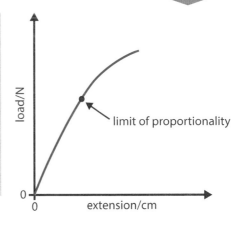

S Momentum

The **momentum** of an object depends on its mass and velocity.

$$p = m \times v$$

where p is momentum in kg m/s; m is mass in kg; and v is velocity in m/s.

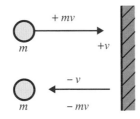

> **Key Point**
>
> Momentum is a vector quantity. When an object changes direction its momentum changes even if the velocity and mass don't change.

The resultant force, F, on an object is defined as the rate of change of momentum.

$$F = \frac{\Delta p}{\Delta t} \text{ or } \frac{\Delta(mv)}{\Delta t}$$

The **impulse** of a force is the product of the force and the change in time, Δt, and has units N s.

$$\text{impulse} = F\Delta t$$

> **Key Point**
>
> When using the principle of conservation of momentum, one direction is chosen as positive so that changes of direction of the objects can be taken into account.

The **principle of conservation of momentum**: the total momentum before a collision is the same as the total momentum after a collision.

> **Quick Test**
>
> 1. A student adds a load to a spring that is 4 cm long. They measure the new length of the spring to be 9 cm. What is the extension of the spring?
>
> **S** 2. When a 10 N load is added to a spring the extension is 0.05 m. What is the spring constant of this spring?
>
> **S** 3. A bowling ball has a mass of 6 kg. It is rolled with a velocity of 8 m/s. Calculate the momentum of the ball.

Energy

Learning aims:

- Name different stores of energy.
- Describe how energy is transferred between stores.
- Apply the principle of conservation of energy.
- **S** Interpret Sankey diagrams.

Syllabus links:
1.7.1.1–1.7.1.3;
S **1.7.1.6**

Energy stores

Energy is measured in Joules. We can describe different **energy stores**.

	Energy stored ...
kinetic	... by a moving object
gravitational potential	... due to an object's position in a gravitational field
chemical	by chemical bonds
elastic (strain)	when an object is stretched or squashed
nuclear	in the nucleus of an atom
electrostatic	by charges moving closer and further away from each other
internal (thermal)	by the total kinetic and potential energies of the particles of an object

> **Key Point**
>
> Energy stores and calculations allow us to determine whether something is possible. Physical processes, such as applying forces, make things happen.

Energy can be transferred between stores.

Energy transfer mechanism	caused ...
mechanical work done	when a force moves an object
electrical work done	when charges move due to potential difference
heating	due to a temperature difference and movement of particles
waves electromagnetic	when electromagnetic wave is emitted or absorbed
sound/water/earthquake waves etc.	due to movement of particles and matter

> **Key Point**
>
> Sometimes people talk about energy being 'wasted'. This often means that energy has transferred to a thermal store where it is less useful.

The **principle of conservation of energy** states that energy cannot be created or destroyed. However, it can be transferred and stored in different ways.

For the pendulum, energy is transferred from a gravitational potential store (at A) to a kinetic store (at B) and back to a gravitational potential store (at C). Some energy is transferred to the surroundings by mechanical work done (against air resistance) and by heating (friction at the pivot).

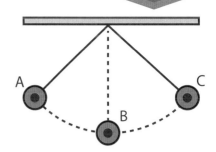

We can represent energy transfers with an **energy flow diagram**.

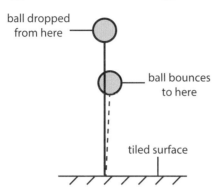

A simple flow diagram to represent the ball dropped onto a tiled floor bounces between point A and point B.

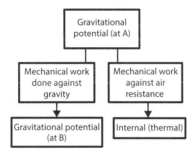

S Sankey diagrams

Sankey diagrams show the transfer of energy between stores. The width of each arrow is drawn to scale.

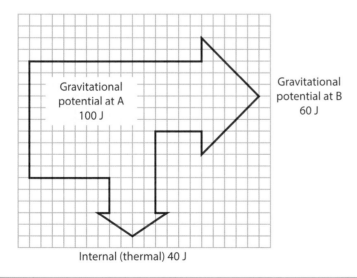

> **Quick Test**

1. Name three energy stores.
2. State the principle of conservation of energy.
3. Draw an energy flow diagram for a parachutist starting when they jump out of the plane and ending when they are falling at a constant speed.

Energy resources

Syllabus links:
1.7.3.1–1.7.3.3;
S **1.7.3.4–1.7.3.6**

Learning aims:

- Describe how useful energy may be obtained, or electrical power generated from different energy resources.

- Understand the concept of efficiency.

- **S** Know that the Sun is the main source of energy for many energy resources.

- **S** Know that energy is released by nuclear fusion in the Sun, and describe fusion research.

Energy resources

Energy resources provide useful energy or generate electrical power. **Fossil fuels** and nuclear fuel are **non-renewable**; all other energy resources are **renewable**.

In a power station:

- fossil fuels, **biofuels** and **nuclear fuel** are used to heat water in a **boiler**
- steam turns a **turbine**
- the turbine rotates a **generator**, which produces an electric current.

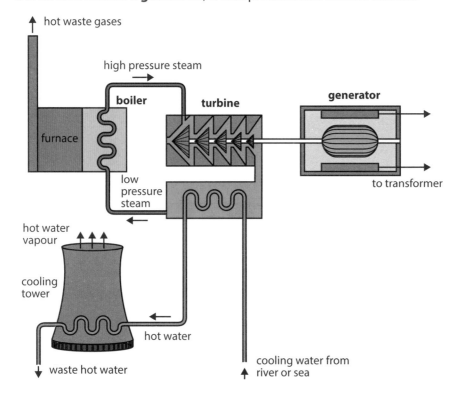

Wind and water in **hydroelectric** dams, **tidal** estuaries and **waves** also cause rotation of a turbine and generator to produce electricity.

Solar cells (photovoltaic panels) use radiation from the Sun to directly generate electric currents.

Solar panels use infrared radiation to heat water for household use.

S Energy is released by **nuclear fusion** in the Sun. The Sun is responsible for all our energy resources, except geothermal, nuclear and tidal.

S Researchers are trying to use nuclear fusion on Earth as another energy resource.

Advantages and disadvantages of energy resources

Energy resource		Availability	Scale	Environmental impact
fossil fuels		large stores	large	Releases carbon dioxide and causes air pollution. Mining is dangerous and polluting.
biofuels		can easily be grown/made	medium	Requires a lot of land.
wind		requires windy areas	small/ medium	Onshore: noise and visual pollution, impact wildlife. Offshore: less impact.
water	waves	limited to coastal areas	small	May impact wildlife.
	tides	limited to coastal areas	small	May impact wildlife.
	hydroelectric		small	Ecosystem loss or damage. Impact on water flow downstream of the dam.
nuclear		large stores	large	Mining is dangerous and polluting. Small amount of highly radioactive waste.
electromagnetic radiation from the Sun	solar (PV) cells	widely available needs suitable positioning	small	Limited
	solar panels	widely available needs suitable positioning	small	Limited
geothermal		limited areas with suitable geology	small	Limited

Efficiency of energy transfers

In most energy transfers some energy will be transferred to internal (thermal) energy stores of objects or their surroundings. The more efficient the energy transfer, the more energy is available for useful purposes.

> **Quick Test**

1. Name three renewable energy resources.
2. Name one energy resource that uses radiation directly from the Sun.
3. Give two disadvantages of fossil fuels.
   S 4. Name the process that releases energy in the Sun.

Calculating energy, work and power

Syllabus links:

S 1.7.3.7; 1.7.1.4–1.7.1.5; 1.7.2.1–1.7.2.2; 1.7.4.1

Learning aims:

- **S** Define and calculate efficiency of energy transfers.
- **S** Calculate kinetic energy and gravitational potential energy.
- Understand that mechanical or electrical working is equal to the energy transferred.
- Calculate mechanical work done.
- Calculate power.

S **Efficiency** of energy transfers can be calculated using these equations:

$$\text{efficiency} = \frac{\text{useful energy output}}{\text{total energy input}} \times 100$$

$$\text{efficiency} = \frac{\text{useful power output}}{\text{total power input}} \times 100$$

> **Key Point**
>
> Efficiency is sometimes written as a ratio rather than a percentage, for example 0.95 instead of 95%.

S Kinetic and gravitational potential energy

All moving objects have energy stored as **kinetic energy**, E_k, given by:

$$E_k = \frac{1}{2}mv^2$$

where E_k is measured in J, m is the mass of the object in kg, and v is the speed of the object in m/s.

Any object above the surface of the Earth has energy stored as **gravitational potential energy**, E_p given by:

$$E_p = mg\Delta h$$

where E_p is measured in J, m is the mass of the object in kg, g is the acceleration of free fall, 9.8 m/s^2, and Δh is the change in height of the object.

> **Key Point**
>
> Remember that Δ means 'change in …'. In some questions, we might not know the change in height so we can use height above the ground instead.

Work

Mechanical working and electrical working both transfer energy between stores.

The energy transferred is equal to the **work done** in each case.

For mechanical working the work done, W, depends on the force applied, F, and the distance moved in the direction of the force, d.

$$W = F \times d$$

> **Key Point**
>
> 1 joule is the energy transferred when a force of 1 newton moves an object a distance of 1 m in the direction of the force.

Power

Power, P, is the work done per unit time. Work done is equivalent to energy transferred so we can also say that power is the energy transferred per unit time. Power is measured in J/s or watts.

$$\text{power} = \frac{W}{t} = \frac{\Delta E}{t}$$

> **Key Point**
>
> Friction forces oppose motion. Energy is transferred from kinetic stores to internal (thermal) stores. Work is done by the frictional forces.

Quick Test

1. A student pushes a box with a force of 15 N. They push it for 1.5 m. Calculate the work done moving the box.
2. An electric motor transfers 50 J of energy in 10 s. Calculate the power of the motor.
S 3. A 0.2 kg ball is rolling down a slope with a speed of 2 m/s. Calculate the kinetic energy of the ball.
S 4. A student lifts a 2 kg box from the ground and puts it on a 1.5 m high shelf. Calculate the gravitational potential energy transferred to the box.

Key Point

1 watt of power is 1 joule of work being done per second, or 1 joule of energy transferred per second.

Pressure

Learning aims:

- Calculate pressure.
- Describe how pressure varies with force and area.
- Describe how pressure varies underneath the surface of a liquid.
- **S** Calculate pressure changes beneath the surface of a liquid.

Syllabus links:
1.8.1–1.8.3;
S 1.8.4

Pressure

Pressure, p, is defined as force, F, per unit area, A.

$$p = \frac{F}{A}$$

> **Key Point**
>
> Pressure is measured in **pascals** (Pa).
> 1 Pa = 1 N/m^2.

Pressure in a fluid

Pressure in a **fluid** (liquid or gas) is caused by the constant motion of the particles. The particles collide with the walls of a container and each other. The force of the many collisions over an area causes pressure.

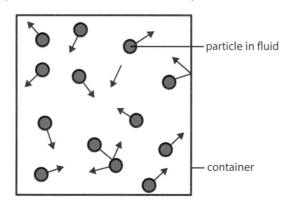

particle in fluid

container

> **S Key Point**
>
> The force due to the particles occurs because there is a change in momentum of the particles as they bounce off the walls of the container.

If a liquid or gas is at rest, the pressure acts equally in all directions.

Pressure difference, height and density

There is an increase in pressure as you go below the surface of a liquid. The pressure depends on:

- depth below the surface
- density of the liquid.

> **Key Point**
>
> A change in depth of 10 m of water will increase pressure by 100 kPa.

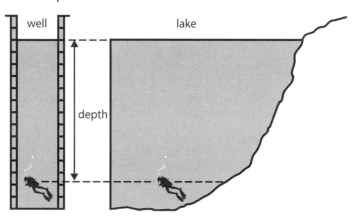

well   lake

depth

The denser a liquid, the greater the increase in pressure below the surface.

S The change in pressure, Δp, between two points in a fluid can be calculated using:

$$\Delta p = \rho g \Delta h$$

where Δp is measured in Pa, ρ is the density of the fluid in kg/m^3, g is the gravitational field strength in N/kg, and Δh is the height difference in m.

Key Point

Density must be given in kg/m^3. If density is in g/m^3, you will need to convert it using $1 \text{ g/cm}^3 = 1000 \text{ kg/m}^3$.

depth/m   pressure/10⁵ Pa

scuba diver

Quick Test

1. Calculate the pressure exerted by a force of 500 N acting on an area of 0.01 m^2.
2. A box is placed on a table. The weight of the box is 10 N. It exerts a pressure of 250 Pa. Calculate the area of the box.
3. What does the pressure in a liquid depend on?
4. S A diver goes underwater to see a coral reef. The density of the water is 1000 kg/m^3. The reef is 6 m below the surface of the water. What is the change in pressure on the diver at this depth?

Physical quantities and measurement techniques

1 A student uses a measuring cylinder to measure the volume of some oil. The diagram shows part of the measuring cylinder.

What is the volume of the oil?

A. 30.4 cm^3 **B.** 32.0 cm^3 **C.** 32.5 cm^3 **D.** 34.0 cm^3 [1]

2 Two students measure the period of a pendulum using a stopwatch.

a The first student times a single oscillation of the pendulum ten times. The readings from the stopwatch were:

2.4 s, 2.3 s, 2.3 s, 2.2 s, 2.2 s, 2.2 s, 2.4 s, 2.2 s, 2.3 s, 2.4 s

What is the average value for the period of the pendulum measured by this student?   [1]

b The second student times ten oscillations once. The reading from the stopwatch was 25.1 s.

Calculate the period of the pendulum measured by this student.   [1]

c Explain why the second student has obtained the more accurate value for the period of the pendulum.   [2]

'Explain' means that you need to support your answer with relevant evidence for full marks.

[Total marks 4]

3 The diagram shows a measuring cylinder used to measure the volume of a small necklace.

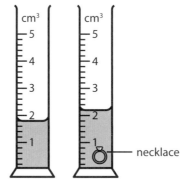

necklace

What is the volume of the necklace?   [2]

> **Show me**

The volume of the water in the measuring cylinder without the necklace is .... cm^3

The volume of the water in the measuring cylinder with the necklace is .... cm^3

The volume of the necklace is .... cm^3 – .... cm^3

Volume = ... cm^3

4 A student is writing lists of vector quantities.

Which list includes only vector quantities?

A. velocity, speed, time

B. velocity, time, acceleration

C. velocity, weight, force

D. weight, mass, force [1]

Motion and speed–time graphs

1 The diagram shows a distance–time graph for an object.

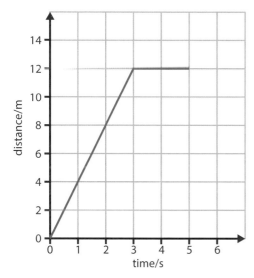

Which row describes the speed of the object during its motion? [1]

	between X and Y	between Y and Z
A.	3 m/s	0 m/s
B.	3 m/s	12 m/s
C.	4 m/s	0 m/s
D.	4 m/s	12 m/s

2 The graph shows the distance–time graphs for three children, A, B, and C, who are playing.

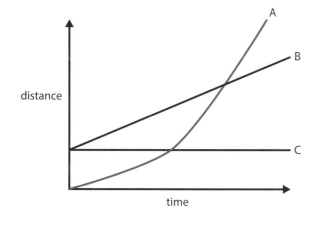

Describe the motion of each child by selecting the correct description from the list below.

constant speed   decreasing speed

increasing speed   stationary

Child A: ....

Child B: ....

Child C: .... [3]

3 ▶ A student has an electric scooter. The diagram shows the speed–time graph of the student on the scooter as they ride along a straight length of road.

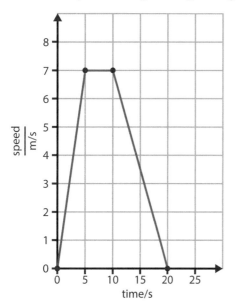

a Calculate the distance that the student has travelled in the 20 s ride. [4]

b Describe the motion of the student between 10 and 20 s. Explain your answer. [2]

> **Show me**
>
> At 10s the student is travelling at .... m/s but at 20 s the student is travelling at
> .... m/s.
>
> Therefore the student is ....

The number of marks for a question indicates the type of answer the examiner is expecting to see.

[**Total marks 6**]

Acceleration and free fall

1 ▶ A cup falls from a table and hits the ground. What is its acceleration as it falls? [1]

S 2 ▶ Two large seeds fall from a tree branch at the same time. The graph shows the speed of each seed as it falls.

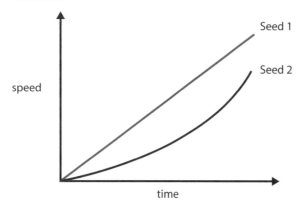

Which row describes the motion of Seed 1 and Seed 2 as they fall?

	Seed 1	Seed 2
A.	constant speed	changing speed
B.	constant acceleration	changing acceleration
C.	changing speed	constant speed
D.	changing acceleration	constant acceleration

3 An aeroplane is moving at 10 m/s on a runway. The plane accelerates until it reaches 70 m/s when it takes off. It takes 30 s to reach this speed.

Calculate the acceleration of the aeroplane. [1]

4 A skydiver jumps out of a plane. Their motion is shown on the speed–time graph.

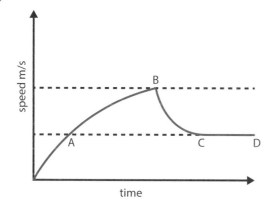

a At the start of the jump (0), the skydiver is at rest. It takes 5 seconds for them to reach a speed of 50 m/s. Calculate their average speed during the first part of the dive. [1]

b At point B the skydiver opens their parachute. Describe their acceleration between:

   i B and C   **ii** C and D. [2]

[Total marks 3]

Mass, weight and density

1 What is the weight of an object?

   A. the amount of matter in an object

   B. the energy needed to lift an object

   C. the force of gravity on the object

   D. the mass of the object [1]

2 A space lander has a mass of 21 kg. It lands on the surface of a comet.

The gravitational field strength on Earth is 9.8 N/kg

The gravitational field strength on the comet is 0.001 N/kg

What is the weight of the space lander on Earth, and what is its weight on the comet?

	On Earth	On the comet
A.	2.1 kg	5000 kg
B.	2.1 N	5000 N
C.	210 kg	0.021 kg
D.	210 N	0.021 N

[1]

3 A Mars rover has a mass of 900 kg on Earth. Earth's gravitational field strength is 10 N/kg.

a Calculate the rover's weight on Earth. [1]

b The rover lands on Mars. On Mars the gravitational field strength is 3.7 N/kg.

    i Copy and complete the following sentence.

        The rover's mass on Mars is .... as the rover's mass on Earth. [1]

    ii Calculate the weight of the rover on Mars [2]

> **Show me**
>
> Use the equation $g = \dfrac{weight\ (W)}{mass\ (m)}$
>
> Rearrange to make W the subject of the equation
>
> weight = gravitational field strength × mass
>
> weight = ... N/kg × .... kg
>
> weight = ... N

[Total marks 4]

S **4** A student wants to make a density column. She has the following liquids.

Liquid	Density
liquid soap	1.1 g/cm^3
vegetable oil	0.9 g/cm^3
water	1 g/cm^3

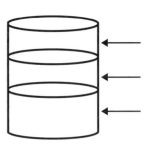

She carefully pours the liquids into a glass.

    i Copy and complete the diagram showing the order of the liquids. [2]

    ii Explain why you have put the liquids in the order you have shown. [2]

[Total marks 4]

Effects of forces

1 A cook is pushing a trolley. He applies a force of 140 N as shown in the diagram on page 33. There is a force of 10 N due to friction in the opposite direction.

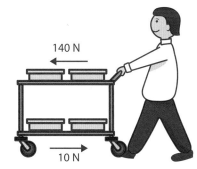

What is the resultant force on the trolley?

A.   14 N

B.   130 N

C.   140 N

D.   1400 N

[1]

> When forces are acting in opposite directions, one of them will have a negative sign. To find the resultant force we add the two forces together.

2 A toy has a rubber ball at the centre and a rope on either side. Two children are pulling on the toy, one holding each rope horizontally at point A and point B as shown. Child A pulls with a force of 5 N.

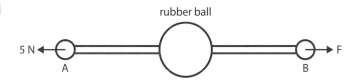

a The ball at the centre of the toy does not move.

  i What is the value of the force that Child B is pulling with? [1]

  ii Suggest what change to the ball the forces cause. [1]

b Child A now pulls with a force of 3 N in the direction shown by the arrow.

  i If Child B is still pulling with the same force as in **(a) (i)**, state the resultant force acting on the ball. [1]

  ii Describe the motion of the ball. [1]

  [Total marks 4]

3 A student gives a toy car an initial push and then takes their hand off the car. The car rolls along the surface. After a few seconds the car slows down and stops.

Which diagram represents the forces acting on the car just before it stops.

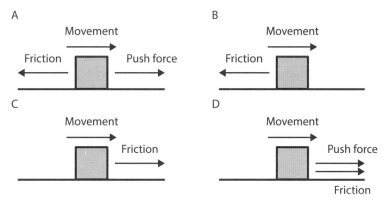

[1]

S **4** Two students push a trolley across the playground. The students push with a force of 20 N and 10 N. There is a force of friction of 15 N in the opposite direction. The forces acting on the trolley are shown in the diagram.

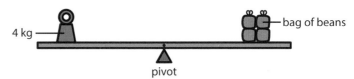

a **i** Calculate the resultant force acting on the trolley. [2]

> **Show me**
>
> Total of students pushing force = 20 N + 10 N = ... N
>
> Friction force is in the OPPOSITE direction. Force is a vector, so we use '–' to show the direction.
>
> Friction force = – .... N.
>
> Resultant force is the sum of all the forces = ... N+ .... N

ii State which direction the trolley will move because of this resultant force. [1]

b The mass of the trolley is 10 kg. Calculate the acceleration of the trolley while it is being pushed. [1]

[Total marks 4]

Turning effect of forces

1 An object of 4 kg is placed on a uniform beam. The beam is balanced by four identical bags of beans.

An identical bag of beans is added to the other four bags. The positions of the object and the bags do not change.

What mass must be added to the 4 kg object to keep the beam balanced? [1]

A. 0.5 kg **B.** 1 kg **C.** 2 kg **D.** 4 kg

2 A student writes the following statement:

"An object is in equilibrium when the turning effect of the forces acting on it is zero."

This statement is incorrect. What should the student have written? [2]

3 A gardener has put some soil into a wheelbarrow. To lift the handle of the wheelbarrow the gardener applies an upward force of 120 N as shown.

Calculate the moment of the force. [2]

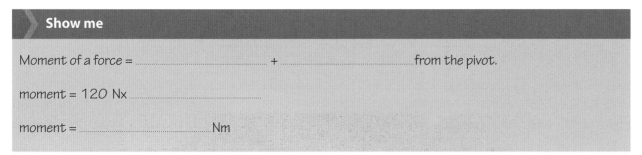

> **Show me**
>
> Moment of a force = ... + ... from the pivot.
>
> moment = 120 N× ....
>
> moment = ... Nm

4 A student uses a metre rule to investigate the principle of moments. The experimental set-up is shown.

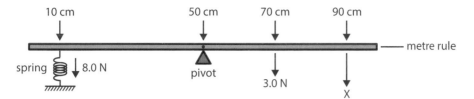

a   State the principle of moments. [1]

b   Calculate the value of X. [4]

[Total marks 5]

Centre of gravity

5 A teacher has two vases that are a similar shape, as shown. Vase A has a very narrow base and a wide top opening. Vase B has a wide base and a narrow top opening.

Suggest which vase will be more stable.

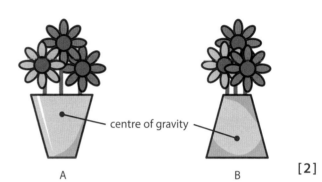

[2]

The key word 'suggest' means that you have to apply your knowledge about centre of gravity and stability to decide which vase is likely to be more stable.

S Circular motion

6 A student is spinning a ball on a rope in a circle above their head.

a   What is the name of the centripetal force acting on the ball? [1]

b   The student starts to spin the ball faster. State how the centripetal force will change. [1]

[Total marks 2]

Springs

1 Two spherical masses are hung on two identical spring balances.

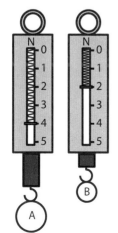

What can be deduced about objects A and B?

A.   They have equal volumes and equal weights

B.   They have equal volumes and different weights

C.   They have different volumes and equal weights

D.   They have different volumes and different weights [1]

2 A student plots an extension–load graph for a spring. They are then given an object with an unknown weight. When they hang the object on the spring the extension of the spring is 22 mm. Use the graph to determine the weight of the object.

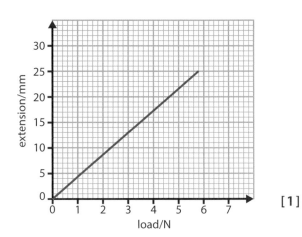

[1]

S **3** A student hangs a mass of 200 g on a spring.

The unstretched length of the spring is 3 cm.

When the mass is hung on the spring the length of the spring is 3.8 cm.

Calculate the spring constant of the spring. [4]

> **Show me**

Mass in kg =...................................kg

Weight = m × g =...................................× 9.81 N/kg =...................................N

Extension = new length − original length = ...− ....cm

Spring constant = $\dfrac{force}{extension}$ = ...

Spring constant = ...N/cm

Momentum

S **4** A cyclist is travelling at a velocity of 2 m/s. The combined mass of the cyclist and the bike is 70 kg. The cyclist then accelerates to a velocity of 5 m/s in the same direction.

What is the change in momentum of the cyclist and bike?

A. 140 kg m/s

B. 175 kg m/s

C. 210 kg m/s

D. 350 kg m/s [1]

5 A child rolls a ball of mass 0.1 kg towards a wall. The ball has a velocity of 1 m/s. The ball hits the

SUPPLEMENT wall and bounces back in the opposite direction with a velocity of 0.8 m/s.

The ball is in contact with the wall for 0.002 s.

a Calculate the change in momentum of the ball. [2]

b State the impulse in this change in momentum. [1]

c Calculate the average force between the ball and the wall. [2]

[Total marks 5]

When calculating change in momentum, it is important to take account of changes in direction by using a minus sign.

6 ▶ A toy train, A, rolls along a level track at a velocity of 2 m/s. It collides with a stationary train carriage, B, and joins with it.

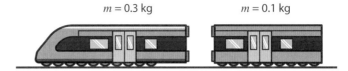

$m = 0.3$ kg $\qquad$ $m = 0.1$ kg

a Calculate the momentum of the toy train before the collision. [2]

b Calculate the speed of the joined train and carriage immediately after the collision. [3]

[**Total marks 5**]

Energy

1 ▶ A biomass-fired power station generates electricity. Which row represents the energy store of the biomass and the moving turbine.

	Biomass	**Moving turbine**
A.	chemical	gravitational potential
B.	nuclear	kinetic
C.	chemical	kinetic
D.	nuclear	gravitational potential

[1]

2 ▶ A parachutist jumps out of a plane. After 30 s of falling they open their parachute and reach terminal velocity. Complete the energy flow diagram for this part of their fall.

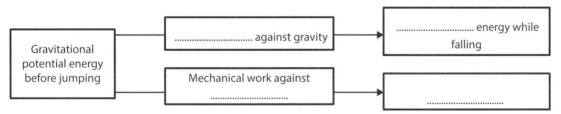

[4]

S 3 A parachutist jumps out of a plane. At the start of the jump they have a gravitational potential energy of 2 000 000 J. Just before they open their parachute, they have a kinetic energy of 125 000 J and a gravitational potential energy of 800 000 J.

a State the principle of conservation of energy. [1]

b Use the principle of conservation of energy to calculate the energy transferred to internal (**thermal**) stores during the first part of the parachutist's fall. [4]

> **Show me**

Energy before = 2 000 000 J

Energy after = gravitational potential energy + kinetic energy + internal energy

= .... J+ .... J+ internal energy

But energy before = energy after

Therefore, we can write

Energy before = ... energy + ... energy + ... energy

We can rearrange this equation to make internal energy the subject:

Internal energy = Energy before − (gravitational potential energy + kinetic energy)

Internal energy = ... J− (.................... J+ .... J)

Internal energy = ... J

[Total marks 5]

S 4 A teacher uses a battery-powered handheld fan to cool down on a hot day. The fan blows air towards the teacher. After using the fan for 10 minutes the teacher notices that the fan casing is warmer. The Sankey diagram shows the energy transfers of the fan.

Use the diagram to calculate the amount of energy transferred to each energy store. [2]

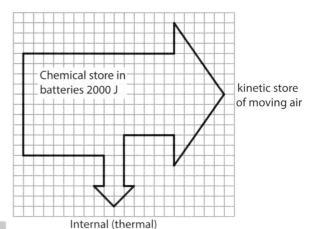

Chemical store in batteries 2000 J

kinetic store of moving air

Internal (thermal)

The widths of the arrows on a Sankey diagram are drawn to scale.

Energy resources

1 Which energy resource is used in power stations to boil water to make steam? [1]

    A. Biomass   **C.** Infrared radiation

    B. Hydroelectric dam   **D.** Wind

2 Solar cells use light from the Sun to generate electricity. Which of the following does **not** rely on the Sun?

    A. Biomass   **C.** Nuclear

    B. Fossil fuels   **D.** Wind [1]

3 Wind turbines generate electrical power when the turbine blades are rotated by the wind.

a Name the energy store of the turbine blades. [1]

b Suggest one advantage of generating electrical power using wind turbines compared to using a nuclear power station. [1]

c The owner of a block of flats wants to use renewable energy to generate electrical power for the building. Suggest one disadvantage of using wind turbines compared to using solar cells (photovoltaic panels) for the owner. [1]

[Total marks 3]

4 A wind turbine produces 2 MW of electrical power. The total power transferred by the wind is 5 MW

Calculate the efficiency of the turbine. [1]

Calculating energy, work and power

1 A child makes a track for her toy cars to roll down.

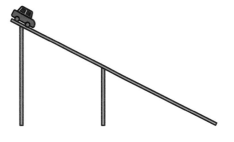

a The child lifts a toy car to the top of the track. The top of the track is 1 m above the floor. The toy car has a mass of 0.05 kg.

Calculate the gain in gravitational potential energy of the car. [2]

b The child releases the car from rest at the top of the track. As the car reaches the bottom of the track it has a speed of 3 m/s.

Calculate the kinetic energy of the car at the bottom of the track. [2]

c **i** Calculate the efficiency of the energy transfer. [3]

    ii Suggest one reason why the value you calculated in **(c) (i)** is not 100%. [1]

[Total marks 8]

2 Two students are stacking textbooks in a classroom. They lift each book from the desk and put it on a shelf. Each student stacks the same number of identical books. Student D takes 6 minutes to stack the books. Student E takes 4 minutes to stack the books.

Which statement about the students is correct?

A. Student D does less useful work than Student E.

B. Student D does more useful work than Student E.

C. Student D has less useful power than Student E.

D. Student D has more useful power than Student E. [1]

3 A horse pulls a cart with a resultant force of 1500 N along a 500 m track.

Calculate the work done by the horse. [1]

4 A crane on a building site lifts a load of tiles 5 m vertically. The tiles weigh 1000 N.

a Calculate the work done on the box by the crane. [1]

b It takes the crane 50 seconds to lift the tiles. Calculate the power of the crane. [2]

[Total marks 3]

Pressure

1 A company makes a measuring instrument that can measure the pressure in a liquid. The instrument is lowered to a depth, h, into four identical tanks of liquid as shown. In which tank will the pressure measurement on the instrument be largest?

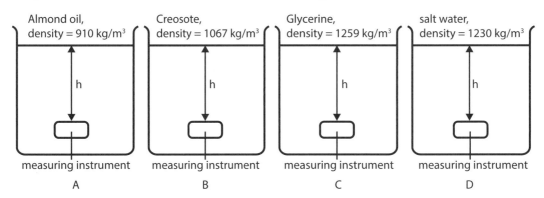

Almond oil, density = 910 kg/m³	Creosote, density = 1067 kg/m³	Glycerine, density = 1259 kg/m³	salt water, density = 1230 kg/m³
h	h	h	h
measuring instrument	measuring instrument	measuring instrument	measuring instrument
A	B	C	D

[1]

2 An empty glass beaker has a weight of 0.5 N. Its base has an area of 0.01 m². It is placed on a bench.

Calculate the pressure on the bench due to the empty beaker. [1]

3 The water pressure at the bottom of a 2 m deep swimming pool is 20 kPa. The pool has an area of 1250 m².

Calculate the force of the water on the bottom of the swimming pool. [3]

4 A tractor and driver have a combined weight of 16 kN. The four tyres
have a total area of 0.04 m^2 in contact with the ground.

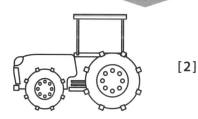

a Calculate the pressure exerted by the tractor on the ground. [2]

b The driver wants to drive over a makeshift bridge. The bridge can
withstand a pressure of 500 000 Pa. The driver thinks that it is safe to
drive over the bridge.

Explain why the driver is correct. [1]

[**Total marks 3**]

5 A scuba diver dives to a coral reef, which is 30 m below the surface of the ocean. The density of the
sea water is 1020 kg/m^3.

Calculate the increase in pressure on the scuba diver as they dive to the coral reef. [2]

> **Show me**

The equation we need is $\Delta p = \Delta gh$

Substitute in the values we know:

$\Delta p =$ .... × 9.8 N/kg × ....

and calculate the change in pressure

$\Delta p =$ ....

States of matter and the kinetic particle model of matter

Syllabus links:
2.1.1.1–2.1.1.2;
2.1.2.1–2.1.2.5;
S 2.1.2.6–2.1.6.8

Learning aims:

- Know that matter can change between three states of matter, each of which has different properties.
- Use the terms 'melting', 'evaporation', 'condensation' and 'solidification' to describe the processes by which matter changes between states.
- Use the kinetic particle model of matter to explain the structure and behaviour of solids, liquids and gases.

States of matter

The three **states** of matter are **solid**, **liquid** and **gas**.

State	Solid	Liquid	Gas
Properties	<ul><li>Fixed shape</li><li>Fixed volume</li><li>Not easily compressed</li><li>Does not flow easily</li></ul>	<ul><li>No fixed shape – takes shape of container it is in</li><li>Fixed volume</li><li>Not easily compressed</li><li>Flows easily</li></ul>	<ul><li>No fixed shape – takes shape of container it is in</li><li>No fixed volume – will spread out and fill all space in a container</li><li>Easily compressed</li><li>Flows easily</li></ul>
Arrangement and separation	Regular pattern, very closely packed together, **particles** held in place	Randomly arranged, closely packed together, particles able to move past each other	Randomly arranged, widely spaced, particles able to move freely
Diagram			
Motion of particles	Vibrate around fixed positions	Move around each other in a random motion	Move faster and randomly (range of speeds in all different directions)

Changes of state:

Melting: solid changes into a liquid

Evaporation: liquid changes to a gas

Condensation: gas changes into a liquid

Solidification: liquid changes into a solid

The kinetic particle model

The properties and behaviour of solids, liquids and gases can be explained using the kinetic particle model of matter.

- All matter is made up of particles, which are constantly moving.
- The higher the temperature of a substance, the more kinetic energy the particles in it have and the faster they move.

Evidence for the kinetic particle model

Evidence for the kinetic particle model of matter comes from the observation of **Brownian motion**. This is the **random motion** of **microscopic** particles, such as pollen grain, suspended in a fluid.

The microscopic particles in a fluid are moved around by many random collisions with the even smaller, lighter **atoms** or **molecules** that make up the fluid.

All particles in a substance, whether they are atoms, molecules, ions or electrons, have **electrostatic forces** acting between them, which vary with the distance between them.

The pressure due to a gas is the force per unit area caused when its particles collide with a surface.

> **Key Point**
>
> The explanation for Brownian motion is that the microscopic particles have lots of random collisions with the smaller particles in the gas or liquid they are in.

> **Key Point**
>
> The lowest possible temperature matter can have is −273°C (**absolute zero**). At this temperature, the particles of matter have zero kinetic energy.

> **Quick Test**
>
> 1. What is the term for a change in state from liquid to gas?
> 2. What is the term for a change in state from gas to liquid?
> 3. What happens to the speed of motion of the particles in a solid as its temperature increases?
> 4. Describe the arrangement of particles in a liquid.
> 5. What is the evidence for the kinetic particle theory?

Gases and temperature

Syllabus links:
2.1.3.1–2.1.3.2;
S 2.1.3.3

Learning aims:

- Describe the effect on the pressure of a gas of changing temperature or volume.
- **S** Recall and use the equation $pV = $ constant.
- Convert temperatures between kelvin and degrees Celsius.

Pressure and temperature at constant volume

If the volume of a fixed mass of gas is kept constant, increasing the **temperature** increases the pressure. This is because:

- increasing the temperature increases the speed of the particles
- faster moving gas particles collide with the walls of a container more frequently and with more force.

Pressure and volume at constant temperature

If the temperature of a fixed mass of gas is kept constant, decreasing the volume increases the pressure. This is because:

- the particles have a smaller distance to travel between collisions, so they will collide more frequently with the walls of a container

S If the temperature and mass of a gas are kept constant, its pressure and volume are related by this equation:

pressure $\times$ volume = constant

$pV = $ constant

where $p = $ pressure in Pa (or N/m^2) and $V = $ volume in m^3.

The equation $pV = $ constant can also be written as $p_1 V_1 = p_2 V_2$, where p_1 and V_1 are the initial pressure and volume, and p_2 and V_2 are final pressure and volume.

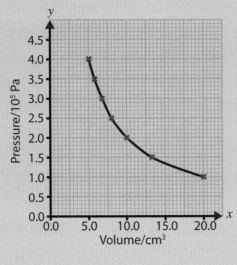

Example 1   Here is an example.

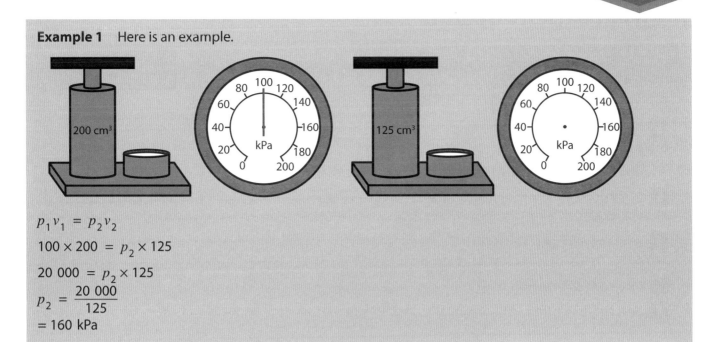

$$p_1v_1 = p_2v_2$$

$$100 \times 200 = p_2 \times 125$$

$$20\,000 = p_2 \times 125$$

$$p_2 = \frac{20\,000}{125}$$

$$= 160 \text{ kPa}$$

Converting temperatures between Kelvin and Celsius

Temperature (*T*) in **kelvin** (K) is related to temperature (*θ*) in **Celsius** (°C) by the equation:

T(in K)=*θ*in(°C) + 273

> ### Key Point
>
> - To change temperature from K to °C, subtract 273.
> - To change temperature from °C to K, add 273.

> ### Quick Test
>
> 1. What happens the pressure of a gas if its temperature decreases?
> 2. What happens to the pressure of a gas if its volume increases?
> 3. Convert 60°C to kelvin
> 4. What is the equation that links the pressure of a gas and its volume at a constant temperature?
> 5. An aerosol can has a volume of 75 cm^3. It contains gas at a pressure of 450 kPa. Calculate the volume of this gas when all of it is allowed to expand into the atmosphere at a pressure of 100 kPa. Assume the temperature remains constant.

Thermal expansion and specific heat capacity

Syllabus links:
2.2.2.1–2.2.2.2;
S 2.2.1.3 ; 2.2.2.1;
S 2.2.2.2 - 2.2.2.4

Learning aims:

- Describe some real-world impacts of thermal expansion.
- **S** Explain the expansion of materials as their temperature rises in terms of the motion and arrangement of particles.
- Recall that increasing the temperature of an object increases its internal energy.
- **S** Recall that an increase in temperature of an object means an increase in the average kinetic energies of its particles.
- **S** Define specific heat capacity as the energy required to increase the temperature of 1 kg of a substance by 1°C
- **S** Recall and use the equation $c = \dfrac{\Delta E}{m\Delta\theta}$
- **S** Describe how you could measure the specific heat capacity of a solid and a liquid.

Thermal expansion of solids, liquids and gases

Nearly all solids and liquids expand as they get hotter.

Gases also expand if the pressure is kept constant.

> **S** A substance will expand when heated because as the temperature increases its particles move around more and take up more space.
>
> For every degree increase in temperature, solids expand less than liquids, which expand less than gases. This is because:
> - particles in a solid are held in fixed positions so they cannot move apart too much
> - forces between particles in a liquid are weaker than the particles in a solid, so particles in a liquid can move farther apart for same increase in energy
> - particles in a gas fill the container they are in. If a gas is in a flexible container, like a balloon, its volume will expand if the gas is heated but the pressure on it is kept the same.

Applications and consequences of thermal expansion

- The **thermal expansion** of mercury is used in thermometers.
- Railway tracks have expansion gaps between different sections to allow the rails to expand when hot.
- Large bridges are built with expansion joints to allow them to get longer on hot days.

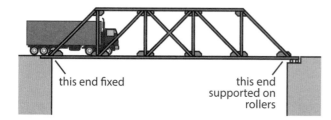

this end fixed   this end supported on rollers

Specific heat capacity

If the temperature of a substance increases, so does its internal energy.

> **S** Increasing the temperature of a substance increases the average kinetic energies of the particles in the substance.
>
> The **specific heat capacity**, c, of a substance is the energy in joules required to increase the temperature of 1 kg of a substance by 1°C.
>
> Specific heat capacity can be calculated using the equation $c = \dfrac{\Delta E}{m\Delta\theta}$ where
>
> ΔE is energy in joules (J), m is mass in kilograms (kg) and $\Delta\theta$ is the change in temperature in degrees Celsius (°C).

Practical skills

To find the specific heat capacity of a solid or liquid:

- heat the substance using an electric heater of known power output
- calculate the energy supplied to the substance using the equation energy transferred = power × time taken ($E = P\Delta t$)
- measure the change in temperature using a thermometer
- measure the mass using a top-pan balance
- put these values in the equation $c = \dfrac{\Delta E}{m\Delta\theta}$

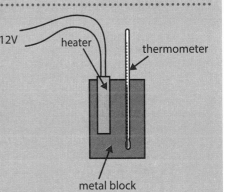

12V   heater   thermometer

metal block

Key Point

To reduce the error in the experimental value for c, minimise energy transfer to the surroundings by:
- ensuring that the substance is well-insulated by wrapping it in an insulating material
- putting a lid on the container if heating a liquid.

Quick Test

1. Why does a substance expand when heated?
2. Which expands most when heated: a solid, a liquid or a gas?
3. How is thermal expansion used in thermometers?
4. What is the specific heat capacity of a substance?

Melting, boiling and evaporation

Syllabus links:
2.2.3.1–2.2.3.5;
S 2.2.3.6–2.2.3.8

Learning aims:

- Describe melting/solidifying and boiling/condensing in terms of energy transfers without changing temperature.
- Recall melting and boiling temperatures for water.
- Describe particle behaviour during changes of state.
- Know the effect of evaporation on the temperature of a liquid.
- **S** Describe how boiling and evaporation differ.
- **S** Describe effect on evaporation of temperature, surface area and air movement over a surface.
- **S** Explain why an object in contact with an evaporating liquid cools down.

Energy transfers during change of state

When a substance changes state its temperature does not change.

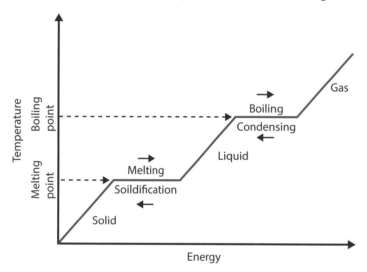

> ### Key Point
>
> At standard atmospheric pressure (100 kPa), solid water (ice) melts at 0°C and liquid water boils at 100°C.

- Energy put into a substance while it melts or boils does not change the average kinetic energy of its particles, but makes the particles move further apart.
- Energy given out by a substance while it solidifies or condenses does not change the average kinetic energy of its particles, but makes the particles move closer together.

Key temperatures

Melting point: temperature at which a substance changes from solid to liquid

Boiling point: temperature at which a substance changes from liquid to gas

Particle behaviour during change of state

When a substance changes state the arrangement and movement of its particles change so that:

- particles get closer together during **solidification** or condensation
- particles break away from the surface of a liquid when it evaporates.

> **S Key Point**

Evaporation and boiling are not the same thing:
- Evaporation:
  - Particles on the surface of a liquid escape.
  - Can happen at any temperature because there are always some particles with enough energy to do this.
  - It is why you can smell dry substances like scented candles.
- Boiling:
  - Particles throughout a liquid have enough energy to leave it.
  - It is why bubbles of gas form inside a liquid when it boils.
  - Only happens at the boiling temperature of the substance.

Cooling by evaporation

Evaporation:

- occurs when more energetic particles from the surface of a liquid break away
- causes a liquid to cool down because the average kinetic energy of the particles left in the liquid is reduced, so the temperature falls.

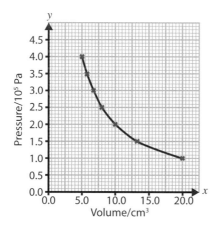

S An object in contact with an evaporating liquid will cool down because, as the liquid cools down, there will be energy transfer from the thermal energy store of the object to the cooler liquid, cooling down the object.

The rate of evaporation of a liquid can be increased by increasing:

- temperature – because the average kinetic energy of particles is greater at higher temperatures so there are more particles with enough energy to escape the liquid
- surface area – because the larger the exposed surface area of a liquid, the more particles can escape from it
- air movement – because the more air movement above a liquid, the more molecules are carried away from the liquid and cannot re-enter it.

> **Quick Test**

1. What happens to the temperature of a solid when it is melting?
2. What is the melting and boiling point of water?
   S 3. Explain the difference between evaporation and boiling.
   S 4. State three ways to increase the rate of evaporation from a liquid.

Transfer of thermal energy: conduction, convection

Syllabus links:
2.3.1.1;
S 2.3.1.2–2.3.1.4;
2.3.2.1–2.3.2.2

Learning aims:

- Describe experiments showing properties of good/bad thermal conductors.
- **S** Describe thermal conduction in solids.
- **S** Use particle theory to describe, why thermal conduction is bad in gases and most liquids.
- **S** Know that many solids can conduct thermal energy better than thermal insulators, but worse than thermal conductors.
- Explain convection as a thermal transfer method in liquids and gases in terms of density changes.

Conduction

Good thermal conductors transfer thermal energy quickly.

Bad thermal conductors do not transfer thermal energy quickly and are known as **thermal insulators**.

S Thermal **conduction** in solids:
- When one end of a solid is heated, the atoms vibrate more than at the cooler end.
- Vibrations are passed from atom to atom via their chemical bonds, transferring thermal energy from the hot end to the cold end.

S Metals are good thermal conductors because thermal energy is also transferred by free (delocalised) electrons, which move quickly and collide with metal ions.

S Gases and most liquids are bad thermal conductors because:
- in liquids, the chemical bonds between particles are weaker than in a solid, so vibrations are not passed along from particle to particle very well
- in gases, the particles are far apart with negligible forces between them.

S The thermal conductivity of solids varies and there are many solids that conduct thermal energy better than thermal insulators, but less well than good thermal conductors.

> **Practical skills**

To demonstrate good and bad thermal conductors:

1. Heat rods made of different materials.

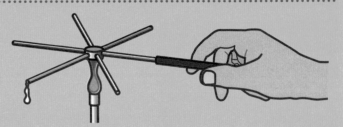

- The rods:
  - are all the same length and thickness
  - have the same amount of wax stuck on the far end.
- Heat the centre of the apparatus. Thermal energy is transferred along the rods.

- Wax melts more quickly from the better thermal conductors.
- Alternatively, heat separate rods of the same dimensions individually and time how long it takes for the wax to melt. The rod with the shortest time is the best conductor.

2. Use a cylinder made of wood and metal.

- Wrap a piece of paper tightly around the cylinder so there is wood on one side and metal on the other
- Hold this just above a Bunsen flame.
- The paper on the wooden side will discolour first. On the metal side, thermal energy is transferred away from the paper into the metal.
- Wood is a thermal insulator so thermal energy is not conducted away from the paper and it starts to burn.

Convection

Convection: the main method of thermal energy transfer in fluids (liquids and gases).

Convection can only happen in fluids because the particles can move around.

- When a fluid is heated the particles gain energy and move around faster and move further apart.
- Hot fluid is less dense than the surrounding cooler fluid.
- The hotter, less dense fluid rises and cooler more dense fluid takes its place.
- This process repeats, setting up a convection current, which transfers thermal energy throughout the fluid.

> **Key Point**
>
> Heat does not rise. The hot, less dense fluid rises. Many insulators trap air in small pockets to restrict its movement and slow down thermal energy transfer.

> **Practical skills**
>
> To show convection:
>
> - place a few crystals of potassium permanganate in a beaker of water
> - heat the bottom of the beaker on one side
> - the potassium permanganate dissolves and travels up in the warm, less dense water
> - a purple trail in the water shows the convection current.

> **Quick Test**
>
> 1. What is the main way in which thermal energy is transferred inside a liquid or a gas?
> S 2. Why are metals good thermal conductors?
> S 3. Why are gases poor thermal conductors?

Transfer of thermal energy: radiation

Learning aims:

- Know that energy transfer by thermal radiation (infrared radiation emitted by all objects) does not require a medium.
- Recall factors affecting the emission, absorption and reflection of thermal radiation.
- S Know that the temperature of an object depends on the rate at which it receives and transfers energy.
- S Recall how incoming radiation and radiation emitted from the Earth's surface affect the Earth's temperature.
- S Know how to distinguish between good and bad emitters/absorbers of infrared radiation through experiments.
- S Describe factors affecting the rate of emission of radiation
- S Explain everyday and complex applications of the different types of thermal radiation.

Thermal radiation

All objects absorb and emit thermal **radiation**, which:

- is part of the electromagnetic spectrum known as **infrared** radiation
- does not need particles and can travel through a **vacuum**.

Type of surface	As an emitter of radiation	As an absorber of radiation
dull black	good	good
bright shiny	poor	poor

S The temperature of an object depends on the rates at which it receives energy and transfers energy away.

rate of receiving energy = rate of transferring energy	temperature constant
rate of receiving energy > rate of transferring energy	temperature increase
rate of receiving energy < rate of transferring energy	temperature decrease

> ### Key Point

The temperature of the Earth is affected by factors that control the balance between incoming radiation and radiation emitted from its surface.
- The Earth:
  - absorbs infrared radiation emitted by the Sun
  - emits (longer wave) infrared radiation from its surface.
- Greenhouse gases in the atmosphere (e.g. carbon dioxide, methane and water vapour) absorb infrared radiation emitted by the Earth and re-emit it in all directions.
- This 'greenhouse effect' keeps the Earth warmer than it would otherwise be.
- The average temperature of the Earth is increasing due to increased amounts of greenhouse gases released into the atmosphere by human activity.

> **S Practical skills**

To show the difference between good and bad **absorbers/emitters** of infrared radiation:

- take two containers, which are identical except one is black and the other is white
- fill both containers with the same amount of cool water at the same temperature
- measure and record the temperature of water in each container using identical thermometers
- place the containers so that they are the same distance away from a heater
- use a stopwatch to measure a period of time and then record the temperatures again
- the water in the white container should now have a lower temperature than the black one Repeat the experiment using hot water and with the heater turned off.
- This time the white container should have a higher temperature than the black one..

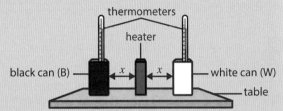

> **S Key Point**

The **rate of emission** of infrared radiation from an object depends on its surface area and surface temperature.
- higher surface area → higher rate of emission
- higher surface temperature → higher rate of emission

Consequences of thermal energy transfer

Thermal energy transfer can be used to explain everyday applications.

- Cooking using metal pans uses conduction to transfer energy.
- Radiators heat a room mainly due to convection currents in air.

S More than one type of thermal energy transfer is significant in many situations.

- A fire transfers thermal energy by emitting infrared radiation and by convection.
- Car radiators help to cool down car engines. Thermal energy from the engine is transferred to a liquid by conduction. The warm liquid enters the radiator, which transfers thermal energy away to the surroundings by radiation. To maximise thermal energy transfer by radiation, car radiators are usually painted a dull colour and have lots of 'fins' so they have a large surface area. Insulated flasks can prevent thermal energy loss by having a vacuum between the inside bottle and outside case. This prevents conduction and convection.

> **Quick Test**

1. What type of thermal energy transfer can take place through a vacuum (empty space)?
2. What type of electromagnetic radiation is thermal radiation?
3. Why are kitchen pans usually made from metals?
4. Why are pan-handles for cookware often made of wood or plastic?
5. What are the main ways in which a radiator transfers thermal energy to a room?

States of matter and the kinetic particle model of matter

1 An ice cube is placed on a saucer and left out at room temperature. After a short time, the ice starts melting and there is some liquid water around the ice in the saucer.

a State what is meant by the term 'melting'. [1]

'State' in a question like this requires you to recall and write down a definition.

b Compare the arrangement and separation of particles in solid and liquid water. [2]

'Compare' in a question like this requires you write down similarities and/or differences between the things you are being asked to compare.

> **Show me**

Particles in a solid are arranged in a regular pattern but are .... arranged in a liquid; particles in a solid are .... packed together but a little .... closely packed in a liquid.

[Total marks 3]

2 The space above a cup of hot water contains some water vapour.

a State the process by which a liquid turns into a gas. [1]

b Describe the arrangement, movement and separation of the molecules in water vapour. [3]

c In the box below, draw a diagram to show the arrangement and separation of the particles in a liquid [2]

[Total marks 6]

Gases and temperature

1 The diagram shows a medicine syringe. You can trap air in it by putting your finger over the open end.

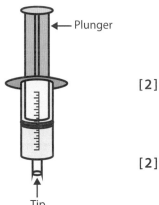

a Explain, in terms of particles, why the pressure of the trapped air increases when you push down the plunger. [2]

S b When the plunger is fully extended, the volume of air inside the syringe is 10 m^3 and the pressure is 1.0×10^5 Pa. Its temperature has not changed.

Calculate the pressure of the air when it is squashed to a volume of 4 cm^3 [2]

'Calculate' requires you to recall and write down an equation before using it to find a numerical answer.

> **Show me**
>
> Use equation $p_1 V_1 = p_2 V_2$
>
> Re-arrange to make p_2 the subject of the equation:
>
> $p_2 = p_1 V_1 \div V_2$ (................... × ....) ÷ .... = ... Pa.

[Total marks 4]

2 A football, which contains a fixed mass of air, is left outside on a cold night. State and explain, in terms of particles, how the pressure of the air inside the football changes as it cools down. [3]

Thermal expansion and specific heat capacity

1 A block of aluminium has a mass of 2.5 kg. It absorbs 22 500 J of thermal energy. The specific heat capacity of aluminium is 900 J / (kg°C).

What is the temperature rise of the metal? [1]

A. 40°C **B.** 30°C **C.** 20°C **D.** 10°C

> **Show me**
>
> Use the equation $c = \dfrac{\Delta E}{m\Delta\theta}$
>
> Rearrange to make $\Delta\theta$ the subject: $\Delta\theta = \dfrac{\Delta E}{mc}$
>
> Put in numbers: $\Delta\theta =$ .... = ... °C

2 ▶ The image shows a large bridge, which is fixed at one end and supported on rollers at the other end. This is so that the bridge can expand safely in hot weather.

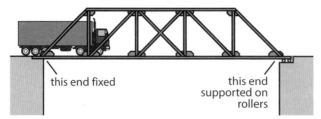

this end fixed

this end supported on rollers

a Explain, in terms of molecules, why a solid expands when heated. [2]

b Explain, in terms of molecules, why a liquid expands more than a solid when heated. [2]

[Total marks 4]

Melting, boiling and evaporation

1 ▶ Explain why sweating helps cool you down. [4]

> **Show me**

As sweat ...., faster moving particles leave the surface of the sweat, so average
.... energy of particles of sweat is reduced, so temperature of sweat
is .... and energy is .... from hotter body to cooler sweat, cooling
down the body.

2 ▶ A student melts a beaker of candle wax and records the temperature of the wax as it changes with time.

Here is the graph of their results.

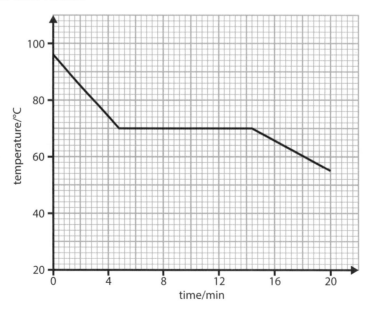

Use the graph to determine the melting point of the wax. [1]

The temperature of a substance does not change when it is changing state.

Transfer of thermal energy

1 In some hot countries, people paint the roofs of their houses white. State why this is a good idea. [1]

Shiny white surfaces are excellent reflectors of thermal radiation.

2 A student has four containers, which are the same shape and size but are painted different colours. They put equal amounts of hot water at the same temperature into them. In which container will the water cool down the quickest?

A. Matt black

B. Matt white

C. Shiny black

D. Shiny white [1]

3 A student buys a new winter coat, which is very warm. Unfortunately, they rip the coat and find that it has a layer of fleece material inside and that the inside of the outer shell of the coat is shiny and silver. Explain how these features helped keep the student warm. [2]

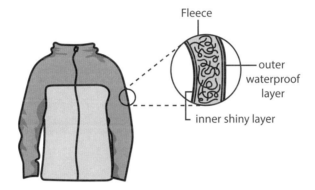

Show me

The fleece material traps .... , which is a poor conductor, ...
thermal energy transfer away from the student's body. The shiny material reflects ....
radiation back towards the student's body.

General properties of waves

Learning aims:

- Know that waves transfer energy but not matter.

- Describe wave motion and the features of a wave.

- Be able to remember and use the equation for wave speed, $v = f\lambda$.

- Know properties and examples of transverse and longitudinal waves

- Describe reflection, refraction and diffraction of waves and how to use a ripple tank to show these behaviours.

- **S** Describe the impact of wavelength and gap size on diffraction.

Types of wave

All waves are vibrations about a fixed point.

Waves transfer energy without transferring matter.

- **Longitudinal** waves travel parallel to the direction of vibrations, e.g. sound waves, seismic P-waves.

- **Transverse** waves travel at right angles to the direction of vibrations, e.g. electromagnetic waves, surface water waves and seismic S-waves.

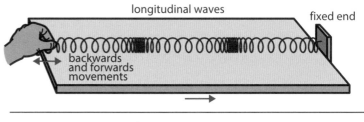

longitudinal waves

backwards and forwards movements

fixed end

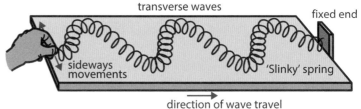

transverse waves

sideways movements

fixed end

'Slinky' spring

direction of wave travel

Wave features

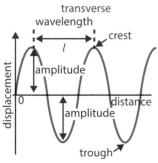

transverse wavelength

crest

l

amplitude

displacement

0

distance

amplitude

trough

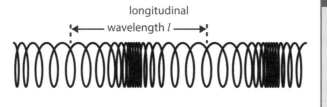

longitudinal

wavelength l

> ### Key Point
>
> Wave speed, frequency and wavelength are related by:
> $v = f \times \lambda$
> where v = speed in m/s,
> f = frequency in Hz,
> λ = wavelength in m.

- Crest (peak) / trough - the highest and lowest points on a wave compared to rest position.

- Amplitude (metres, m) – maximum displacement from rest position.

- Wavelength (metres, m) – distance between two adjacent peaks/troughs.

- Frequency (hertz, Hz) – number of waves passing a point in a second.

- Wave speed (m/s) – distance travelled by a wave in one second.

- Wavefront – line in diagrams representing peaks of a wave as seen from above.

Wave behaviour

A ripple tank (right) can show the behaviour of waves.

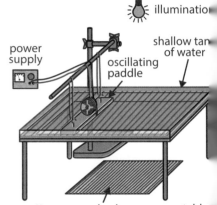

illumination

shallow tank of water

power supply

oscillating paddle

wave patterns on a viewing screen or table

Reflection: when a wave bounces off a surface.

The angle of reflection, r, is equal to the angle of incidence, i.

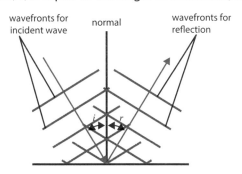

> **Key Point**
>
> Angles of incidence and reflection are measured from the **normal**, the line at right angles to the surface.

Refraction: when the direction of a wave changes because of a change in its speed.

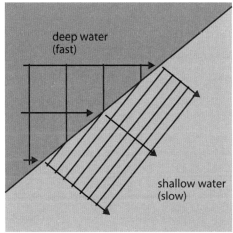

Diffraction: when a wave spreads out at a narrow gap or at an edge.

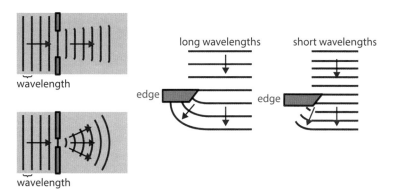

> **S Key Point**
>
> Diffraction is most noticeable when the size of the gap is similar to the wavelength of the waves.

> **S Key Point**
>
> Long wavelengths spread out more when waves curve around an edge.

> **Quick Test**
>
> 1. What is a longitudinal wave? Give an example.
> 2. What is a transverse wave? Give an example.
> 3. What is refraction?
> 4. What is diffraction?
> 5. **S** When is diffraction of a wave most noticeable?

Light – reflection and refraction

Learning aims:

Syllabus links:
3.2.1.1–3.2.1.3:
S 3.2.1.4 ;
3.2.2.1–3.2.2.5;
S 3.2.2.6–3.2.2.9

- Know the meaning of the terms normal, angle of incidence, angle of reflection, angle of refraction.

- Use the law of reflection and describe the formation of an image by a plane mirror

- **S** Construct simple ray diagrams to measure and calculate reflection by plane mirrors.

- Describe the passage of light through transparent materials and an experiment to show the refraction of light using shaped blocks.

- Define the term critical angle.

- Describe internal reflection, total internal reflection and the critical angle.

- **S** Define refractive index, n and use the equations: $n = \dfrac{\sin i}{\sin r}$ and $n = \dfrac{1}{\sin c}$.

- **S** Describe some uses of optical fibres.

Reflection of light

Light rays reflected from a plane (flat) mirror obey the **law of reflection**:

angle of incidence (i) = angle of reflection (r)

A plane mirror produces images of objects in front of it. These images are laterally inverted, the same size and distance from the mirror as the object and virtual, so cannot be projected on a screen.

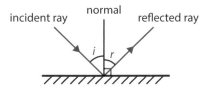

S To draw a ray diagram showing how an image in a mirror is formed:

1. Draw the object and image the same distance from the mirror.
2. Line up a ruler from the eye to the top of the image and draw a line from the eye to the mirror – this is a reflected ray.
3. Extend this line using dashes to the top of the image.
4. Draw the incident ray back to the top of the object.
5. Repeat this process with the bottom of the image.

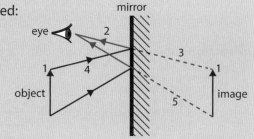

Refraction of light

When light crosses the boundary from one medium to another at an angle, its speed and direction change:

- towards the normal, if the light rays slow down (going into a more dense medium, such as from air to glass)

- away from the normal, if the light rays speed up (going into a less dense medium, such as from glass to air).

> **S Key Point**
>
> The **refractive index**, n, of a medium is the ratio of speed of light in a vacuum to speed of light in that medium.
>
> $$n = \frac{\text{speed of light in a vacuum (or air)}}{\text{speed of light in the medium}} \qquad n = \frac{\sin i}{\sin r}$$
>
> where i = angle of incidence and r = angle of refraction.

To show refraction of light:

- place a block on a sheet of paper and draw around it
- use a ray box to shine a beam of light into the side of the block
- draw crosses to mark the path of the ray into and out of the block
- remove the block and draw a line joining these two points – the refracted ray
- draw a line joining the crosses showing the incident and refracted ray
- draw a line at right angles to the outline of the block where the two lines meet
- use a protractor to measure the angles of incidence (*i*) and refraction (*r*)
- repeat for different angles of incidence.

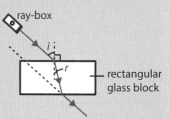

Critical angle and total internal reflection

When light crosses from one medium into another some light is always reflected back. This is called internal reflection.

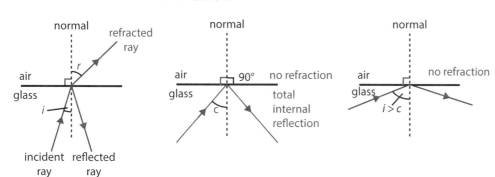

> **Key Point**
>
> The **critical angle** is the angle of incidence when the angle of refraction is 90°.

S The critical angle, *c*, for a material with refractive index *n* can be calculated using:

$$n = \frac{1}{\sin c}$$

> **Key Point**
>
> **Total internal reflection**: no light is refracted at the boundary between two mediums, but is all reflected back.

Internal reflection occurs when light travels into a material with a lower refractive index (e.g. from glass to air), or when the angle of incidence is greater than the critical angle.

Total internal reflection is used in binoculars and reflectors in car headlights.:

S Optical fibres

An optical fibre is a long, thin strand of glass coated in a material with a lower refractive index.

Optical fibres allow signals of light to travel long distances and around corners. They are used for telecommunications and endoscopes.

> **Quick Test**
>
> 1. What is the law of reflection?
> 2. What is a 'normal' line?
> 3. What is the critical angle?
> 4. What is total internal reflection?
> **S** 5. What is the formula for calculating the refractive index of a substance?

Lenses and dispersion of light

Learning aims:

Syllabus links:
3.2.3.1–3.2.3.5;
S 3.2.3.6–3.2.3.8 ;
3.2.4.1–3.2.4.2;
S 3.2.4.3

- Describe how converging and diverging lenses affect a parallel beam of light.
- Know the meaning of focal length, principal axis and principal focus (focal point) and describe the characteristics of images.
- Draw ray diagrams to show the formation of a real image by a converging lens.
- Know how a virtual image is formed.
- **S** Draw ray diagrams to show the formation of a virtual image by a converging lens.
- **S** Describe using a lens as a magnifying glass and how lenses can correct vision problems.
- Describe the dispersion of light and know the colours of the visible spectrum.
- **S** know that monochromatic light is electromagnetic radiation of one frequency.

Lenses

A lens is a piece of transparent glass or plastic that refracts light to form an image. The image may be **real** (on the opposite side of the lens to where the rays originate and able to be projected on a screen) or **virtual** (on the same side of the lens where the rays originate and not able to be projected on a screen).

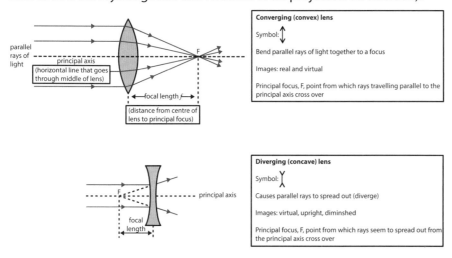

Converging (convex) lens

Symbol: ↕

Bend parallel rays of light together to a focus

Images: real and virtual

Principal focus, F, point from which rays travelling parallel to the principal axis cross over

Diverging (concave) lens

Symbol:)(

Causes parallel rays to spread out (diverge)

Images: virtual, upright, diminished

Principal focus, F, point from which rays seem to spread out from the principal axis cross over

Images

Ray diagrams show us the properties of the image formed by a lens.

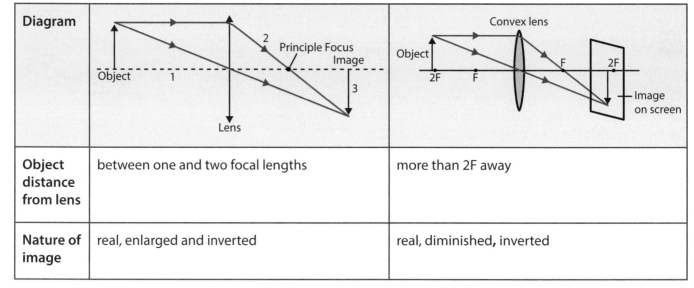

Diagram		
Object distance from lens	between one and two focal lengths	more than 2F away
Nature of image	real, enlarged and inverted	real, diminished, inverted

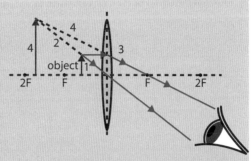

S A converging lens can be used as a magnifying glass if the object is at a distance less than *f* from the lens.

1. Draw a ray from the top of the object through the **centre** of the lens.
2. Draw a dashed line continuing this line upwards.
3. Draw a ray from the top of the object to the lens, parallel to the **principal axis**, then continue it at an angle passing through the **principal focus**.
4. Draw a dashed line continuing this ray upwards.
5. Draw the image arrow straight up from the principal axis to where the dashed lines meet.

The image is virtual, magnified and upright.

Correcting vision

Short-sightedness: the focus point of the eye lens is in front of the retina so it cannot focus on distant objects. Can be corrected using a diverging lens.

Long-sightedness: the focus point of the eye lens is beyond the retina so it cannot focus on closer objects. Can be corrected using a converging lens.

Dispersion of light

Dispersion is the splitting up of white light into the seven colours of the visible spectrum by passing it through a **prism**.

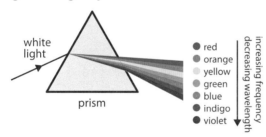

Remember the colours of the spectrum using the acronym ROYGBIV.

Each colour has a different wavelength (and frequency) and is refracted by a different amount by the glass. Violet is refracted the most, red is refracted the least

The light is refracted twice – on entering the glass and on leaving – causing the light to split up.

S All colours making up white light are part of the electromagnetic spectrum.

Monochromatic light is light that has a single frequency (or wavelength).

> **Quick Test**

1. What do diverging lenses do to rays of light?
2. What is a 'virtual' image?
3. What kind of lens can be used to correct long-sightedness?
4. What is the name given to the splitting up of white light by a prism?
5. **S** What is monochromatic light?

Electromagnetic spectrum

Syllabus links:
3.3.1–3.3.5;
S 3.3.6–3.3.10

Learning aims:

- Know regions of electromagnetic spectrum in order of frequency and wavelength **S** and that they travel at the same speed of 3.0×10^8 m/s in a vacuum.
- Describe uses of the different parts of the electromagnetic spectrum and the harmful effects of excessive exposure to electromagnetic radiation.
- **S** Know the role of electromagnetic radiation in systems of communications.
- **S** Know how a digital and analogue signals differ, and explain the benefits of digital signalling.
- **S** Know that sound transmission can be digital or analogue.

Regions of the electromagnetic (EM) spectrum

EM waves:

- transverse and transfer energy from a source
- move through a **vacuum** at the same speed
- **S** travel at 3.0×10^8 m/s in a vacuum and approximately the same in air
- form a continuous spectrum separated into seven regions.

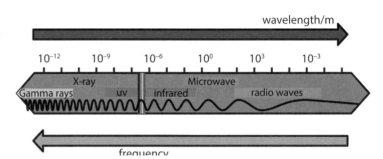

Electromagnetic spectrum uses

Wave	Use	S Reason	Danger
radio	• communication – radio/television transmissions • astronomy • radar • radio frequency identification (RFID)	• can travel long distances and pass through walls and buildings	
microwave	• communication – satellite television, mobile phones (cell phones), Bluetooth, wireless internet • cooking (microwave ovens)	• can penetrate Earth's atmosphere, pass through walls (signal weakened when this happens) • only require a short aerial for transmission and reception	• can cause internal heating of body cells at high intensity
infrared	• electric grills • short range communications, e.g. remote control for television • intruder alarms • thermal imaging • optical fibres	• both infrared and visible used for optical fibres because they can pass through glass and carry high rates of data	• can cause burns

Wave	Use	S Reason	Danger
visible	• seeing • photography • illumination • optical fibres	• both infrared and visible used for optical fibres because they can pass through glass and carry high rates of data	
ultraviolet	• security marking • detecting fake bank notes • sterilising water • sun-tanning		• can cause damage to surface cells and eyes, leading to skin cancer, eye conditions, e.g. cataracts and retinal damage
X-rays	• medical scanning • security scanners	• goes through soft tissue but not bone	• can damage/mutate cells and cause cancer because they are highly ionising radiations
gamma	• sterilising (food and medical equipment) • detection and treatment of cancer	• highly ionising so kills bacteria	

Satellite communications

Artificial satellites use microwaves for communication. They may be in low Earth orbit (LEO) or a higher **geostationary** orbit.

S Digital and analogue signals

Electrical signals can be **digital** or **analogue**. Analogue signals vary continuously with time and can take any value. Digital signals have only two values: high and low (or on and off). Digital signals are used by devices to store and process information accurately. Digital signals allow more data to be transferred more accurately.

S Transmission of sound

Sound waves can be transmitted as **digital** or **analogue** signals.

Sound waves are analogue waves so have to be converted to and from digital signals if using digital technology to transmit sound.

> **Quick Test**

1. What are the two types of satellite used for communications?
2. Which EM waves can harm living cells?
3. Which EM waves can be used for a TV remote control?
   S 4. Why are microwaves used for Bluetooth?
   S 5. What is an advantage of using digital signals over analogue ones?

Sound

Learning aims:

- Know that sound waves are longitudinal and produced by vibrating sources.
- **S** Describe how sound waves travel through compressions and rarefactions.
- State the range of frequencies humans can hear.
- Know that sound waves need a medium and state the speed of sound in air.
- **S** Know relative speeds of sound in solids, liquids and gases.
- Describe how amplitude and frequency can change loudness and pitch.
- Know that an echo is a reflection of sound waves and describe how echoes can be used to determine the speed of sound in air.
- Know that a sound with a frequency more than 20 kHz is defined as ultrasound.
- **S** Describe uses of ultrasound.

Syllabus links:
3.4.1–3.4.9;
S 3.4.10–3.4.11

Sound waves

- Produced by a vibrating source.
- Need a medium to travel through (cannot travel through a vacuum).
- Longitudinal.
- Speed of between 330 m/s and 350 m/s in air.
- **S** Travel faster in solids than in liquids, and faster in liquids than in gases.

> **S Key Point**
>
> Sound waves travel through a medium via **compressions** (where molecules are squashed together in a region of higher density) and **rarefactions** (where molecules are spread out in a region of lower density).

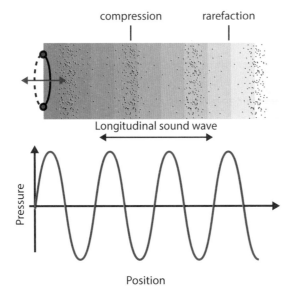

Longitudinal sound wave

Finding the speed of sound in air

An **echo** is the reflection of a sound wave and can be used to find the speed of sound in air like this:

1. Stand a measured distance of several hundred metres away from a wall.
2. Clap two pieces of wood together to make a loud noise and start a timer at the same time.

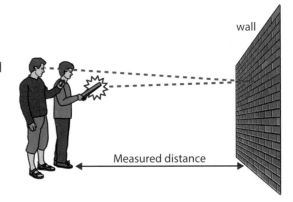

3. Stop the stopwatch when an echo is heard.
4. Use the equation speed $= \dfrac{\text{distance}}{\text{time}}$ to calculate the speed of sound.

   Remember: distance travelled by sound is TWICE the distance to the wall.

Pitch, frequency, amplitude and loudness

Humans can hear sounds in the range 20 Hz to 20 000 Hz.

Pitch

- **high** pitch sounds → **high** frequency (short wavelength)
- **low** pitch sounds → **low** frequency (long wavelength)

Loudness

- **loud** sounds → **big** amplitude
- **quiet** sounds → **small** amplitude

> **Key Point**
>
> **Ultrasound** is sound of frequency above 20 000 Hz (20 kHz).

S Uses of ultrasound

Sonar: to measure depth of ocean

- An ultrasound wave transmitted from the ship is reflected from the sea floor.
- The speed of ultrasound in water is known.
- Time taken for the sound to return is recorded.
- Distance = speed × time used to calculate distance travelled by ultrasound.
- Distance to sea floor $= \dfrac{1}{2} \times$ distance calculated.

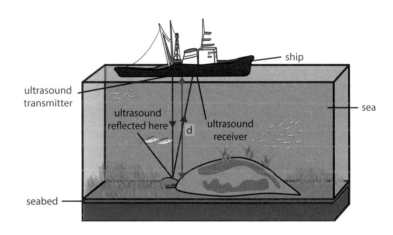

Medical scanning: Ultrasound provides a non-invasive, safe way to image internal organs and unborn babies because it passes through living tissue without harming it.

- A transducer produces and detects a beam of ultrasound sent into the body.
- A special gel is applied to the skin, which improves the contact with the transducer and the transmission and detection of ultrasound.
- Ultrasound is reflected at the boundaries between the different tissues (e.g. between bone and flesh) in its path.
- The computer uses the information from the different reflected waves to construct an image.

Industrial scanning: Ultrasound can be used to detect cracks in objects like pipes and building materials. Ultrasound waves are reflected from cracks in materials.

> **Quick Test**
>
> 1. What is an echo?
> 2. What property of a sound wave is related to its loudness?
> 3. What is ultrasound?
> S 4. Give two uses for ultrasound.
> S 5. Why is ultrasound safe to use to scan unborn babies?

General properties of waves

1 Which arrow shows the wavelength of the wave?

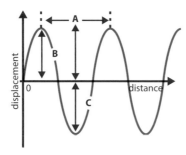

[1]

2 Copy and complete the diagram below to show what happens when the wave passes through the gap in the barrier.

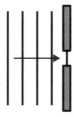

[3]

3 A metal bell vibrates 33 000 times a minute when it has been struck, making a sound that travels through air at a speed of 330 m/s. Calculate the wavelength of the sound the bell makes. [3]

> **Show me**

Use the wave equation: speed = frequency × wavelength

First, notice that frequency is not given in the question so calculate it from the information that the bell vibrates 33 000 times a minute.

Frequency = no. of vibrations per second = (total no. of vibrations ÷ total amount of time in seconds)

So, frequency = ... ÷ .... = ... Hz

Next, rearrange the wave equation to make wavelength the subject of the equation:

wavelength = speed ÷ frequency

wavelength = ... ÷ .... = ... m

4 A sound wave travels at a speed of 330 m/s in air. If the frequency of the wave is doubled, what effect would this have on the wavelength of the wave? [1]

5 **a** Waves can be made on a spring by holding one end and moving it up and down, as shown in **Fig. 1**.

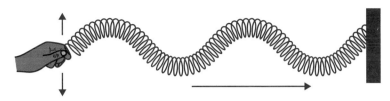

i) What type of wave is shown in **Fig. 1**? [1]

ii) How could the person producing the wave increase the frequency of the wave? [1]

iii) How could the person producing the wave increase the amplitude of the wave? [1]

b Waves can also be made by moving a spring backwards and forwards, as shown in **Fig. 2**?

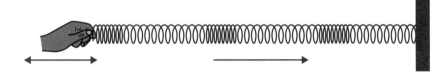

i) What type of wave is shown in this diagram? [1]

ii) Give an example of a wave that travels in this way? [1]

c What is transferred by all waves, regardless of the type of wave? [1]

Light – reflection and refraction

1 Which of these statements about the image in a plane mirror is incorrect?

A. It cannot be projected onto a screen.

B. It is as far behind the mirror as the object is in front.

C. It is laterally inverted.

D. It is smaller than the object. [1]

2 › A ray of light is travelling from glass into air, as shown in the diagram.

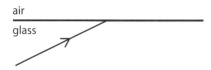

The angle of incidence is greater than the critical angle. Complete the diagram to show what happens to the ray of light. [1]

The critical angle is the angle of incidence when the angle of refraction for a ray of light is 90°. Above this angle, there is total internal reflection.

> **Show me**

First, draw a dashed line (the normal) at right angles to the boundary where the ray meets it.

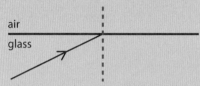

Then, draw the reflected ray so it makes the same angle with the normal as the incident ray.

Lenses and dispersion of light

1 › Short-sightedness is a condition where people cannot see distant objects clearly. The lenses in the eyes of people with this condition cannot form an image on the retina. Instead it is formed in front of the retina. The image seen is not in focus.

What type of lens can be used to correct this? [1]

S 2 › The diagram below shows an object placed in front of a converging lens. F marks the principal focus of the lens. The width of each little square represents a distance of 0.5 cm.

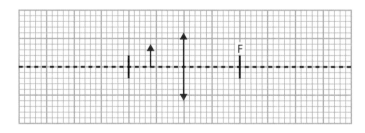

a What is the focal length of the lens? [1]

b Complete the diagram to show how rays from the arrow would form an image. [3]

c Describe the image formed. [3]

Virtual images cannot be projected onto a screen and are formed on the same side of the lens as where rays originate.

> **Show me**

To complete the diagram, because the object is less than F away from the lens, do the following:

1. Draw a ray from the top of the object through the **centre** of the lens, then continue it at an angle passing through the principal focus.

2. Draw a dashed line continuing this line upwards.

3. Draw a ray from the top of the object to the lens, parallel to the principal axis, then continue it at an angle passing through the principal focus.

4. Draw a dashed line continuing this ray upwards.

Draw the image arrow straight up from the principal axis to where the dashed lines meet.

[Total marks 7]

3 Explain the difference between a real image and a virtual image. [3]

4 Complete the sentences about how images are formed by a convex lens using words from the list. Each word can be used once, more than once, or not at all.

distant   **focus**   **near**   **parallel**   **principal axis**   **principal focus**

Light rays from .... objects are effectively .... When a

convex lens focuses light from these objects, the image will be formed at the ....

If the object is in line with centre of the lens, the image will be formed on the .... [4]

Electromagnetic spectrum

1 Which of these is not a property of microwaves?

   A. can travel through a vacuum

   B. electromagnetic

   C. longitudinal

   D. transverse [1]

2 Which of the following electromagnetic waves do not present a danger to human health?

   A. gamma

   B. infrared

   C. microwave

   D. radio [1]

S **3** ⟩ Describe how a digital signal is different from an analogue signal. [2]

> **Show me**

An analogue signal is .... but a digital signal can only take one of ....
values, on or .... / high or ....

Sound

1 ⟩ The graphs below represent sound waves. Which of the graphs represents the lowest, quietest sound?

> The loudness of a sound is related to its amplitude and the pitch of a sound to its frequency – loud sounds have big amplitudes and high sounds have high frequencies.

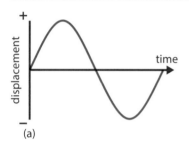
(a)

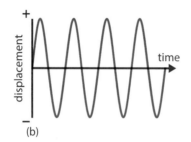
(b)

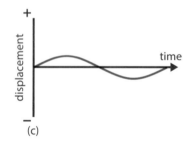
(c)

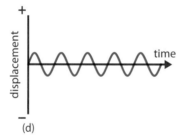
(d)

[1]

S **2** ⟩ Which statement best describes the relative speeds of sound in solids, liquids and gases?

  A. Sound travels faster in gases than liquids, and faster in liquids than solids.

  B. Sound travels faster in liquids than gases, and faster in gases than solids.

  C. Sound travels faster in solids than liquids, and faster in liquids than gases.

  D. Sound travels the same speed in all three mediums. [1]

3 A ship measures the depth of the ocean below it by sending out a pulse of ultrasound and timing how long it takes to get back to a detector.

The speed of ultrasound in water is 1600 m/s.

The pulse takes 1.2 seconds to be detected.

Calculate the depth of the water [3]

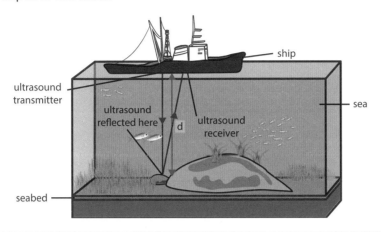

Show me

Depth of water = distance to the ocean floor so use the equation: distance = speed × time

Since the time taken for the pulse to travel to the ocean floor and back is 1.2 seconds, the time for it to reach the floor is:

time = 1.2 ÷ ....

Put in numbers: distance to floor = ... × .... = ... m.

Magnetism

Learning aims:

- Know when magnets attract and repel each other.
- Give some uses of permanent magnets and electromagnets.
- Compare magnetic and non-magnetic materials.
- Describe experiments to show the shape and direction of a magnetic field.
- **S** Use ideas about magnetic fields to explain magnetic forces

Syllabus links: 4.1.1–4.1.9; S 4.1.10–4.1.11

Forces between magnets

The ends of a freely rotating magnet point towards Earth's north and south poles.

The end pointing north is the **north-seeking (N) pole**; the other end is the **south-seeking (S) pole**.

Opposite poles (N–S or S–N) **attract** and like poles (N-N or S-S) **repel**.

Uses of magnets

Type of magnet	Permanent	Electromagnet
Always **magnetised**?	yes	no, only magnetised when an electric current passes through it
Uses	devices such as motors, loudspeakers and microphones	scrap metal yards and recycling centres use them to pick up and then drop magnetic materials

Magnetic and non-magnetic materials

A **magnetic material** can be magnetised inside a **magnetic field**. This is called **induced magnetism**.

Some magnetic materials (such as steel, neodymium, ferrite ceramic or alcino) become permanent magnets.

Others (such as soft iron) become **temporary magnets**. They are only magnetised in a magnetic field. They are always attracted to other magnets.

Non-magnetic materials cannot be magnetised.

> ### Key Point
>
> Temporary magnets always attract. Permanent magnets can attract or repel.

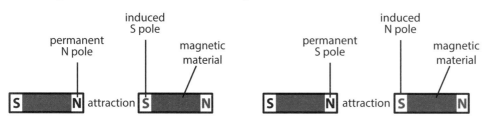

Magnetic fields

A magnetic field is a region where a magnetic pole experiences a force.

A **magnetic field line** shows the direction that the force acts on a north-seeking pole.

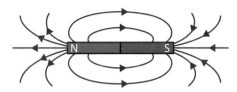

> **Key Point**
>
> Magnetic field lines always start on a N pole and end on a S pole.

> **Practical skills**

Show the shape of the field by using these two methods.

Iron filings	Compass
• Place some paper on top of the magnet. • Sprinkle iron filings over the paper and gently tap the paper.	• Place the magnet on some paper. • Place a compass near the magnet's N pole and draw dots at each end of the arrow. • Move the compass so the arrow's tail lines up with where the head was and draw a new dot at the arrow's head. • Repeat until you reach the S pole and join the dots.

S Interaction of magnetic fields

The strength of a magnetic field is shown by how close the field lines are together.

When two or more magnetic fields interact, they exert a force on each other.

> **Quick Test**
>
> 1. State one advantage of an electromagnet over a bar magnet.
> 2. What is the difference between a temporary and a permanent magnet?
> 3. Explain how a compass can show the direction of a magnetic field.
> S 4. Explain where the magnetic field is the strongest for a bar magnet.

Electric charge

Syllabus links:
4.2.1.1–4.2.1.6;
S 4.2.1.7–4.2.1.10

Learning aims:

- Know when charged objects attract and repel each other.
- Describe experiments to show charging by friction.
- Explain the difference between conductors and insulators.
- **S** Describe electric field patterns around some simple charged objects.

Forces between charges

There are two types of charge: **positive** (+) and **negative** (−).

Opposite charges (+ − or − +) attract. Like charges (− − or + +) repel.

> **S** Charge is measured in **coulombs, C**.

> **Key Point**
>
> Remember that magnets have a N or S pole; they do not have a + or − pole.

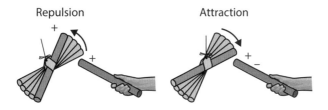

Repulsion   Attraction

Charging by friction

When you rub two solids together, electrons (which are negatively charged) can move from one solid to the other.

An object that gains electrons becomes negatively charged. A positively charged object has lost electrons.

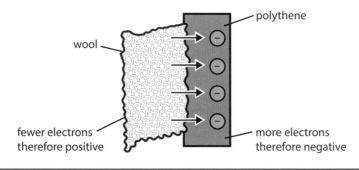

polythene

wool

fewer electrons
therefore positive

more electrons
therefore negative

> **Key Point**
>
> When you charge a solid by friction, only the negative charge (electrons) moves.

> **Practical skills**
>
> To investigate charging by friction by rubbing different rods with a cloth:
>
> - suspend one rod so it can rotate and bring another rod close to it
> - if they repel they are charged the same; if they attract they are charged oppositely.

Conductors and insulators

Charge moves freely inside an electrical **conductor**. Metals such as copper are good electrical conductors because electrons move freely inside them.

Charge cannot move easily inside an **insulator** such as plastic. Plastic is used to surround electrical devices to stop electric shocks.

Test a material by placing it in an electric circuit. The lamp lights if it is a conductor because a current can flow.

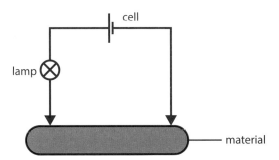

S Electric fields

An **electric field** is a region where a charge feels a force. Field lines show the direction the force would act on a positive charge.

Negative point charge

Positive point charge

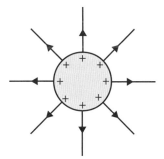
Positively charged sphere

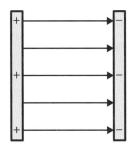
Two oppositely charged plates

> **Quick Test**

1. A polythene rod is rubbed with a cloth and the cloth becomes positively charged. Explain what has happened to the electrons.
2. Why are metals good electrical conductors?
S 3. Explain the difference between the electric fields of a negative point charge and a positive point charge.

Current, potential difference and electromagnetic force

Syllabus links:
4.2.2.1–4.2.2.4;
S 4.2.2.5–4.2.2.6;
S 4.2.3.1–4.2.3.5;
S 4.2.3.6–4.2.3.7

Learning aims:

- What electric current is and how to measure it.

- Describe the difference between d.c. and a.c.

- Define potential difference (p.d.) and electromagnetic force (e.m.f.) and know how to measure them.

- S Recall and use the equations for current, p.d. and e.m.f.

Electric current

An electric **current** is a flow of charge.

Current is measured in **amperes** (A) using an **ammeter** connected in series.

Ammeters are **analogue** (a pointer on a scale) or **digital**. Select the correct range so that the current lies within it.

In **direct current (d.c.)** charge always moves the same way; in **alternating current (a.c.)** it changes direction.

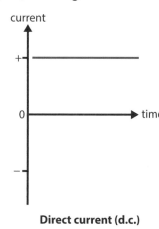

Direct current (d.c.)   Alternating current (a.c.)

S Electrons flow around a circuit from the negative to the positive terminal of a power supply (source). However, we say that **conventional current** goes the opposite way.

> **Key Point**
>
> Conventional current goes around a circuit in the opposite direction to the electrons.

S Calculating the current

Current (I) is charge (Q) passing per unit time (t).

$$\text{current} = \frac{\text{charge}}{\text{time}} \qquad I = \frac{Q}{t}$$

Current (I) is measured in amperes (A), charge (Q) in coulombs (C) and time (t) in seconds (s).

Electromotive force and potential difference

Charge does work when it moves through a component (such as a lamp).

The **potential difference (p.d.)** across a component is the work done by a unit charge moving through.

Electromotive force (e.m.f.) is the work a source does moving a unit charge around a complete circuit.

E.m.f. and p.d. are measured using a **voltmeter** connected in parallel to the component (p.d.) or source (e.m.f).

Voltmeters are analogue or digital and you need to select the correct range. P.d. and e.m.f. are in **volts (V)** and they are often called 'voltage'.

> **Key Point**
>
> An electromotive force is measured in volts (not Newtons).

S Calculating the p.d. and the e.m.f.

Use the following equations to calculate the p.d. and the e.m.f.

$$\text{p.d.} = \frac{\text{work done}}{\text{charge}} \qquad V = \frac{W}{Q}$$

$$\text{e.m.f.} = \frac{\text{work done}}{\text{charge}} \qquad E = \frac{W}{Q}$$

P.d. (V) and e.m.f. (E) are measured in volts (V), work done (W) in joules (J) and charge (Q) in coulombs (C).

A 12 V battery drives a current of 2 A around a circuit for 120 s. How much work does it do?

Charge, $Q = It = 2 \times 120$ C

Work, $W = EQ = 12 \times 120 = 1440$ J

> **Quick Test**
>
> 1. How does a current flow in metal wires?
> 2. What is the difference between d.c. and a.c.?
> 3. A battery with an e.m.f. of 12 V pushes charge through two non-identical lamps around a circuit. If the p.d. across one lamp is 8 V, what is the p.d. across the other one?
> S 4. The p.d. across a motor is 2 V. How much work is done when a current of 2.5 A flows through it for 1 minute?

Resistance, electrical energy and electrical power

Syllabus links:
4.2.4.1–4.2.4.3;
S 4.2.4.4–4.2.4.5;
S 4.2.5.1–4.2.5.4

Learning aims:

- Describe how a wire's resistance depends on length and cross-sectional area.
- **S** Recall and explain current–voltage graphs of resistors, filament lamps and diodes.
- Know and use the resistance, energy and electrical power equations.

Determining resistance

A component's **resistance** (R) is a measure of how hard it is for charge to flow through it.

$$\text{resistance} = \frac{\text{potential difference}}{\text{current}} \qquad R = \frac{V}{I}$$

Resistance (R) is measured in **ohms** (Ω), p.d. (V) in volts (V) and current (I) in amperes (A).

Resistance, length and cross-sectional area

> **Practical skills**

Use this circuit and the equation to investigate the resistance of a metallic wire. The **variable resistor** sets the current.

....

- The longer the wire, the larger the resistance.
- The larger the cross-sectional area, the smaller the resistance.

S Resistance is proportional to length and inversely proportional to cross-sectional area.

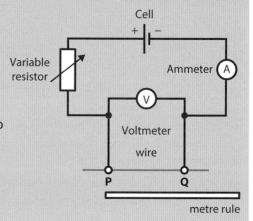

S Current–voltage graphs

- **Resistor:** straight line – resistance stays the same.
- **Filament lamp:** curve – resistance increases for larger currents. It gets hot so it is harder for electrons to move through (since its ionic lattice vibrates more).
- **Diode:** the diode only conducts in one direction (above 0.7 V).

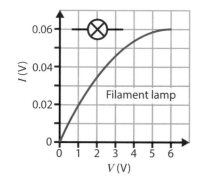

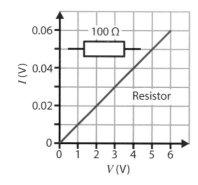

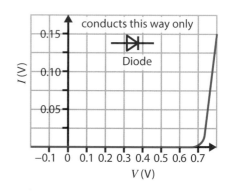

Energy, power and the kilowatt-hour

Energy transfers from the source to the components and then to the surroundings.

Electrical power is energy transferred (by **electrical working**) per unit time.

Electrical power = current × voltage (e.m.f. or p.d.) $P = IV$

Electrical power (P) is measured in watts (W), current (I) in amperes (A) and voltage (V) in volts (V).

> **Example 1**   A 12 V source powers a current of 3 A. Calculate the work done per unit time.
>
> ....
>
> $P = IV = 3 \times 12 = 36$ W

Since energy transferred = power × time:

electrical working = current × voltage × time $E = IVt$

Electrical working (E) is measured in joules (J), current (I) in amperes (A), voltage (V) in volts (V) and time (t) in seconds (s).

The cost of mains electricity depends on the energy transferred. It uses a more convenient unit than joules – the **kilowatt–hour (kWh)** .

energy in kilowatt-hours = power in kW × time in hours

> **Key Point**
>
> Remember to convert power from W to kW when calculating kWh.

> **Quick Test**
>
> 1. A current of 0.20 A flows through a 50 Ω resistor. What is the p.d.?
> **S** 2. A wire has a resistance of 20 Ω. Calculate its resistance if it has four times the cross-sectional area (but the same length).
> 3. Explain why the current–voltage graph for a filament lamp curves.
> 4. 1 kWh costs 25 cents. Calculate the cost of powering five 100 W lightbulbs for 16 hours.

Electrical symbols and series circuits

Syllabus links:
4.3.1.1;
S **4.3.1.2; 4.3.2.1–**
4.3.2.4;

Learning aims:

- Draw standard electrical symbols and describe the behaviour of the components.
- Calculate the combined e.m.f. of sources in series.
- State that current is the same everywhere in a series circuit.
- Calculate the combined resistance of resistors in series.

Electric symbols

You need to recognise and draw these symbols that are used in electric circuit diagrams.

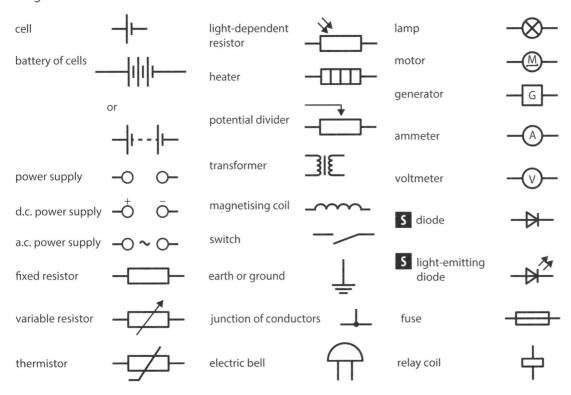

- A **thermistor** is a device whose resistance decreases when the temperature increases.
- A **light dependent resistor (LDR)** is a device whose resistance decreases when the intensity of light shining on it increases.
- A **relay** is an electromagnetic switch. It is often used for remotely switching on a circuit with a large and dangerous current, by switching a circuit with a small and safe current.
- A magnetising coil is an electromagnet.
- **S** A diode only conducts in one direction (current can only flow in the direction of the arrow). It is often used to convert a.c. to d.c.
- **S** A **light-emitting diode (LED)** is a diode that produces light. Light is only produced when the diode is conducting.
- Potential dividers and transformers are explained later in this section.

> **Key Point**
>
> When drawing circuits, use the standard symbols and join them together with straight lines.

Series circuits

A **series circuit** is an electric circuit where all the sources and components are connected in a single loop.

If sources of e.m.f. are connected in series in the same direction, their e.m.f.s add together. If they are connected oppositely, their e.m.f.s subtract.

The current in a series circuit is the same everywhere.

To calculate the total resistance of the components in a series circuit, you add them together.

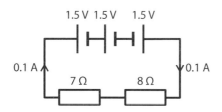

> **Key Point**
>
> Current does not decrease as you go around a series circuit – it is the same everywhere.

In this series circuit the total e.m.f. = 1.5 V + 1.5 V − 1.5 V = 1.5 V

The total resistance = 7 Ω + 8 Ω = 15 Ω

The current $I = \dfrac{V}{R} = \dfrac{1.5}{15} = 0.1$ A

> **Quick Test**
>
> 1. Draw the symbols for a thermistor and an LDR. Describe how you would make their resistance as large as possible.
> S 2. A light emitting diode is connected in series to an a.c. supply. Explain what you will see if the supply alternates at a low frequency.
> 3. A 5 V d.c. supply is connected in series to a 2 V a.c. supply. Calculate the maximum and minimum e.m.f. produced in total by these supplies.
> 4. A series circuit consists of a source, a 20 Ω resistor and a lamp. The overall resistance is 100 Ω. What is the resistance of the lamp?

Parallel circuits

Learning aims:

- Explain the advantage of connecting lamps in parallel.
- Describe how the current changes around a parallel circuit.
- Understand how adding a parallel resistor changes the total resistance.
- **S** Use the rules for p.d. in a parallel circuit.

Syllabus links:
4.3.2.5–4.3.2.7;
S **4.3.2.8(a);**
S **4.3.2.8(c);**
S **4.3.2.9–4.3.2.10**

Connecting lamps in parallel

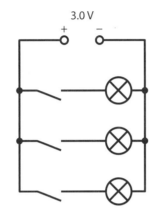

3.0 V

This is a **parallel circuit**. The black circles are **junctions** where connecting wires join. A **branch** is a section between the junctions.

Each lamp lights if the switch next to it is closed.

> **Key Point**
>
> Components in parallel can be switched on and off separately from each other.

Current in a parallel circuit

The current from the source equals the sum of the branch currents.

- The current from the source is larger than the current in any branch.
- **S** The sum of the currents entering a junction = the sum of the currents leaving.

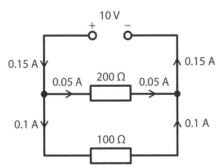

10 V

Resistance in a parallel circuit

Adding a resistor in parallel decreases the overall resistance.

S Calculate the overall resistance using the equation:

$$\frac{1}{R_T} = \frac{1}{R_1} + \frac{1}{R_2}$$

R_T is the overall resistance in ohms (Ω); R_1 and R_2 are the resistances of the two resistors in parallel.

Example 1 Calculate the combined resistance of a 20 Ω and a 60 Ω in parallel.

Sequence	Calculation
Write the equation.	$\dfrac{1}{R_T} = \dfrac{1}{R_1} + \dfrac{1}{R_2}$
Substitute the values.	$\dfrac{1}{R_T} = \dfrac{1}{20} + \dfrac{1}{60}$
Calculate the right-hand side of the equation.	$\dfrac{1}{R_T} = \dfrac{1}{15}$
Re-arrange to find R.	$R = 15 \ \Omega$

> **Key Point**
>
> The overall resistance is smaller than the smallest resistance of each branch. The current from the source is larger than any current through a branch.

[S] Potential difference in a parallel circuit

The p.d. across each branch is the same as the p.d. across the whole combination.

Example 2 Calculate the currents at the ammeters.

The p.d. across the combination = 12 V.

Therefore the p.d. across the 40 Ω resistor = 12 V.

$I = \dfrac{V}{R} = \dfrac{12}{40} = 0.3 \ A$ (ammeter A_1)

p.d. across the 60 Ω resistor = 12 V.

$I = \dfrac{V}{R} = \dfrac{12}{60} = 0.2 \ A$ (ammeter A_2)

Sum of currents entering a junction = sum of current leaving, so A_3 reads $0.3 \ A + 0.2 \ A = 0.5 \ A$.

> **Quick Test**
>
> 1. Why are household lights connected in parallel?
> 2. A 1 Ω and a 1000 Ω resistor are connected in parallel. Is their total resistance less than 1 Ω or greater than 1000 Ω?
>
> [S] 3. An 80 Ω and 120 Ω resistor are connected in parallel to a 12 V power supply. Calculate:
>   a) the overall resistance
>   b) the current through each resistor
>   c) the current flowing into the power supply.

Potential dividers and electrical safety

Learning aims:

- **S** Explain the use of a potential divider.
- State common hazards of mains electricity and how to use it safely.
- Select the correct rating for a fuse or a trip switch.

Syllabus links:

S 4.3.2.8(b) ; 4.3.3.1;

S 4.3.3.2–4.3.3.3 ;

4.4.1–4.4.5

S Potential divider circuits

A **potential divider** is a circuit with components in series. The total p.d. is divided up between them.

For two resistances:

$$\frac{V_1}{R_1} = \frac{V_2}{R_2}$$

where V_1 is the p.d. across resistance R_1 and V_2 is the p.d. across resistance R_2.

Example 1

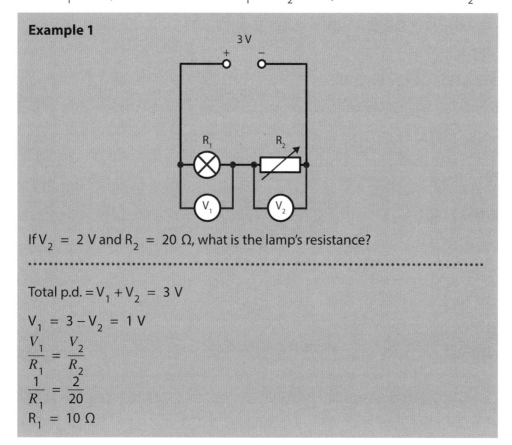

If $V_2 = 2$ V and $R_2 = 20\ \Omega$, what is the lamp's resistance?

Total p.d. $= V_1 + V_2 = 3$ V

$V_1 = 3 - V_2 = 1$ V

$$\frac{V_1}{R_1} = \frac{V_2}{R_2}$$

$$\frac{1}{R_1} = \frac{2}{20}$$

$$R_1 = 10\ \Omega$$

Hazards of mains electricity and ways to prevent them

Hazard	How to prevent
fire (heating effect of currents)	Don't overload the current by plugging multiple devices into the same socket.
	Uncoil extension leads so they don't overheat.
electric shock	Use **insulation** and Earth wires.
	Check insulation undamaged.
	Check objects are dry.

Wires in a mains circuit

Switches, **fuses** and **trip switches** are connected to the live wire. This ensures the high p.d. is disconnected when switched off.

Fuses, trip switches and earth wires

If the current becomes too large, a fuse's wire melts and breaks the circuit.

Trip switches behave in the same way but you can reset them.

Example 2

For a supply of 220 V which fuse is best for a 500 W appliance: 1 A, 3 A or 13 A?

....

Operating current: $I = \dfrac{P}{V} = \dfrac{500}{220} = 2.3$ A

So, a 3 A fuse is best. (A 13 A fuse would work but would let an unsafe current through.)

Devices with non-metal cases are **double insulated**. Two layers of insulation are between live wires and the outside.

Other appliances need an earth wire connected to the metal case. If the case becomes live, a large current flows through the earth wire and the fuse melts, making the appliance safe.

> **Quick Test**

 1. A 1200 Ω resistor, a 400 Ω resistor and a source are in series. The p.d. across the 400 Ω resistor is 4 V. What is the source's e.m.f.?
> 2. Which fuse is best for a 1000 W, 110 V drill: 1A, 3A or 13A?
> 3. Explain how an earth wire keeps metal appliances safe.

Electromagnetic induction and the a.c. generator

Syllabus links:
4.5.1.1–4.5.1.3;
S 4.5.1.4–4.5.1.5;
S 4.5.2.1–4.5.2.2

Learning aims:

- Know how an e.m.f. is induced and what factors affect its magnitude.
- **S** Determine the direction of the e.m.f.
- **S** Describe a simple a.c. generator and explain its e.m.f.–time graph.

Inducing an e.m.f.

Electromagnetic (EM) induction is when an e.m.f. is generated in a conductor due to the interaction between the conductor and a magnetic field.

The conductor acts as a source of e.m.f. and can drive a current around a circuit.

> **Key Point**
>
> An e.m.f. is generated when a conductor cuts through magnetic field lines, or the magnetic field changes.

> **Practical skills**

To demonstrate EM induction:

- connect a wire to a sensitive ammeter
- move the wire through a horseshoe magnet at right angles to the field.

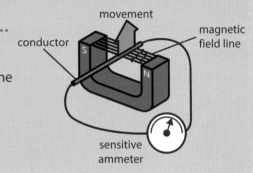

Increase the e.m.f. by:

- increasing the speed of movement
- using a stronger magnet
- wrapping the wire into a coil around one arm of the magnet and increasing the number of turns.

S The direction of the e.m.f.

When an e.m.f. is generated it produces an electromagnetic effect that opposes its production. For example, there will be a magnetic force opposing the motion of the wire.

To determine the direction of the e.m.f., use Fleming's right-hand rule. Position your right hand as shown. The second finger points in the direction of the e.m.f.

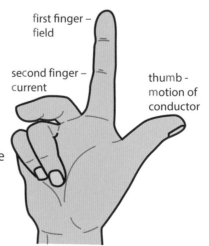

> **Key Point**
>
> The thumb shows the direction the conductor is moving in relative to the magnetic field.

S The a.c. generator

An **a.c. generator** produces an alternating e.m.f. by EM induction. Make one by rotating a coil in a magnetic field. Alternatively, rotate a magnet near a stationary coil of wire.

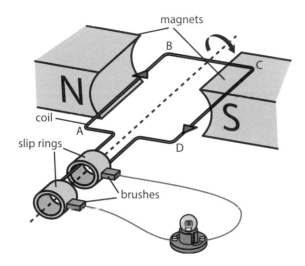

ABCD in the diagram is a coil. The slip rings turn with the coil but the brushes are stationary. This allows electrical contact without the wires getting tangled. You could turn the coil by using a handle.

S E.m.f.–time graph for the a.c. generator

A graph of e.m.f. against time shows peaks and troughs as the e.m.f. changes direction.

Maximum e.m.f. occurs when the coil is horizontal as it cuts the field lines quickest at this point. E.m.f. is zero when the coil is vertical – there is no cutting at this point.

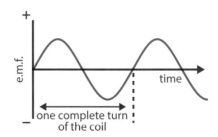

Quick Test

1. A magnet moves towards a conductor.
   a) Explain why an e.m.f. is induced.
   b) State two ways of increasing the e.m.f.

S 2. A horseshoe magnet moves to the right towards a stationary conductor. Which way would you point your thumb for Fleming's right-hand rule?

S 3. Explain why e.m.f. generated by a rotating coil is alternating.

S 4. State two differences in the e.m.f.–time graph if the coil rotates faster.

Magnetic effect of a current

Syllabus links:
4.5.3.1–4.5.3.3;
S 4.5.3.4–4.5.3.5

Learning aims:

- Describe the magnetic fields around a current-carrying wire and solenoid.

- **S** Describe how the strength of these fields varies and what happens when the current changes direction.

- Explain how magnetic effects are used in relays and loudspeakers.

Current-carrying wires

Electromagnets work because an electric current produces a magnetic field.

The magnetic field produced by a straight wire carrying a current is a set of circles. The circles all go the same way, and this depends on the direction of the current.

> **S** The magnetic field's strength decreases the further it is from the wire – shown by the field lines getting further apart.
>
> The diagram shows how you can use your right hand to determine the direction of the field.

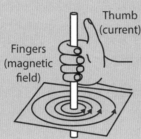

Thumb (current)

Fingers (magnetic field)

Solenoids

A **solenoid** is a long coil. When a current passes through it, its magnetic field is like that of a bar magnet. However, the field also passes through the middle where it is strong and uniform. Use plotting compasses and iron filings to investigate the shape and direction of the field.

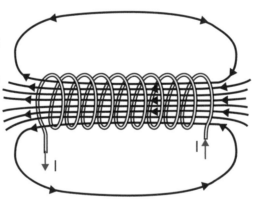

> **Key Point**
>
> Plotting compasses show the direction of the field as well as its shape.

> **S** The strength and direction of the field depends on the size and direction of the current.

The field is much stronger inside the solenoid than outside – shown by the field lines being very close together.

To determine the field's direction:

- curl the fingers of your right hand in the direction the current goes around the solenoid

- your thumb points in the direction of the field lines through the middle.

> **Key Point**
>
> The thumb and fingers mean opposite things for the straight wire and the solenoid.

Relays

An electromagnet is a solenoid with soft iron inside. A current through the solenoid produces a magnetic field, which makes the iron become a temporary magnet. If you turn the current off, the iron immediately de-magnetises.

A relay is an electromagnet plus a switch. The switch closes when the electromagnet is on and opens when it is off.

Relays are often used to operate switches carrying dangerous currents by using switches carrying safe currents.

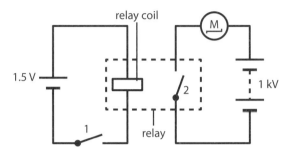

Close switch 1 and switch 2 automatically closes, operating the 1 kV motor.

Loudspeakers

Loudspeakers use the magnetic field of a current to produce sound waves. An alternating current through the coil produces an alternating magnetic field. This interacts with the magnet's magnetic field to produce an alternating force on the cone. The cone vibrates causing sound waves.

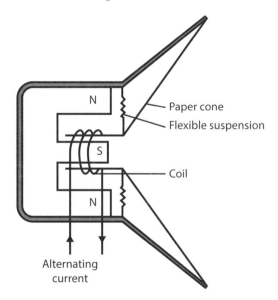

> **Quick Test**
>
> 1. **a)** What is the shape of the magnetic field around a current-carrying wire?
>   **b)** What happens when the current changes direction?
> **S 2.** What direction would the magnetic field lines go for a current coming straight out of the page?
> **S 3.** Give two differences between the magnetic field inside and outside a solenoid carrying a current.
> 4. What is a relay?
> 5. Why doesn't a loudspeaker work if the current is d.c.?

Force on a current-carrying conductor and the d.c. motor

Syllabus links:
4.5.4.1;
S 4.5.4.2–4.5.4.3;
4.5.5.1;
S 4.5.5.2

Learning aims:

* Describe an experiment to show a magnetic force on a current-carrying conductor.
* **S** Determine the direction of the magnetic force.
* Know how to build a basic electric motor and how to make it go faster.
* **S** Explain how the motor keeps rotating in the same direction.

Investigating the force on a current-carrying conductor

> **Practical skills**

To investigate the magnetic force on a current-carrying conductor set up the apparatus shown in the diagram.

The direction of the force is reversed if:

* the current is reversed
* the field direction is reversed (by turning the magnet round).

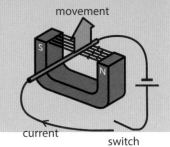

S Fleming's left-hand rule

Use Fleming's left-hand rule to determine the direction of the magnetic force.

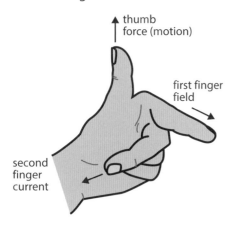

> **Key Point**
>
> In electromagnetic induction, a movement of the conductor generates a current. Here, a current through the conductor produces movement.

Beams of charged particles

A beam of charged particles also feels a force in a magnetic field. Moving charge is the same as a current. Remember, the second finger needs to point in the direction of conventional current. If the particles are negatively charged, this is in the opposite direction to their motion.

> **Key Point**
>
> Conventional current is in the same direction of motion for positive particles but opposite for negative particles.

The d.c. motor

Place a coil of wire inside a magnetic field and magnetic forces can cause it to turn. This is a motor. Make the motor spin faster by increasing:

- the current
- the number of turns in the coil
- the strength of the field.

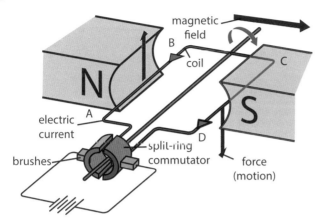

> **S** Fleming's left-hand rule shows that the force on side AB will be up, and the force on CD will be down. The coil turns clockwise.
>
> The brushes and **split-ring commutator** ensure the coil keeps spinning the same way.
> - The stationary brushes provide electrical contact.
> - The commutator rotates with the coil and scrapes past the brushes.
> - 90° later, the coil is vertical and the gaps between the split rings are level with the brushes. The coil loses electrical contact but keeps spinning under its own momentum.
> - As the coil turns further, each side of the commutator contacts with the other brush.
> - This ensures the force on the side of the coil nearest the N pole is always upwards.

> **Quick Test**
>
> 1. Describe one difference between an experiment that shows the force on a current-carrying conductor and one that shows electromagnetic induction.
> 2. State three things that make a motor turn faster and two things that make it spin in the opposite direction.
> **S** 3. A beam of electrons moves to the left through a magnetic field directed into the page. What direction is the magnetic force on the beam?
> **S** 4. Explain why a motor will not spin if its coil is connected directly to a power supply rather than via brushes and a split-ring commutator.

Transformers

Learning aims:

Syllabus links:
4.5.6.1–4.5.6.5;
S 4.5.6.6–4.5.6.8

- Describe the components of step-up and step-down transformers.

- Use the equations for transformers.

- Explain why transformers are used in the transmission of electrical power.

Step-up and step-down transformers

A **transformer** uses electromagnetism to change voltages.

A **step-up** transformer changes voltages from low to high and a **step-down** transformer from high to low.

It consists of two coils of wire wrapped around an iron core.

The **primary** coil is at the input side; the **secondary** coil is at the output.

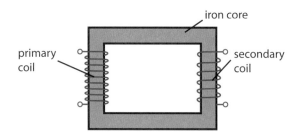

Transformer equations

Use this equation to calculate how the voltage changes:

$$\frac{V_P}{V_S} = \frac{N_P}{N_S}$$

V_P and V_S are the voltages across the primary (P) and secondary (S) coils. N_P and N_S are the number of turns in the coils.

> **Key Point**
>
> $\dfrac{N_P}{N_S}$ is also called the turns ratio of the transformer.

Example 1 A transformer changes a voltage from 240 V to 12 V. N_p = 500. Calculate N_s.

Sequence	Calculation
Substitute values in the equation.	$\dfrac{240}{12} = \dfrac{500}{N_S}$
Simplify and rearrange.	$20 = \dfrac{500}{N_S}$ $N_S = \dfrac{500}{20}$
Calculate the answer.	$N_S = 25$

S A transformer works using a combination of electromagnetism and EM induction.

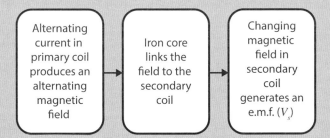

Transformers also change the current. For a 100% efficient transformer, power out = power in. Therefore (since $P = IV$)

$$I_p V_p = I_s V_s$$

The higher the voltage, the lower the current.

Transmitting electrical power

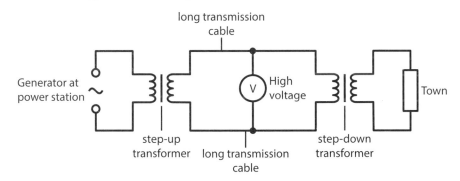

Transformers are used in electrical transmission systems.

This is more efficient – the cables heat up less and less power is wasted. However, it uses high voltages, which can be dangerous.

- A step-up transformer increases the voltage and a lower current flows along transmission cables.
- A step-down transformer reduces the voltage to safe levels.

S To calculate the power loss in a cable use:

$$P = I^2 R$$

P is the power loss in watts (W), I is the current in amperes (A) and R is the cable's resistance in ohms (Ω).

> **Key Point**
>
> Transmitting power at high voltage means that the current is low, which doesn't heat the cables as much.

> **Key Point**
>
> You normally can't use $P = IV$ as you won't know V, which is the voltage across the length of the cable

> **Quick Test**

1. Explain the difference between a step-up and step-down transformer.
2. A primary coil has 100 turns. How many turns does a secondary coil need to increase a voltage from 20 V to 1000 V?
3. State one advantage and one disadvantage of transmitting electrical power at high voltages.
 S 4. A voltage is increased from 240 V to 132 000 V. By what factor is the power loss in the cables reduced?

Magnetism

1 Which of these materials can be used to make a permanent magnet?

   A. copper   **C.** steel

   B. soft iron   **D.** sulfur   [1]

2 The diagram shows a magnet and a circle showing the location of a compass.

Draw an arrow in the circle to show the direction the compass points.

[1]

3 The diagram shows two iron nails hanging from the N pole of an electromagnet. The flat ends of the nails are repelling each other.

a The iron nails were unmagnetised before the electromagnet was switched on.

Explain why they don't fall down to the ground.   [2]

> **Show me**

The iron nails become .... magnets. This means they are .... to the electromagnet.

Make sure you use the key terms correctly in your explanations. These are given in **red and bold** in each topic.

b Explain why the flat ends of the nails repel each other.   [2]

c In another experiment, the electromagnet was connected so that its south pole was at the bottom. Again, two iron nails were hung from the bottom. Explain what happens to the nails this time.   [2]

[Total marks 6]

4 The diagram shows a picture of two magnetic fields.

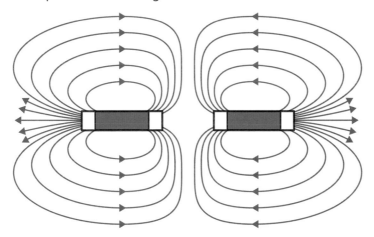

a Explain whether the magnets are attracting or repelling. [3]

S **b** On the diagram, show two regions where the magnetic fields are the strongest. [2]

S **c** Describe why magnets attract or repel each other. Use ideas about magnetic fields in your answer. [2]

[Total marks 7]

Electric charge

1 A polythene rod has a negative charge. Which one of these objects will repel the rod?

A. A magnetic north-seeking pole

B. A magnetic south-seeking pole

C. A negatively charged piece of amber

D. A positively charged acetate rod. [1]

2 A cloth rubs an acetate rod and the rod becomes positively charged. Which row of the table is correct?

A.	Cloth is neutral	Protons move from the cloth to the rod
B.	Cloth is negatively charged	Electrons move from the cloth to the rod
C.	Cloth is positively charged	Protons move from the rod to the cloth
D.	Cloth is negatively charged	Electrons move from the rod to the cloth

[1]

3 An electron is in an electric field. It experiences a force to the right.

Draw an arrow on the diagram to show the direction of the electric field. [1]

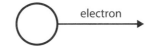

electron

4 Two uncharged conducting spheres (A and B) stand on insulating bases and touch each other. A negatively charged polythene rod is brought close to sphere B as shown.

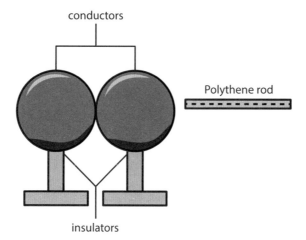

a Explain the difference between conductors and insulators [2]

b A and B are separated while the polythene rod is held in position. The rod is then taken away from the experiment. For each sphere, explain whether it is left positively or negatively charged or if it is uncharged. [4]

[Total marks 6]

Current, potential difference and electromagnetic force

1 Explain what the terms a.c. and d.c. mean and the difference between them. [3]

2 The diagram shows an ammeter display reading a constant current.

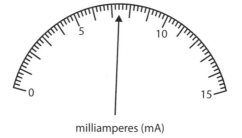

milliamperes (mA)

a What type of ammeter is this? [1]

b State the size of the current to 1 decimal place. [1]

c The range of the ammeter was changed to 0–1 mA. Explain what would happen to the display if it was trying to measure the same current as before. [2]

[Total marks 4]

3 A circuit was set up consisting of a cell, a lamp and a resistor as shown.

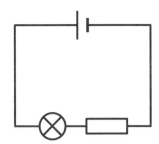

The cell does 2 J of work pushing a unit charge around the circuit. The unit charge does 1.5 J of work when it passes through the resistor.

a Draw a voltmeter on the circuit to measure the p.d. across the resistor. [2]

b What value is the p.d. across the resistor? [1]

c What is the e.m.f. of the source? [1]

d Calculate the p.d. across the lamp. [1]

[**Total marks 5**]

4 A 2 kV source pushes a current of 100 mA through a component for 10 minutes.

a Charge is measured in C. What word does 'C' stand for? [1]

b Calculate the charge that passes through the component in 10 minutes. [4]

c Calculate the total work done by the source. [3]

> Remember that a 'k (kilo)' in front of a unit means '1000' and an 'm (milli)' means '1/1000'.
> 1 kV = 1000 V, 1 mA = 1/1000 = 0.001 A

[**Total marks 8**]

Resistance, electrical energy and electrical power

1 Which circuit could you use to measure the resistance of the resistor?

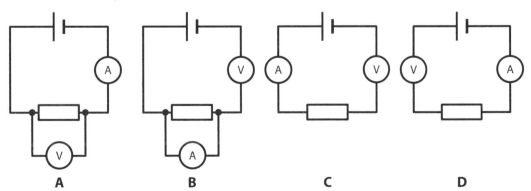

[1]

2 A lamp is connected in series with a resistor and a 1.5 V cell. The p.d. across the lamp is 0.90 V and the current through the lamp is 0.12 A.

a Calculate the lamp's resistance. [2]

b What is the power of the lamp? Give your answer to 2 decimal places. [2]

c How much electrical work does the cell do in 20 seconds? [2]

[Total marks 6]

3 **a** Define the kilowatt-hour. [2]

b A 2500 W washing machine operates for 210 minutes. Calculate how much the electrical energy costs. Cost of 1 kWh = $0.60. [4]

> Make sure you convert the power and the time to the correct units.

[Total marks 6]

S **4** A student plots a current–voltage graph for an unknown component.

a Explain why the student needs to include a variable resistor in their circuit. [2]

b Here is a table of the student's results:

Voltage/V	−2.0	−1.0	0.0	1.0	2.0
Current/A	0.0	0.0	0.0	0.5	2.8

Explain what component the student is measuring. [2]

In another experiment, the student finds that the resistance of a filament lamp increases as the current increases.

c Explain why a filament lamp behaves in this way. [3]

[Total marks 7]

Electrical symbols and series circuits

1 Four identical 1.5 V cells are connected in series. However, one cell is connected the wrong way round.

What is the combined e.m.f. of these cells?

A. 0 V

B. 1.5 V

C. 3.0 V

D. 4.5 V [1]

2 A simple hairdryer circuit consists of an a.c. power supply, a heater, a motor and a switch connected in series. Draw a circuit diagram for this circuit, including the correct symbols. [5]

3 In this circuit the p.d. across the 80 Ω resistor is 3.0 V.

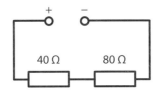

a What is the total resistance in the circuit? [1]

b Calculate the current passing through the 80 Ω resistor. [2]

c Calculate the p.d. across the 40 Ω resistor. [3]

[Total marks 6]

Parallel circuits

1 Three lamps, each of resistance 40 Ω, are connected in parallel in a circuit.

a State one advantage of connecting lamps in parallel rather than in series. [1]

b A student thinks that the total resistance of the circuit is 120 Ω. Explain whether the student is correct. [2]

[Total marks 3]

2

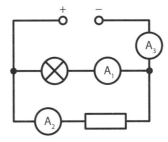

In this circuit, A_1 reads 2.5 A and A_2 reads 1.5 A.

a What does A_3 read? Explain your answer. [2]

b Another lamp is connected in parallel. Explain whether the readings on ammeters A_1, A_2 and A_3 increase, decrease or stay the same. [5]

[Total marks 7]

3 A circuit is set up using a 12 V source and three resistors as shown.

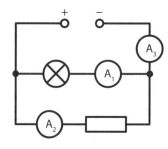

a Calculate the total resistance in the circuit. [3]

> **Show me**

The 40 Ω and 60 Ω resistors are in parallel. Let their combined resistance = R.

$$\frac{1}{R_T} = \frac{1}{R_1} + \frac{1}{R_2} = \frac{1}{40} + \frac{1}{60} = \text{......................}$$

Therefore, R = ... Ω

R is in series with the 16 Ω resistor.

So, the total resistance = ... + ... = ... Ω

b Which two resistors have the same p.d. across them? [1]

c Calculate the current through the 16 Ω resistor. [2]

[Total marks 6]

Potential dividers and electrical safety

1 Explain why it is dangerous to plug lots of devices into the same plug socket. [3]

2 **a** Explain how a fuse works and how it acts as a safety device. [4]

b A 13 A fuse is used in a plug for a lamp. The lamp has a power of 20 W and the voltage is 220 V.

Explain why the 13 A fuse could be dangerous and what should be done
to make the lamp safer. [3]

c Which wire should switches be placed in: the live, neutral or earth wire? Explain your answer. [2]

d The lamp is double insulated. Explain what this means and why it doesn't need an earth wire. [3]

[Total marks 12]

S **3** Two 50 Ω resistors are connected in series to a 12 V power supply. Use the potential divider
equation to show that the p.d. across each resistor is 6 V. [4]

4 **a** If the length of a metallic wire doubles, what happens to its resistance? [1]

A circuit is set up as shown. Points **A** and **B** are halfway and three quarters of the way down the wire respectively.

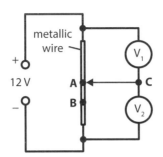

The middle of the voltmeters V_1 and V_2 (labelled **C**) is connected to the metallic wire at point **A** using a crocodile clip.

b Explain why the resistance of the metallic wire above point **A** is the same as the resistance below it. [1]

c The crocodile clip is moved so that the middle of the voltmeters (**C**) is connected to point **B**.

Explain why $V_1 = 9\,V$ and $V_2 = 3\,V$. [4]

d Where would you connect the crocodile clip so that $V_2 = 9\,V$? [1]

[Total marks 7]

Electromagnetic induction and the a.c. generator

1 A metallic wire is in a magnetic field. State **two** ways in which you can induce an e.m.f. in the wire. [2]

2 The N pole of a magnet is moved towards a coil. The ends of the coil are connected to a light emitting diode (**LED**) to complete an electric circuit.

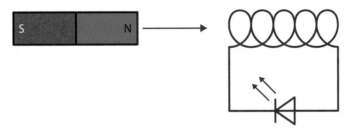

a Explain why the LED lights when the magnet is moved towards the coil. [2]

b When an induced current is flowing, the coil acts as an electromagnet. Explain whether the side closest to the magnet would be the N or S pole. [3]

c Explain what happens to the LED when the magnet is pulled back to the left. [3]

[Total marks 10]

3 A magnet is rotated near a coil of wire.

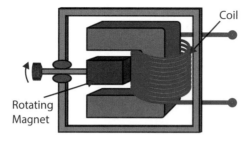

a Sketch a graph to show how the induced e.m.f. varies with time. [2]

The coil was replaced with a new one that had more turns and the magnet was rotated in exactly the same way as before.

b On the same set of axes used in (a), sketch and label a new graph to show how the e.m.f. varies with time for the new coil. [2]

[Total marks 4]

Magnetic effect of a current

1 Which device uses electromagnetism to control a switch automatically?

A. loudspeaker C. relay

B. motor D. thermistor [1]

2 a Describe an experiment using iron filings to determine the pattern of a magnetic field around a straight wire that is carrying a current. [3]

b How would you determine the direction of the field? [2]

[Total marks 5]

3 a Sketch a diagram to show the shape and strength of a magnetic field around a wire. Assume that the wire carries a current directly into the page. [3]

b State **two** ways in which your diagram would change if the current was larger and it flowed in the opposite direction. [3]

[Total marks 6]

Force on a current-carrying conductor and the d.c. motor

1

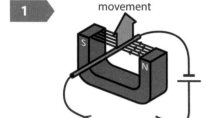

When the switch is closed, the conductor moves up.

Explain what direction the conductor moves if the cell is connected the other way round **and** the magnetic field is reversed. [2]

2 What happens if you place a coil, carrying a current, in a magnetic field?

    A. It does nothing.   **C.** It moves sideways.

    B. It expands.   **D.** It turns.   [1]

3 A beam of positive ions and a beam of negative ions are fired into a magnetic field.

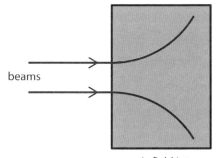

beams

magnetic field into page

a Explain why the beams deviate in opposite directions when they enter the field.   [2]

b Explain which beam deviates downwards: the negative ions or the positive ions? Explain how you arrived at your answer.   [4]

[Total marks 6]

Transformers

1 **a** A transformer for a phone charger needs to change the voltage from 220 V to 18 V. The primary coil has 990 turns. Calculate how many turns the secondary coil must have.   [3]

b What else is needed (other than the coils) to make a transformer?   [1]

[Total marks 4]

2 A cable is delivering electrical power to a factory.

a The resistance of the cable is 100 Ω. Calculate the power loss when a current of 100 A passes through it. Give your answer in MW.   [3]

b After the losses, the cable delivers 0.25 MW of power to the factory. What is the efficiency of this system?   [3]

Engineers install transformers, which reduce the current in the cable to 10 A. The cable delivers 0.25 MW of power to the factory as before.

c Calculate the efficiency of this new system. Give your answer as a percentage to the nearest whole number.   [2]

d Explain one disadvantage of using this method.   [2]

[Total marks 10]

The nuclear model of the atom

Learning aims:

- Describe atomic structure.
- Know how ions are formed.
- Describe nuclear structure and state the charges of nucleons.
- Use $^A_Z X$ notation to describe isotopes and nuclear reactions.

Syllabus links:

5.1.1.1–2; **S** 5.1.1.3 ;
5.1.2.1–5;

S 5.1.2.6–8

The atom

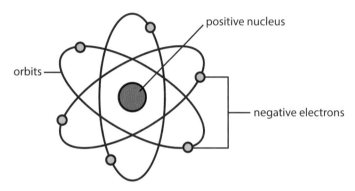

The nuclear model of the atom consists of a tiny positively charged **nucleus**, containing positively charged **protons** (relative charge +1) and neutral **neutrons** (relative charge 0)), surrounded by orbiting, negatively charged **electrons** (relative charge -1).

In a neutral atom there are the same number of protons and electrons. The outermost orbiting electrons of metal atoms can be removed, leaving more protons than electrons, forming a positive **ion**. Non-metal atoms gain electrons, giving more electrons than protons, forming negative ions.

> **Key Point**
>
> Ions are formed by the addition or removal of electrons.

S Alpha (α) particle scattering – evidence supporting the nuclear model

When atoms are bombarded by **α particles** most of the α particles travel straight through the atoms, but a small number are scattered by the nucleus in all directions. This tells us that the nucleus:

- is very small, surrounded by empty space
- contains most of the mass of the atom
- is positively charged.

The nucleus

Each nucleus is defined by the **proton number** (Z) or atomic number. The number of protons plus the number of neutrons in a nucleus is called the **nucleon number** (A) or mass number.

> **S** The proton number, Z, also defines the relative charge of the nucleus. Lithium nuclei have 3 protons, so their relative charge is +3.
>
> The nucleon number, A, defines the relative mass of the nucleus. Protons and neutrons have a relative mass of 1. Lithium-7 has 3 protons and 4 neutrons, making its relative mass 7.

Nuclei with the same number of protons but different numbers of neutrons are called **isotopes.** The $^A_Z X$ **notation** describes the structure of nuclei.

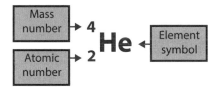

The value $(A–Z)$ = neutron number. Isotopes can also be written with a hyphen, e.g. helium-3 and helium-4.

S Nuclear fission and fusion

Nuclear fission is the splitting up of a large nucleus when it is hit by a neutron. This also releases energy. A typical fission reaction occurring inside a reactor is:

$$^{235}_{92}U + ^1_0 n \longrightarrow ^{137}_{56}Ba + ^{97}_{36}Kr + 2 ^1_0 n$$

The total mass of the products is lower than the total mass of the reactants. This mass difference is converted into energy, which can be converted into electricity by a nuclear power station.

Nuclear fusion is the joining of light nuclei to form heavier nuclei. This process powers the Sun and the mass difference is converted into energy, emitted as light. A typical solar fusion reaction is:

$$^2_1 H + ^2_1 H \longrightarrow ^3_2 He + ^1_0 n$$

Nuclear fusion releases substantially more energy than nuclear fission.

Nuclear equations balance – the total nucleon number (A) on the left-hand side equals the total nucleon number on the right-hand side. The proton numbers (Z) also balance.

> **Quick Test**

1. Beryllium-9 has an atomic number of 4. Calculate the number of neutrons in a beryllium-9 nucleus.
2. Write the $^A_Z X$ notation of a carbon nucleus containing 6 protons and 7 neutrons.
3. What is the charge of a calcium atom that has lost two electrons?
 S 4. Why does the alpha-scattering experiment show that most of an atom is empty space?

Radioactivity and nuclear emissions

Learning aims:

- Know the mechanisms of radioactive decay.
- Describe the processes of radioactive decay **S** using $_Z^A X$ notation equations.
- Describe the properties of alpha (α), beta (β) and gamma (γ) emissions.

Radioactive decay

Radioactive decay is the spontaneous and random change in an unstable nucleus resulting in the emission of α- or β-particles and/or γ-radiation. During radioactive decay, the unstable nucleus changes into a different element.

> **Key Point**
>
> The −1 proton number in the $_Z^A X$ notation of a β-particle is used to show that it is an electron.

S Radioactive decay equations

Isotopes of an element undergo radioactive decay if they have an excess of neutrons in the nucleus and/or the nucleus is too heavy. Following decay, the resulting nucleus is more stable and has fewer neutrons.

Decay	Mechanism	Example decay equation
alpha (α)	The unstable nucleus emits two protons and two neutrons joined together (a helium nucleus). The nucleon number drops by 4 and the proton number drops by 2.	$_{88}^{226}\text{Ra} \longrightarrow {_{86}^{222}}\text{Rn} + {_2^4}\alpha$
beta (β)	One neutron in the unstable nucleus decays into a proton and an emitted electron (the β-particle). neutron → proton + electron The nucleon number remains unchanged but the proton number increases by 1.	$_6^{14}\text{C} \longrightarrow {_7^{14}}\text{N} + {_{-1}^0}\beta$
gamma (γ)	The unstable nucleus rearranges itself and the excess energy is emitted as a γ-ray. The nucleon and proton numbers remain the same.	$_{43}^{99}\text{Tc*} \longrightarrow {_{43}^{99}}\text{Tc} + \gamma$

The properties of nuclear emissions

Radioactive emission is spontaneous and is emitted in random directions. All three types of nuclear radiation are examples of **ionising radiation**, causing damage to living tissue. The relative ionising effects of the three types of radiation are shown in the table on page 109. The level of ionisation of the radiation depends on its:

- **kinetic energy** – the higher the kinetic energy, the greater the ionisation
- electric charge – greater charge causes more ionisation.

> **Key Point**
>
> An asterisk (*) is used to show an unstable nucleus before the emission of gamma rays.

Radiation	Nature	Relative charge	Relative ionising effect	Relative penetrating ability	Range in air
alpha (α)	helium nucleus 2 protons and 2 neutrons	+2	high	stopped by skin or paper	about 5 cm
beta (β)	electron	−1	low	stopped by 3 cm of aluminium	about 1 m
gamma (γ)	short wavelength electromagnetic waves	0	very low	stopped by lead or concrete	unlimited

Radiation	Deflected in electric and magnetic fields?	Charges attracted to
alpha (α)	yes	negative
beta (β)	yes	positive
gamma (γ)	no	neither

The diagram shows the deflection of these particles in a magnetic field (into the plane of the paper).

> **Key Point**
>
> Exam-style questions often ask you to **compare** the properties of the three types of radioactive emission. This means that you have to identify, or comment on, similarities and/or differences between them.

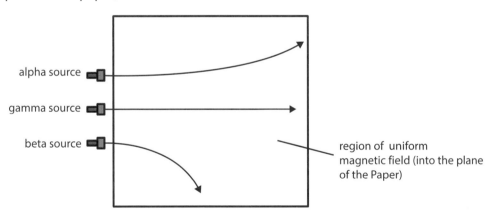

alpha source

gamma source

beta source

region of uniform magnetic field (into the plane of the Paper)

> **Quick Test**
>
> 1. What is radioactive decay?
> 2. Which forms of nuclear emission are absorbed by 3 mm of aluminium?
> **S** 3. Americium-241, $^{241}_{95}$Am, is radioactive and emits α-particles forming an isotope of neptunium, Np. Am-241 is used in smoke detectors. Write the decay equation for this radioactive decay.

Detection of radioactivity and safety

Learning aims:

Syllabus links:
5.2.1.1–4; 5.2.5.1–2;
S 5.2.1.5; 5.2.5.3

- Explain the term 'background radiation' and describe the main sources.

- Explain how radiation can be measured; describe the units; **S** and correct count-rates for background radiation.

- Describe the effects of ionising radiation on living things, and how radioactive materials are stored and handled in a safe way.

- **S** Explain the safety precautions that are needed to avoid radioactive contamination.

Background radiation

Background radiation is the radiation all around us, all the time. Background radiation varies depending on location. There are four main natural sources coming from the environment:

- **radon** gas (in the air)
- rocks and buildings (e.g. from granite)
- food and drink (radiation absorbed from the environment)
- cosmic rays (coming from space).

Other sources of background radiation include:

- medical radiation
- radiation from nuclear power
- radiation from nuclear weapons testing.

The pie chart shows the relative amounts of background radiation from different sources.

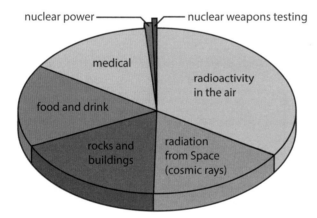

Measuring radiation

Radiation is commonly detected using a device called a Geiger–Müller (G–M) tube. The tube is connected to an electronic counter.

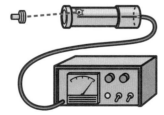

The counter measures the number of detected radioactive particles (the count) per second or per minute – called the **count-rate** (in counts/sec or counts/min).

S Corrected count-rate

As background radiation is all around us, you need to 'correct' any measurements from radioactivity experiments for the local background count-rate. Before a radioactive experiment, measure and record a series of local count-rates without the experiment source. Calculate a mean background count-rate. Do the experiment and:

corrected count-rate = measured count-rate − mean background count-rate

Safety precautions

Ionising radiation can harm living cells. Among other effects, radiation can:

- mutate cells
- kill cells
- cause cancers.

To prevent these effects humans must reduce their exposure to ionising radiation. Radioactive sources must be moved, used and stored in safe ways. Simple steps can be taken to prevent contamination such as:

- only handle radioactive sources using a tool, such as forceps
- avoid pointing radioactive sources at living tissue
- always store radioactive sources inside locked, lead-lined containers
- monitor working areas for radiation levels above local background levels.

> S The amount of radiation energy that living tissue is exposed to is called the **radiation dose**. The dose received by any living tissue can be minimised by:
>
> - avoiding contamination
> - reducing exposure time
> - increasing the distance between the source and the living tissue
> - using shielding (such as lead or concrete).

> **Key Point**
>
> In the exam, you would be told if the count-rate data is corrected or uncorrected. If you need to correct data, you will be given a background figure or be asked to calculate a mean value from given background readings.

> **Quick Test**
>
> 1. What is background radiation?
> 2. List three sources of naturally occurring background radiation.
> 3. Why is ionising radiation dangerous to living tissue?
> S 4. What is the corrected count-rate of a radioactivity experiment?
> S 5. Why would reducing the exposure time to a radioactive source reduce the radiation dose received by living tissue?

Half-life

Learning aims:

Syllabus links:

5.2.4.1; **S** 5.2.4.2–3

- Be able to define and recall the definition of half-life.
- **S** Use data or decay curves to calculate half-life.
- **S** Explain how half-life is used to determine the suitability of isotopes for use in a range of applications.

Defining half-life

The **half-life** of a radioactive sample is the time taken for half the number of nuclei to decay. The diagram shows how the count-rate of a radioactive sample changes with time.

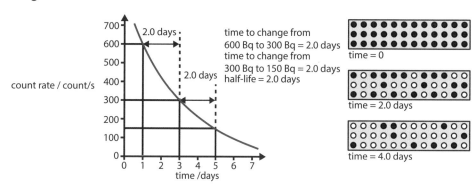

- After 1 day, the count rate is 600 counts/s.
- It takes 2.0 days for this to halve to 300 counts/s.
- During this time, half the number of nuclei have decayed.
- It takes a further half-life, 2.0 days, for the count rate to halve again to 150 counts/s.

> **Key Point**
>
> In any exam question containing a background radiation count-rate measurements, you will be expected to determine corrected count-rates of all given count-rate values.

S Sometimes the background count-rate needs to be subtracted from the measured count-rate. This is called corrected count-rate.

If the measured background count-rate of a laboratory is 8 counts/minute, and a sample has a count-rate of 85 counts/minute, then the corrected count-rate will be (85 − 8) counts/minute = 77 counts/minute.

If a sample has a corrected count rate of 240 counts/minute and 60 minutes later the count rate is 30 counts/min, the half-life can be calculated using a table such as this.

Time	Count rate (counts/minute)
0	240
1 half-life	120
2 half-lives	60
3 half-lives	30

> **Key Point**
>
> Half-life questions typically involve analysing graphical decay curves or data presented in a table. You could be asked to calculate a half-life from a given count rate or a count rate from a given half-life.

Three half-lives is 60 minutes, so one half-life is $\frac{60}{3} = 20$ s.

S Applications of radioactive decay

The main considerations when choosing a suitable radioactive isotope for an application are:

- the relative ionising effects
- penetration of the emitted radiation
- the half-life of the isotope.

Type of radiation	Main applications
alpha (α)	• household fire (smoke) alarms
beta (β)	• measuring and controlling the thicknesses of sheet materials, such as paper, plastics and aluminium
gamma (γ)	• kill bacteria by irradiating food • sterilise equipment (particularly surgical instruments) • diagnosis and treatment of cancer

> **Key Point**
>
> Remember, when answering questions involving the usefulness of a particular source for an application, you should consider all three main properties: half-life; penetration; and the relative ionising effects.

> **Quick Test**
>
> 1. What is the meant by the half-life of a radioactive isotope?
> 2. Look at the decay curve of the sample shown in the graph. The half-life is 2.0 days. What will be the count-rate on day 7 (three half-lives after a count-rate of 600 counts/s on day 1)?
> S 3. Suggest a reason why a beta-emitting source is used to measure and control the thickness of sheet paper produced by a paper-making machine.
> S 4. A radiation source has a count-rate of 160 counts/s. 90 minutes later its count-rate is 40 counts/s. What is the half-life of the source?

The nuclear model of the atom

1 The Earth's atmosphere contains 78% nitrogen (atomic number 7) and 21% oxygen-16 ($^{16}_{8}O$).
Nitrogen has two stable isotopes: nitrogen-14 and nitrogen-15.

a State what is meant by the term isotope. [1]

'State' means express in clear terms.

b State the number of protons in the nucleus of nitrogen-14. [1]

c Copy and complete the table below, comparing the structure of an atom of nitrogen-14 to an atom of oxygen-16.

Atom	Number of protons	Number of neutrons	Number of electrons
Nitrogen-14			
Oxygen-16			

[3]

For 3 marks, there will be one mark per correct column.

S **d** Nitrogen-14 is involved in the fusion reactions of large stars. During this process nitrogen-14 nuclei fuse with protons ($^{1}_{1}H$), forming an isotope of oxygen and emitting a gamma ray (γ). Complete the nuclear equation summarising this reaction.

$$^{\square}_{7}N^{+} + {}^{1}_{1}H \rightarrow {}^{\square}_{\square}O + \gamma$$

[3]
[Total marks 8]

S **2** During alpha (α) particle scattering, most of the α-particles travel straight through the atoms of a target nucleus. A tiny number of α-particles are scattered away from the atoms, and an even smaller number are scattered through very high angles, effectively travelling straight back to the source of α-particles.

Which of these statements is **not** a conclusion of these observations?

A. Atoms have a nucleus.

B. Most of the mass of an atom is contained within the nucleus.

C. The nucleus contains protons and neutrons.

D. The nucleus is positively charged. [1]

If you are not certain about a multiple-choice answer, work by elimination. In this case, eliminate the statements you know to be correct.

Radioactivity and nuclear emissions

1 A student is monitoring the count-rate emitted by a radioactive source. The detector is placed close to the source with a 5 mm gap between them. The count rates with different absorbers in the gap are shown in the table (all adjusted for background).

Absorber in gap	Count rate of detector (cpm)
air	340
paper	120
aluminium	0
lead	0

Which forms of radioactive emission are being emitted by the source?

A. α, β and γ

B. α only

C. α and β

D. β only   [1]

2 The table shows some properties of the three types of nuclear radiation.

Type of radiation	Range in air	Relative ionising effect	Relative penetrating ability
alpha particles	5 cm	high	stopped by skin/paper
beta particles	1 m	medium	stopped by 3 mm of aluminium
gamma rays	unlimited	low	stopped by lead or concrete

Use only information from the table to answer the questions.

a State **two** reasons why alpha particles are often used to treat skin cancers.   [2]

b State **one** reason why gamma ray emitting radioactive sources are frequently used to detect cracks and leaks in underground water pipes.   [1]

c A student investigates the types of radiation being emitted from a sample of radioactive granite rock.

The following apparatus is available to the student:

Radiation detector connected to a counter (Geiger counter)

Other apparatus normally available in a school laboratory can also be used.

Plan an experiment to determine the type or types of nuclear radiation being emitted by the rock.

In your plan, you should:

- list any additional apparatus required
- explain briefly how you would carry out the investigation, including the measurements you would take
- state the key variables to be kept constant
- draw a suitable table, with column headings, to show how you would display your readings (you are not required to enter any readings in the table)
- explain how you would use the results to reach a conclusion. [7]

Questions such as 2(c) appear on Paper 5: Practical Test or Paper 6: Alternative to Practical. You are required to plan a practical procedure, but the question will be scaffolded using bullet points. You should concentrate on addressing each bullet point in turn.

> **Show me**

(c) Marking Point 1: The additional apparatus I require is .... and ....

Marking Point 2: I will measure the .... for .... without any absorbers between the sample and the detector.

Marking Point 3: I will place a sheet of paper between the sample and detector and measure and record ....
....

Marking Point 4: I will .... the measurements for the other ....

Marking Point 5: The key variable that I will keep constant is ....

Marking Point 6: My table will look like:

....	.... units ....
None	
Paper	
Aluminium	
Lead	

Marking Point 7: The paper will stop any .... ; the aluminium will stop

and .... ; the lead will stop any ....

[Total marks 10]

S 3 A radioactive nucleus will decay by emitting nuclear radiation and turn into a different (**daughter**) nucleus of another element. The daughter nucleus is frequently radioactive and will also decay. Some radioactive nuclei are involved with long decay chains, with each subsequent daughter nucleus decaying by the emission of radiation.

Part of one decay chain is shown:

$$^{222}_{86}Rn \longrightarrow ^{4}_{2}\alpha + ^{218}_{84}Po$$

Polonium-218 decays by alpha emission to an isotope of lead (Pb).

The lead isotope decays by beta emission to an isotope of bismuth (Bi).

The bismuth isotope decays by alpha emission to an isotope of thallium (Tl).

Write decay equations for each of these decays. [6]

Detection of radioactivity and safety

1 Background radiation varies with location. The contribution of natural sources of background radiation at two locations is shown.

Source of background radiation	Percentage composition of total background radiation (%)	
	Location A	Location B
radon gas (in the air)	81	50
rocks and buildings	X	14
food and drink	4	11
cosmic rays (from space)	3	10
other radiation sources	5	Y

a Calculate the values of X and Y from the table. [2]

b Explain why new houses at Location A have to have to be built with a radon sump – a device that pumps air out from underneath the floorboards of the house. [2]

[Total marks 4]

2 Which of these outcomes is **not** a possible effect of ionising radiation on living tissue?

A. cancer   **C.** cell division

B. cell death   **D.** cell mutation [1]

3 A student uses a Geiger–Müller (G–M) tube and counter to measure the background radiation count-rate before a radioactivity experiment. They record the count from the G–M tube for 5 minutes and then repeats this twice so they have three readings in total. Their measurements are shown.

Measurement	Count in 5 minutes
1	1811
2	1802
3	1787

a **i)** Calculate the mean count in 5 minutes. [1]

> **Show me**
>
> The total count for all three measurements is ....
>
> $\dfrac{\text{Total count}}{3} =$ ....

ii) Calculate the mean count-rate, in counts/s. [1]

> **Show me**

Total number of seconds in 5 minutes = ...

Mean count-rate $= \dfrac{\text{mean count in minutes}}{\text{number of seconds in 5 minutes}} = $ .... counts/s

b During the experiment the student removes a radioactive source from a lead-lined box using a pair of tongs. She then mounts the source in a holder, pointing away from her. Explain why this technique will make the student safer during this experiment. [3]

Questions such as 3(b) appear on Paper 5: Practical Test or Paper 6: Alternative to Practical. You may be asked to identify risks and suggest/analyse appropriate safety precautions for a practical procedure.

[**Total marks 5**]

S 4 A student makes the following measurements of the background radiation count-rate in a laboratory before investigating how the count-rate of gamma rays varies with distance away from a gamma ray source. These are their measurements.

Measurement	1	2	3	4	5
Background count-rate (counts/min)	27	30	32	24	27

a Calculate the mean background count-rate, in counts/min. [1]

The apparatus for the experiment is shown.

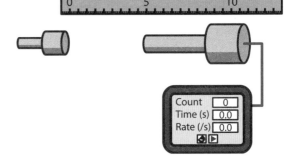

The student's measurements are shown.

Distance from source (cm)	1	3	5	7	9
Count-rate (counts/min)	1044	334	134	118	70

b Use your answer to (a) to calculate the corrected count-rate at each distance. [1]

c i) Plot a graph of corrected count-rate (*y*-axis) against distance (*x*-axis). [4]

ii) Draw a suitable best-fit curve. [1]

iii) Describe the pattern shown in the graph. [2]

Questions such as 4(c) appear on Paper 5: Practical Test or Paper 6: Alternative to Practical. You are required to plot a graph of a set of practical or given data on a blank grid. You should ensure that you:
- write the correct label on each axis, with the correct unit
- have a scale that covers over half of the plottable area
- plot the points accurately
- draw a smooth best-fit line.

[**Total marks 9**]

Half-life

1 The graph shows how the count rate of a sample of polonium-201 changes with time.

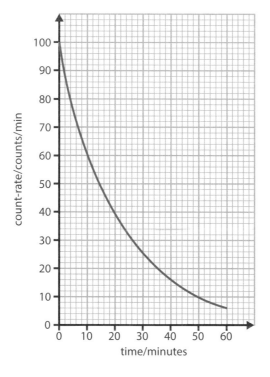

a **i)** Use the graph to determine the half-life of polonium-201. [1]

The half-life of a radioactive source is the time taken for the number of nuclei OR the count-rate to halve.

ii) The count-rate after 60 minutes is 6 counts/minute. Estimate the count rate after 75 minutes. [1]

S **b** Polonium-210, another isotope of polonium, has been used as a power source in satellites. It has a half-life of 138 days. Initially the corrected count-rate of one Po-210 power source was 6400 counts/s. Calculate the time for the corrected count rate to drop to 200 counts/s. [2]

[Total marks 3]

2 Iodine-131 is used to treat thyroid cancer. One sample has an initial corrected count-rate of 880 counts/minute. 24 days later, the count rate is 110 counts per minute. What is the half-life of iodine-131?

A. 24 days **B.** 16 days **C.** 8 days **D.** 4 days [1]

[Total marks 1]

3 The diagram shows a radioactive source acting as a tracer to find a leak in a pipe.

The isotope sodium-24 (Na-24) is often used as a source for leak testing. $^{24}_{11}$Na is a beta emitter.

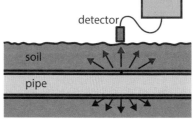

a Complete the decay equation for Na-24.

$$^{24}_{11}\text{Na} \longrightarrow {}^{\square}_{12}\text{Mg} + {}^{\square}_{\square}\beta$$

[2]

b A water engineer uses a radiation detector/counter to determine the site of a leak in a pipe. The engineer first takes a series of measurements to determine the local background count. The measurements are shown in the table.

Measurement number	1	2	3	4	5	Mean
Count-rate (counts/s)	8	9	8	7	9	

i)   Calculate the mean background count-rate. Give your answer to 1 significant figure.   [1]

The water engineer monitors the count-rate of a sample of sodium-24 for 60 hours. The measurements are shown in the table.

Time (hours)	0	10	20	30	40	50	60
Uncorrected count-rate (counts/s)	328	210	135	88	58	40	28
Corrected count-rate (count/s)							

ii)   Using your answer to **(b) (i)**, calculate the corrected count-rate values.   [1]

> **Show me**

Corrected count-rate = uncorrected count-rate – mean background count-rate (from (b) (ii))

iii)   Plot your corrected count-rate values on a grid similar to this and draw a suitable best-fit curve.

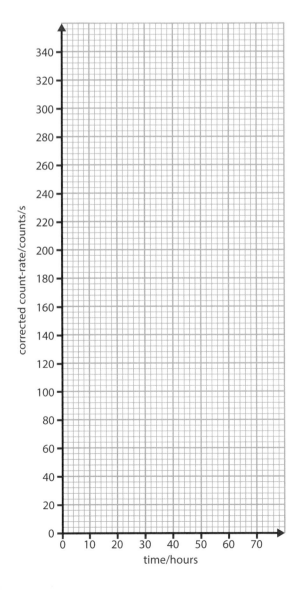

[3]

iv) Use the graph to determine the half-life of Na-24, in hours. Give your answer to 2 significant figures. [1]

c The water engineer has three radioisotopes to choose from when performing the leak test.

Isotope	Radiation emitted	Half-life	Penetration	Relative ionisation effect
Copper-66	beta	307 s	stopped by 3 mm of aluminium sheet	medium
Radon-211	alpha	14.6 hours	stopped by a sheet of paper	high
Cobalt-60	gamma	5.3 years	will travel through several cm of lead	low

Using only information from the table and the diagram, suggest a reason why each of these isotopes should **not** be chosen for this application. [3]

'Suggest' means that, in order to make proposals or put forward considerations, you need to apply your knowledge and understanding to a situation where there is a range of valid responses. In this case you need to consider the properties of each of the three given isotopes and relate them to the diagram, showing the radiation leaking into the soil surrounding the leak site.

[Total marks 11]

Earth and the Solar System

Syllabus links:
6.1.1.1–3; 6.1.2.1–2

Learning aims:

- Explain how the relative motion of the Earth, Moon and Sun leads to day/night, months and seasons.
- Describe the structure of the Solar System.
- Describe the formation of the Solar System.

The motion of the Earth and the Moon

The motion of the Earth and Moon around the Sun leads to yearly changes, day/night, months and the **seasons**. It explains the apparent motion of the Sun and the Moon, as seen from Earth.

The Earth:

- **orbits** the Sun at a distance of 150×10^6 km, once every 365 days (1 year).
- rotates on its axis every 24 hours – leading to day and night.
- rotates on its axis at an angle of 23° to the plane of the Solar System – leading to seasons.

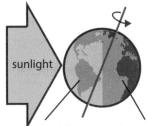

the Earth spins around its axis every 24 hours

sunlight

this side of the Earth is facing towards the Sun – it is day here

this side of the Earth is facing away from the Sun – it is night here

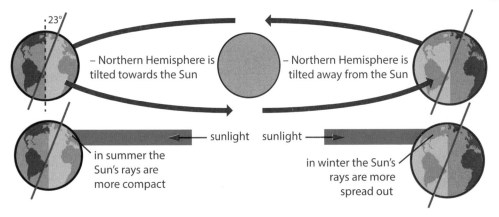

23°

– Northern Hemisphere is tilted towards the Sun

– Northern Hemisphere is tilted away from the Sun

in summer the Sun's rays are more compact

sunlight   sunlight

in winter the Sun's rays are more spread out

The Moon:

- orbits the Earth at a distance of 384 400 km once every 27 days – leading to the Moon's **phases** (observed from Earth).
- rotates on its axis once every 27 days, so we always see the same side of the Moon.

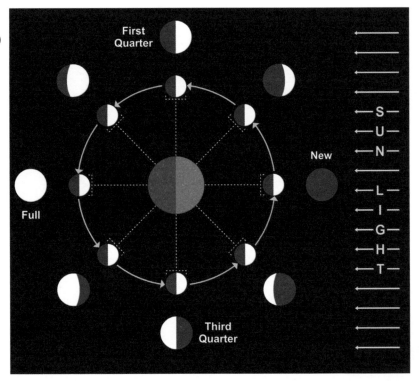

First Quarter

New

Full

Third Quarter

S
U
N

L
I
G
H
T

The Solar System

The **Solar System** contains:

(a) one **star**, the Sun

(b) eight **planets**, orbiting the Sun, in order away from the Sun: Mercury, Venus, Earth, Mars, Jupiter, Saturn, Uranus and Neptune

(c) nine **minor planets** (objects that are neither planets nor comets, orbiting the Sun): Pluto, Haumea, Ceres, Makemake, Sedna, Eris, Gonggong, Quaoar and Orcus; and the **asteroids** in the asteroid belt

(d) **moons** (natural **satellites**) that orbit the planets/dwarf planets

(e) smaller Solar System bodies, such as **comets**

> **Key Point**
>
> You need to memorise the order of the planets away from the Sun. You could use a mnemonic: **M**y **V**ery **E**ducated **M**um **J**ust **S**erved **U**s **N**achos.

Formation of the Solar System

- The Solar System formed from an **interstellar** gas and dust cloud, containing many elements, 4.6 billion years ago.

- Rotation and gravity caused the gas and dust cloud to collapse forming the Sun and an **accretion disc**.

- Gravity caused material within the accretion disc to clump together and this formed into the Solar System objects.

- The Sun's gravity is strongest closest to the Sun, and the temperature is highest, causing the first four inner planets to become small and rocky, and most of the gases to be blown off.

- The outer planets are large and gaseous as the Sun's gravity is weaker, and the temperature is lower.

> **Key Point**
>
> Satellites can be natural (moons) or artificial (e.g. communications satellites).

> **Quick Test**
>
> 1. In terms of the motion of the Earth, what is the difference between a year and a day?
> 2. Why do we have 12 full moons per year?
> 3. What is the difference between a moon and a comet?
> 4. Name the four planets closest to the Sun and explain why they are small and rocky.

Orbits and using planetary data

Learning aims:

Syllabus links:

6.1.2.3–6; S 6.1.1.4; 6.1.2.7–10

- Describe how gravity causes objects to move inside the Solar System.

- S Describe and calculate orbital motion within the Solar System.

- S Analyse and interpret planetary data.

Gravitational fields

Massive objects (e.g. the Sun) have large gravitational fields. Gravity keeps the planets in orbit because the Sun contains most of the mass of the Solar System.

A planet's gravitational field strength:

- at the surface, depends on the planet's mass or **density**

- decreases as the distance from the planet increases.

The Earth's gravitational field holds us to its surface and keeps satellites in orbit.

S Orbital motion

- Some objects (e.g. Venus) have nearly circular orbits around the Sun.

- The Sun's gravitational attraction, and rotational movement, cause most objects to have elliptical orbits, with the Sun at one focus.

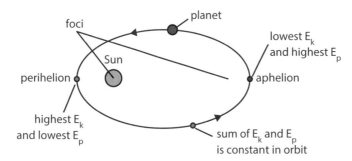

- Planets in an elliptical orbit travel faster when closer to the Sun. The total energy of a planet is the sum of its **kinetic energy** (E_k) and **gravitational potential energy** (E_p). This remains constant throughout the orbit but kinetic energy and gravitational potential energy interchange.

- The strength of the Sun's gravitational field decreases with distance away, as does planetary orbital speed.

- In a circular orbit the **orbital speed**, v, is:

$$v = \frac{2\pi r}{T}$$

where r is the mean orbital radius and T is the orbital period.

> **Key Point**
>
> You need to be able to recall and use the equation for orbital speed. Practise rearranging the equation to calculate r or T.

S Planetary data

Planet	Mass /10^{24} kg	Mean orbital distance from Sun /10^6 km	Closest distance to Sun /10^6 km	Furthest distance to Sun /10^6 km	Orbital duration or period /Earth days	Mean surface temperature /°C	Density /kg/m^3	Surface gravitational field strength/N/kg
Mercury	0.33	57.9	46.0	69.8	88.0	167	5427	3.7
Venus	4.87	108.2	107.5	108.9	224.7	464	5243	8.9
Earth	5.97	149.6	147.1	152.1	365.2	15	5514	9.8
Mars	0.64	227.9	206.6	249.2	687.0	−65	3933	3.7
Jupiter	1900	778.6	740.5	816.6	4331	−110	1326	23.1
Saturn	570	1433.5	1352.6	1514.5	10747	−140	687	9.0
Uranus	87	2872.5	2741.3	3003.6	30589	−195	1271	8.7
Neptune	100	4495.1	4444.5	4545.7	59800	−200	1638	11.0

Key patterns:

- As the distance away from the Sun increases:
  - orbital duration (or period) increases
  - mean surface temperature decreases (with the exception of Venus).
- The small rocky inner planets are low mass/high density; the outer large, gaseous planets are high mass/low density.

> **Key Point**
>
> Be prepared to analyse data in both tabular and graphical formats.

Distances in the Solar System

These are frequently given in light-seconds or light-minutes (the distance that light travels in one second or one minute).

The mean time taken for light to travel from the Sun to the Earth:

$$\text{time of signal travel} = \frac{\text{mean distance}}{\text{speed of light}} = \frac{149.6 \times 10^6 \text{ km}}{300\,000 \text{ km/s}} = 498.7 \text{ s} = 8.3 \text{ minutes}$$

> **Quick Test**
>
> 1. What does the surface gravitational field strength of the Earth depend on?
> 2. Why do planets orbit the Sun?
> S 3. Why does a planet's orbital speed increase as it gets closer to the Sun?
> S 4. Use the data from the table to calculate the mean orbital speed of Venus in km/h. 1 day = 24 hours.

Stars

Learning aims:

- Describe the Sun as a star.
- Describe the features of galaxies.
- **S** Describe the life cycles of different types of star.

Syllabus links:
6.2.1.1; 6.2.2.1;
6.2.3.1; S 6.2.1.2;
6.2.2.2–3

The Sun as a star

The Sun is:

- a medium sized star
- 73% hydrogen, 25% helium and 2% other elements.

Most of its energy is radiated as infrared, visible light and ultraviolet.

> **S** The Sun, like all stars, is powered by nuclear fusion reactions that release energy, emitted as electromagnetic waves. Like other stable stars, the nuclear reactions involve the fusion of hydrogen into helium.

> **Key Point**
>
> A common misconception is that the Sun only emits light. The Sun emits all parts of the electromagnetic spectrum, but emits very large quantities of infrared, visible light and ultraviolet.

S Stellar life cycles

The life cycle of a star is dictated by its original mass.

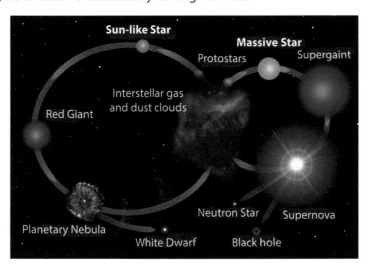

- All stars are 'born' within interstellar gas and dust clouds containing hydrogen.
- **Protostars** form when the temperature of an interstellar cloud increases as it collapses inwards due to internal gravitational attraction.
- When the temperature of the protostar reaches 15 million °C nuclear fusion starts and the star becomes stable – the inward force of gravitational attraction is balanced by the outward force due to the high temperature in the centre of the star.
- All stars eventually run out of hydrogen fuel and start to fuse heavier elements, such as helium, releasing more energy.
- Most stars (including the Sun) expand to form **red giants** and more massive stars expand to form **red supergiants**.
- When a red giant runs out of nuclear fuel it collapses, forming a **planetary nebula** (cloud) with a **white dwarf star** at its centre.

- When a red supergiant runs out of nuclear fuel it explodes as a **supernova**, forming a nebula containing hydrogen and new heavier elements.

- The supernova of a very massive red supergiant can leave behind a **neutron star** or (for the most massive red supergiants) a **black hole** at its centre.

- The remnant nebula from a supernova may form new stars with orbiting planets.

The Sun and galaxies

- Large collections of stars 'close' to each other in space are called **galaxies**.

- Galaxies are made up of many billions of stars.

- The enormous astronomical distances involved with space are measured in **light-years** – the distance travelled by light in (the vacuum of) space in one year.

- **S** One light-year is equal to 9.5×10^{15} m.

- Our galaxy is called the Milky Way, a spiral galaxy with a diameter of 100 000 light-years.

- Galaxies are vast and the other stars that make up the Milky Way are very much further away from the Earth than the Sun is from the Earth.

- The Milky Way is only one of many billions of galaxies that make up the Universe.

> ### Key Point
>
> A common examination question is to compare the end-of-life pathways of low mass, Sun-like stars and high mass stars. 'Compare' questions require you to identify or comment on the similarities and/or differences.

Quick Test

1. The Sun emits electromagnetic radiation in all parts of the electromagnetic spectrum but most of the radiation is emitted in which three parts of the spectrum?
2. What is meant by the term 'galaxy'?
S 3. Which physical factor determines whether the supernova of a red supergiant produces a neutron star or a black hole?
S 4. Our nearest neighbour star, Proxima Centauri, is 4.2 light-years away. How many kilometres is 4.2 light-years?

The Universe

Syllabus links:
6.2.3.2–4;
S 6.2.3.5–11

Learning aims:

- Explain how redshift gives evidence for the expansion of the Universe and supports the Big Bang Theory.
- **S** Link redshift to the speed of recession of a galaxy.
- **S** Describe the Cosmic Microwave Background Radiation (CMBR) as evidence for the Big Bang Theory and the expansion of the Universe.
- **S** Define and use the Hubble Constant, H_0, to determine distances within the Universe and use it to determine the age of the Universe.

Redshift and the Big Bang Theory

The **Big Bang Theory** proposes that the Universe came into being approximately 14 billion years ago, the result of an enormous explosion out of nothing. The Universe started from a single point and has been expanding outwards every since, at an increasing rate.

Light emitted by stars travels towards the Earth through this expanding space and gets stretched as it travels. This means that the wavelength of the light gets longer, towards the red end of the visible spectrum. This is called **redshift**.

The light emitted by all the galaxies in the Universe is redshifted, meaning that they are all moving away from the Earth. This is direct evidence for the Big Bang Theory.

> **S** The speed, v, of a galaxy moving away from Earth can be determined by measuring the change in wavelength of the light emitted by the galaxy, due to redshift.

> **Key Point**
>
> A common misconception is that the Universe is expanding into something else. This is false: the space of the Universe is expanding outwards. There is nothing 'outside' the Universe.

S The Cosmic Microwave Background Radiation (CMBR) and the Big Bang Theory

At the moment of the Big Bang, vast quantities of energy, in the form very short wavelength gamma rays, were emitted in all directions. Since the Big Bang, the space of the Universe has expanded and the gamma rays have redshifted so much that they now have microwave wavelengths. This is the **Cosmic Microwave Background Radiation (CMBR)** and is observed at all points in space, and has a very specific characteristic frequency.

S The Hubble constant, measuring cosmic distances and the age of the Universe

The enormous distances, d, to distant galaxies can be measured independently by measuring the brightness of supernovae within the galaxy. The speed, v, that a galaxy is moving away from Earth can be measured using the redshift of light from the galaxy. Plotting a graph of v against d produces a linear relationship:

$$H_0 = \frac{v}{d}$$

where H_0 is the **Hubble constant**, equal to 2.2×10^{-18} per second.

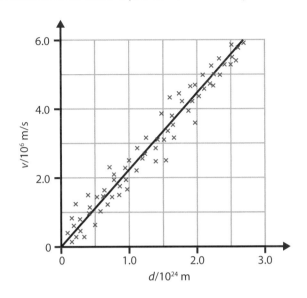

> **Key Point**
>
> The value of the Hubble constant, H^0, changes over time as the accuracy of the measurements of v and d improves.

The age of the Universe, in seconds, can then be estimated by:

$$\frac{1}{H_0} = \frac{d}{v}$$

All this evidence supports the Big Bang Theory for all the mass and energy in the Universe to be present at a single point, approximately 14 billion years ago.

Quick Test

1. What is the Big Bang Theory?
2. Why is the redshift of light evidence for the Big Bang Theory?
S 3. What is the Cosmic Microwave Background Radiation?
S 4. The Black Eye Galaxy, M64, is 17.3×10^6 light-years away from Earth. What is the speed of the galaxy away from Earth in light-years/second?

Earth and the Solar System

1 Which of the following is a large gaseous planet?

   A. Mercury   **C.** Uranus

   B. Mars   **D.** Venus   [1]

2 The diagram shows the apparent path of the Sun across the Earth's sky in the Northern Hemisphere on 21 June and 21 December of each year.

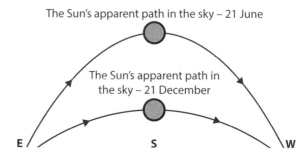

a State the time taken, in days, for the Earth to orbit the Sun once.   [1]

b   **i)** Explain why, at the location shown in the diagram, the Sun appears to travel across the Earth's sky once every day.   [2]

     ii) Explain the difference in the path of the Sun on 21 June compared to 21 December.   [2]

                                                          [Total marks 5]

3 The order of the planets away from the Sun is:

   A. Mercury > Venus > Earth > Jupiter > Mars > Saturn > Neptune > Uranus

   B. Mercury > Venus > Earth > Mars > Jupiter > Saturn > Neptune > Uranus

   C. Mercury > Venus > Earth > Mars > Jupiter > Saturn > Uranus > Neptune

   D. Mercury > Venus > Earth > Uranus > Jupiter > Mars > Saturn > Neptune   [1]

4 The Solar System formed 4.6 billion years ago.

a Number the stages in the formation of the Solar System in time order. The first and last stages have been done for you below.

An accretion disc formed around the Sun.	
An interstellar cloud of gas and dust started to rotate and collapse.	1
Material at the centre of the interstellar cloud collapsed to form the Sun.	
Small rocky planets formed close to the Sun and large gaseous planets formed further away.	
Material inside the accretion disc started to collapse and form planets.	
The present day Solar System.	6

                                                                       [2]

b Explain why small, rocky planets formed close to the Sun but large and gaseous planets formed in the outer Solar System.   [2]

> You need to 'explain why', which means you have to link what happens to the reason. Use words that link one part of each sentence to the next part such as 'because'.

                                                                        [Total marks 4]

Orbits and using planetary data

1 The gravitational field strength of the Sun…

   A. …decreases with distance away from the Sun.

   B. …increases with the mass of each planet.

   C. …increases with distance away from the Sun.

   D. …stays constant with distance away from the Sun. [1]

2 The Mars Odyssey satellite observes the surface of Mars and acts as a communication link between the Mars Curiosity Rover and Earth.

a Name the force that keeps the Mars Odyssey satellite in orbit around Mars. [1]

b State why Mars' gravitational field strength at its surface is less than the Earth's gravitational field strength at its surface. [1]

c The mean distance of Mars from Earth is 225×10^6 million kilometres. Radio signals received and emitted from the Mars Odyssey satellite travel at the speed of light, 300 000 km/s.

   i) Calculate the time taken for a radio signal to be sent from Earth to the Mars Odyssey satellite. Give your answer in seconds.

> **Show me**
>
>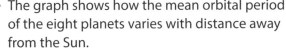
> $$\text{time taken} = \frac{\text{distance travelled}}{\text{speed}} = \frac{\square \text{ km}}{\square \text{ km/s}} = \square \text{ s}$$

   ii) Suggest a reason why it is impossible for an operator on Earth to remotely 'drive' the Mars Curiosity Rover in real time. [1]

   [Total marks 6]

3 The graph shows how the mean orbital period of the eight planets varies with distance away from the Sun.

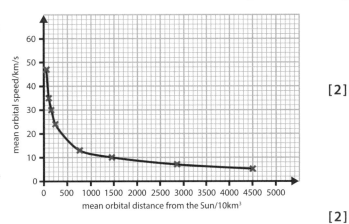

a Describe the pattern in the graph. [2]

b The dwarf planet Ceres is situated within the Asteroid belt, and orbits the Sun in an approximately circular orbit with a mean orbital distance from the Sun of 400×10^6 km.

   i) Use the graph to determine the mean orbital speed of Ceres. Give the unit. [2]

   ii) Use your answer to **(b)(i)** to calculate the mean orbital period of Ceres. Give your answer in days.

   1 day = 86 400 s. [4]

c The table shows the densities of the eight planets.

Planet	Mercury	Venus	Earth	Mars	Jupiter	Saturn	Uranus	Neptune
Density (kg/m³)	5427	5243	5514	3933	1326	687	1271	1638

The dwarf planet Ceres has a density of 2160 kg/m^3.

The four inner 'terrestrial' planets are small rocky planets.

The four outer 'Jovian' planets are large gaseous planets.

Justify the reason why planetary scientists believe that Ceres is a hybrid world consisting of rock and frozen water ice. [3]

'Justify' means that you need to support a case with evidence or argument. In this case you should use the data given to support the planetary scientists' view.

[Total marks 11]

S 4 Halley's comet is in a highly elliptical orbit around the Sun, with a period of 76 years. When it is furthest from the Sun its orbital speed is 0.91 km/s, and when it is closest to the Sun its orbital speed is 54.6 km/s.

Which combination correctly describes the total, kinetic and gravitational potential energies of the comet as it gets closer to the Sun?

	Total energy	Kinetic energy	Gravitational potential energy
A.	constant	increases	decreases
B.	constant	decreases	increases
C.	increases	increases	decreases
D.	decreases	decreases	increases

Stars

1 Which is the correct list showing most of the electromagnetic spectrum energy emitted by the Sun?

A. infrared, visible light and ultraviolet

B. radio, visible light and infrared

C. radio, visible light and microwaves

D. radio, visible light and ultraviolet [1]

2 All the stars that we see in the night sky are inside our own galaxy.

a State what is meant by the term 'galaxy'. [1]

'State' means that you have to express an answer in clear terms. Usually this requires a meaning of a term, or to give a value from some given information.

b Our galaxy is a spiral-disc shape, with a diameter of approximately 100 000 light-years.

i) State the name of our galaxy. [1]

ii) The Sun is approximately half-way between the centre and the outer edge of our galaxy. Calculate the distance, in light-years, between the Sun and the centre of our galaxy. [2]

Show me

Distance from centre to the edge of the galaxy = half the diameter of the galaxy = ...(X)....light-years

Distance from centre to the Sun = $\frac{X}{2}$ = ... light-years

[Total marks 4]

3 Which sequence describes the life-cycle of a star like our own Sun?

A. nebula → protostar → star → red giant → planetary nebula → white dwarf

B. nebula → protostar → star → red giant → supernova → white dwarf

C. nebula → protostar → star → red supergiant → supernova → nebula

D. nebula → protostar → star → red supergiant → supernova → neutron star **[1]**

4 In 2023 the European Space Agency (FSA) Gaia Space Telescope discovered the closest black hole to Earth. Gaia BH1 is 1600 light-years away and was discovered due to the unusual motion of its orbiting star, and it has a mass 10 times that of our Sun.

a Describe the stages in the formation of a black hole such as Gaia BH1 from a massive stable star. **[3]**

b Calculate the distance of Gaia BH1 from Earth in kilometres (km).

$$1 \text{ light-year} = 9.5 \times 10^{15} \text{ m}$$ **[2]**

c The graph shows how the mass of the remnant of the collapse of a red giant or red supergiant varies with the initial mass of the stable star that formed it.

The units are in solar masses (where the mass of the Sun = 1 solar mass = 2×10^{30} kg).

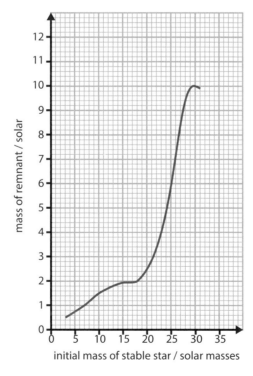

i) Use the graph to determine the initial mass of a star (in solar masses) that produced a black hole remnant with a mass of 10 solar masses. **[1]**

ii) Use your answer to **(c)(i)** to calculate the mass of the stable star that produced Gaia BH1. **[1]**

[Total marks 7]

The Universe

1 Evidence for the Big Bang Theory comes by measuring the redshift of light emitted by distant galaxies.

Which row correctly describes the light emitted by distant galaxies?

	Motion of galaxy	Wavelength
A.	towards Earth	increases
B.	towards Earth	decreases
C.	away from Earth	decreases
D.	away from Earth	increases

[1]

2 The Big Bang Theory proposes that the Universe came into being approximately 14 billion years ago.

a State the origin of the Universe in the Big Bang Theory.

Tick (✓) **one** box.

The Universe has always existed in its present state.	
The Universe started from a single point.	
New parts of the Universe are created between the current galaxies.	

[1]

b State the current evolution of the Universe.

Tick (✓) **one** box.

The Universe is expanding.	
The Universe is not changing.	
The Universe is collapsing.	

[1]

c State the reason why light from distant galaxies is redshifted.

Tick (✓) **one** box.

The light from distant galaxies reduces in energy, which stretches the wavelength of emitted light.	
The Universe is getting cooler, which stretches the wavelength of light emitted by distant galaxies.	
The space of the Universe is expanding, stretching the wavelength of light emitted by distant galaxies.	

[1]

[Total marks 3]

3 The Cosmic Microwave Background Radiation (**CMBR**) was discovered by Arno Penzias and Robert Wilson in 1964.

a State **two** properties of the CMBR. [2]

b Explain how the CMBR is evidence for the Big Bang Theory of the formation of the Universe. [4]

[Total marks 6]

4 M51, the Whirlpool Galaxy is a spiral shaped galaxy in the constellation Canes Venatici.

a Light emitted from the Whirlpool Galaxy is observed to be redshifting and the speed of recession is measured to be 7.04×10^{-11} light-years/s. Calculate the distance of the Whirlpool Galaxy away from Earth, in light-years.

The Hubble constant, H_0, is equal to 2.2×10^{-18} per second.

> **Show me**
>
> $$H_O = \frac{v}{d}$$
>
> $$\Rightarrow d = \frac{v}{H_O} = \boxed{} \text{ light years}$$

[4]

b A distant galaxy is measured to be 2.5×10^{24} m away from Earth, and is moving away with a speed of 6.0×10^6 m/s.

i) Calculate the Hubble constant, H_0, using the data from this galaxy.

$$H_0 = \frac{v}{d} = \frac{\boxed{}}{\boxed{}}/s$$

[3]

ii) Calculate the age of the Universe, in years, using this data. 1 year $= 31.5 \times 10^6$ s.

$$\text{age of the Universe (in seconds)} = \frac{1}{H_0} = \boxed{} \text{ s}$$

$$\text{age of the Universe (in years)} = \frac{\text{age of the Universe (in seconds)}}{\text{number of seconds in one year}} = \boxed{} \text{ years}$$

[5]

'Calculate' means that you have to work out and answer from given facts, figures or information. In these examples, you also have to recall the equations involving the Hubble constant, H_0.

[Total marks 12]

Mixed exam-style questions

1 ▶ Our Solar System was formed about 4.5 billion years ago.

a State which of these astronomical objects is **not** found in our Solar System.

    A. asteroid

    B. comet

    C. galaxy

    D. star   **[1]**

b State the names of the two planets that are further away from the Sun than Jupiter.   **[2]**

c The planets closest to the Sun are smaller than the planets further away. Describe one other difference between these sets of planets.   **[2]**

d Explain why the planets orbit the Sun rather than any other object.   **[2]**

    [Total marks: 7]

2 ▶ A light bulb with a power of 11 W is powered by mains electricity. The e.m.f. of the mains supply is 110 V.

Calculate the resistance of the light bulb when it is operating normally.   **[4]**

> **Show me**
>
> First use the power formula to calculate the current.
>
> $$P = IV, I = \frac{P}{V} = \qquad\qquad = \text{.....................................} \text{ A}$$
>
> Now use the resistance formula to calculate the resistance.
>
> $$R = \frac{V}{I} = \qquad\qquad = \text{.....................................} \ \Omega$$

3 ▶ An atom is made from protons, neutrons and electrons.

a Complete the table to show the relative charges.

	Relative charge
proton	+1
neutron	
electron	

    [2]

b An isotope of plutonium has a proton number of 94 and a nucleon number of 239. Calculate how many neutrons are in each nucleus.   **[1]**

S **c** State the relative charge of a nucleus of the plutonium isotope described in **(b)**.   **[1]**

S d   The plutonium (**Pu**) nucleus was formed by the radioactive decay of a neptunium (**Np**) nucleus.
The atomic number of neptunium is 93. Write the nuclear equation for this process.   [3]

[Total marks: 7]

4   The diagram shows two people (A and B) on a seesaw. The seesaw is in equilibrium.

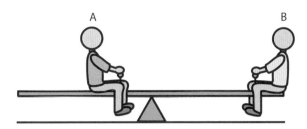

a   State the **two** conditions needed for a system to be in equilibrium.   [2]

b   Explain which person is heavier.   [3]

[Total marks: 5]

5   Here is an incomplete ray diagram used to show the formation of an image using a converging
lens. The focal points, *f*, of the lens are shown. The object is just beyond the focal point on the left
of the lens.

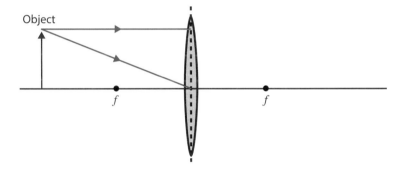

a   Copy and complete the diagram to show the formation of the image.   [3]

b   State **three** properties of the image.   [1]

5 a   Explain what would happen to the size of the image if a new lens, with a slightly higher refractive
index, was used. The distance between the object and the lens and the shape of the lens are the
same as before.   [3]

[Total marks: 7]

6   Calculate which of these distances is the closest to the distance that light travels in a year.

A. 10^{14} m   C. 10^{16} m

B. 10^{15} m   D. 10^{17} m   [1]

7   Ultraviolet light is part of the electromagnetic spectrum.

a   State **two** properties that are common to all electromagnetic waves.   [2]

b   A student states that you can see UV light because the light bulbs glow purple.

   i)   Explain why the student is incorrect.   [1]

   ii) Suggest why the light bulbs are designed to glow when they are switched on.   [2]

c   Explain one use of UV waves.   [2]

[Total marks: 7]

137

8 Americium-241 produces both alpha and gamma radiation.

a Compare the properties of alpha and gamma radiation.

When a question asks you to compare things, you should describe their similarities as well as their differences.

[4]

b Describe an experiment to show that the americium produces alpha and gamma radiation but does not produce beta radiation. [5]

[Total marks: 9]

S **9** Two metal nails can be welded together by melting them where they contact. Electromagnetic induction is used to produce the heating effect.

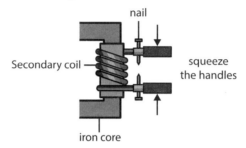

a The coil is connected up so that it acts as a secondary coil in a transformer. Explain how a simple iron-cored transformer works. [3]

b When the handles are squeezed inwards the pointed ends of the nails touch and they quickly become red hot.

   i) Explain why the resistance of the pointed ends of the nails is higher than the other parts of the nails. [2]

   ii) Therefore, explain why the pointed ends of the nails heat up more quickly. Use the formula $P = I^2R$ in your explanation. [2]

c Should the primary coil of the transformer have a large number or a small number of turns to produce the maximum melting effect? Explain your answer. [3]

[Total marks: 10]

10 Here is a speed–time graph for an object falling to the ground on Mars.

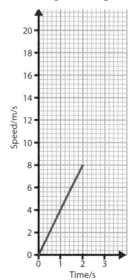

a Use the graph to calculate the distance that the object fell. [3]

Show me

Distance = area under a speed–time graph = $\frac{1}{2}$ × base × height =   =   m.

S **b** Use the graph to calculate the gravitational field strength on the surface of Mars. [2]

S **c** Another object falls to the ground on Earth. Air resistance has no measurable effect on the object's motion. The object also takes 2.0 s to reach the ground.

Add another line to the graph to show the motion of this object. Use the graph to calculate the distance this object falls. [3]

[Total marks: 8]

11 Astronomers can deduce information about the universe from the electromagnetic radiation it produces.

a In the early universe the wavelength of the cosmic microwave background radiation was about 0.0002 mm. However, today it is close to 2 mm. Explain why the wavelength has changed. [2]

S **b** The Sculptor galaxy is 8 million light years from Earth.

i) Explain how astronomers have calculated this distance. [3]

ii) Convert 8 million light years to the equivalent distance in metres. [1]

iii) The redshift, Z, of the light from a galaxy can be calculated from the following equation:

$Z = \frac{v}{c}$

where v is the speed the galaxy is moving away and c is the speed of electromagnetic waves in a vacuum.

Calculate Z for the Sculptor galaxy. [5]

[Total marks: 11]

12 The diagram shows a microwave transmitter and two microwave receivers (A and B).

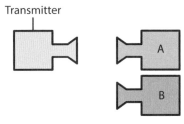

a Explain why receiver A detects the microwaves and receiver B doesn't. [1]

b A metal plate is placed between transmitter and the receivers as shown.

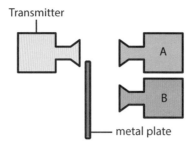

Explain whether the microwaves can now be detected by detector B. [2]

[Total marks: 3]

13 A ray of light is passing out of the surface of a piece of glass as shown in the diagram.

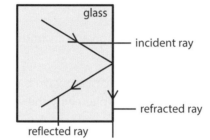

The ray both refracts and reflects. The refracted ray passes along the surface of the glass.

a Label the diagram to show:

i) the normal line [1]

ii) the angle of incidence [1]

iii) the angle of refraction. [1]

b Explain why the angle of incidence equals the critical angle of the glass. [2]

S **c** The refractive index for glass is 1.5. Calculate the angle of reflection for the reflected ray. [3]

[Total marks: 8]

S **14** Physical quantities such as speed, force, mass and energy can be classed as scalars or vectors.

a Describe the difference between a scalar and a vector quantity. [1]

b Other than those quantities identified above, give an example of one scalar quantity and one vector quantity. [2]

c A box is being pulled with a force of 12 N to the right and a force of 5 N upwards as shown in the diagram.

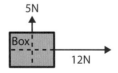

Calculate the size of the resultant force on the box. [3]

> If you use a scale diagram, remember to join the vectors together so the tail of the second vector connects to the head of the first vector.

[Total marks: 6]

15 In hot and dry countries, a pot of food can be cooled down by placing it into another pot. Wet sand is placed into the layer between the two pots. The outer pot is porous so water from the wet sand can seep through to the outside surface.

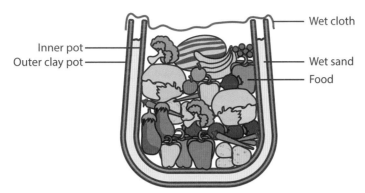

a Explain how the process of evaporation can produce a cooling effect. Use ideas about particles in your answer. [3]

S b Explain why this method of cooling food is only effective if the surroundings are hot and dry. [2]

c State one thing you can do to the pots to make the evaporation faster. [1]

[Total marks: 6]

16 The diagram shows the Earth in part of its orbit around the Sun. The Earth's North and South poles are shown in the diagram.

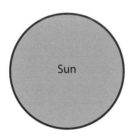
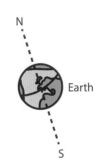

a State which season each hemisphere of the Earth is in. [2]

b Explain why the climate is hotter in the summer than it is in the winter. [3]

S c The Earth takes 3.15×10^7 s to orbit the Sun. The radius of its orbit is 150 million km. Calculate the orbital speed of the Earth. [3]

[Total marks: 8]

17 The diagram shows the inside of the cable used to connect an electrical appliance safely to the mains.

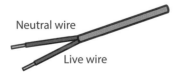

a i) Describe what it means if an appliance is double insulated. [2]

ii) Explain how you know the appliance is double insulated. [2]

b The appliance has a power of 800 W and is connected to a mains supply with a voltage of 220 V. Explain whether a 3 A fuse would be suitable to protect the appliance. [4]

[Total marks: 8]

18 A brick measures 0.10 m $\times$ 0.15 m $\times$ 0.20 m as shown in the diagram. The brick has a mass of 2.0 kg.

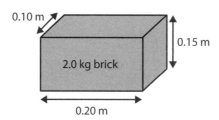

0.10 m
0.15 m
2.0 kg brick
0.20 m

a Calculate the weight of the brick. [2]

b Calculate the maximum pressure the brick can exert on the ground. [3]

[Total marks: 5]

S **19** Two cars have a head on collision on a flat icy road as shown in the diagram. Car A has a mass of 2000 kg and car B has a mass of 2500 kg. Before the collision car A is moving to the right at 20.0 m/s and car B is moving to the left at 19.6 m/s.

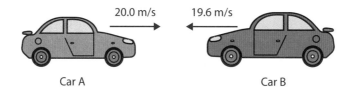

20.0 m/s   19.6 m/s

Car A   Car B

a Calculate the size and direction of the total momentum before the collision. [5]

> **Show me**
>
> Make vectors to the right positive and vectors to the left negative.
>
> Momentum of A = mass × velocity =   ×   =   kgm/s
>
> Momentum of B =   × –19.6 = –   kgm/s
>
> Therefore, total momentum = 40 000 –   =   kgm/s
>
> Direction is to the   (because the value is negative)

b The cars stick together when they collide.

Calculate the size and direction of their combined velocity after the collision. Assume no external friction is acting. [3]

[Total marks: 8]

20 Two types of wave are transverse and longitudinal.

a Describe what is different between how vibrations in a medium cause transverse waves and longitudinal waves. [3]

b Here are some statements about waves. Decide whether they apply to **transverse** waves, **longitudinal** waves or **both** types of wave. The first statement has been answered for you.

  i) They have crests.   **transverse**

  ii) They reflect. [1]

iii) They diffract. [1]

iv) Electromagnetic waves are all of this type. [1]

[**Total marks: 6**]

21 A ball is thrown vertically upwards at 4.0 m/s.

4.0 m/s

At this speed it has 2.4 J in its kinetic energy store.

As the ball rises it slows down to a stop. At the same time, 0.3 J of energy is transferred by heating to the internal energy stores of the surroundings.

a Justify why the ball must have gained 2.1 J of gravitational potential energy when it reaches its maximum height.

> When a 'Justify' question contains a value you need say why it is that particular value.

[2]

S **b** Calculate the mass of the ball. [3]

S **c** Calculate the vertical height the ball rises to before coming to a stop. [3]

[**Total marks: 8**]

22 A student measures the density of a liquid. The diagram shows the measurements that they take.

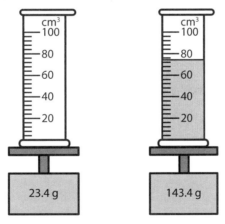

a Calculate the density of the liquid. [4]

b The student drops a small ball made from Perspex onto the liquid.

The density of Perspex is 1180 kg/m^3.

Explain whether the ball floats or sinks in the liquid. [2]

[**Total marks: 6**]

23 The diagram shows apparatus that can be used to locate the centre of gravity on a shaped piece of card.

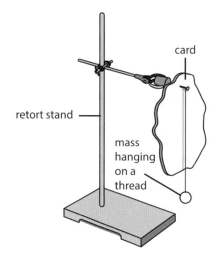

a Describe how the apparatus can be used to find the centre of gravity. [3]

b A pin was clamped so it pointed vertically upwards. The card was placed horizontally on top of the pin. The card's centre of gravity was exactly above the point of the pin, as shown in the diagram.

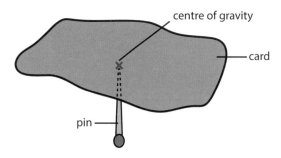

Explain what happens to the card in this position. [2]

[Total marks: 5]

24 The nearest star to the Sun, Proxima Centauri, is just over 4 light years away from the Sun.

a Explain what is meant by a light year. [2]

b Proxima Centauri is in the same galaxy as the Sun.

   i) State the name of this galaxy. [1]

   ii) What is the approximate diameter of this galaxy in light years? [1]

c The wavelengths of light from galaxies a long distance away are longer than the wavelengths of nearer galaxies. Explain what is causing this effect. [2]

[Total marks: 6]

S **25** An electric kettle heats up 1.5 kg of water from 20°C to 100°C in 4.0 minutes.

The specific heat capacity of water is 4200 J/(kg°C).

a Explain why the kettle is not 100% efficient. [1]

b Calculate the useful power of the kettle. [4]

> **Show me**

Temperature change $\Delta\vartheta$ = ...

Useful energy supplied to the water, $\Delta E = mc\Delta\vartheta$ = ...

Useful power = useful energy ÷ time = ...

You need to convert the time to seconds.

c The kettle is 80% efficient.

    i)   Calculate the total power supplied to the kettle.   **[2]**

    ii)   Calculate the energy supplied to the kettle in kW h.   **[3]**

                                               [Total marks: 10]

26 Transformers are used in electricity distribution systems, to make the systems more efficient.

Identify which of the following is the correct way to send electrical power effectively and efficiently through electrical cables.

	Current (through the cable)	Voltage (between the cable and the Earth)
A.	large	large
B.	large	small
C.	small	large
D.	small	small

                                                                       [1]

27 People need frictional forces to walk along a pavement.

a Explain what would happen if you tried to walk along a pavement and there was no friction   **[2]**

This person is walking along a pavement where there is friction.

b Draw an arrow on the diagram to show the direction of the force of friction on one of the person's feet.   **[1]**

c Some runners have shoes with spikes that dig into the ground. Explain how this helps them to accelerate faster.   **[3]**

                                                               [Total marks: 6]

28 > Here is an incomplete series circuit, which includes a 12 V power source and a resistor.

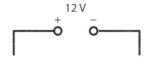

(a) Complete the diagram and include the two measuring instruments that are used to determine the resistance. [3]

(b) The current flowing out of the power source is 0.80 A. Calculate the resistance of the resistor. [2]

(c) A 7.5 Ω resistor is added in parallel to the resistor in the diagram. Explain why the current flowing out of the power source is now larger than 0.80 A. [1]

S (d) Calculate the combined resistance of the two resistors. [2]

[**Total marks: 8**]

29 > Here is a picture of a bar magnet.

(a) Copy the diagram and draw magnetic field lines that show the shape and direction of the magnetic field. [3]

S (b) How would the diagram be different if the magnet was stronger? [1]

[**Total marks: 4**]

30 > Here is a graph showing how the count rate of a radioactive material varies with time. The count rate has been corrected for background radiation.

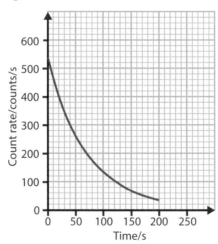

(a) Calculate the half-life of the radioactive material. [3]

(b) A larger sample of the same material has a count rate of 2000 counts/s. Calculate how long it would take for the count rate to fall to 250 counts/s.

Use the value of the half-life you calculated in part (a). [2]

> **Show me**
>
> Time for the count rate to fall from 2000 counts/s to 1000 counts/s = 1 half-life = ... s
>
> Time for the count rate to fall from 1000 counts/s to 500 counts / s = ... s
>
> Time for the count rate to fall from 500 counts/s to 250 counts/s = ... s
>
> So the total time = ... s

[Total marks: 5]

31 The diagram shows a geostationary satellite that is used by direct broadcast satellite television stations.

a i) State the type of electromagnetic waves that are used to communicate between satellites and the Earth. **[1]**

ii) State **two** other uses for this type of electromagnetic wave. **[2]**

b Explain the advantage of using a geostationary satellite compared to a low orbiting satellite. **[2]**

c Two satellite TV stations use the geostationary satellite to communicate with each other. The signal between the stations travels a total distance of 75 000 km. Calculate the time it takes for the signal to travel that distance. Assume that the waves always travel through a vacuum. **[3]**

[Total marks: 8]

32 The diagram shows a box on a ramp. The box is at rest.

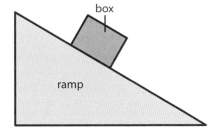

Each row of the table describes some of the forces that might be acting on the box. Identify which row of the table is correct.

	Solid friction	Air resistance	Weight
A.	0 N	greater than 0 N	greater than 0 N
B.	greater than 0 N	0 N	greater than 0 N
C.	0 N	0 N	0 N
D.	greater than 0 N	greater than 0 N	greater than 0 N

[1]

S **33** The diagram shows a power source, which drives a large current through the wire when the switch is closed. The wire passes through a magnetic field produced by a horseshoe magnet.

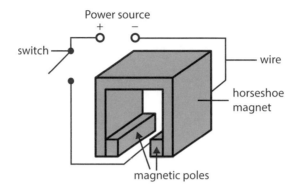

a A force is exerted on the wire because there are two magnetic fields that interact with each other. Explain why there are two magnetic fields when the switch is closed. **[1]**

b Describe how you can determine the direction of the magnetic field of the horseshoe magnet if you know the directions of the force and the current. **[4]**

c When the switch is closed the wire lifts upwards off the table. Label the diagram to indicate where the N and S poles are on the magnet. **[1]**

[Total marks: 6]

34 The Sun radiates energy as electromagnetic waves.

a There are three regions of the electromagnetic spectrum where most of the Sun's energy is radiated. Two of these are **ultraviolet** and **visible light**. What is the third region? **[1]**

b The three types of electromagnetic waves have similarities and differences.

i) State one similarity between all three types of wave. **[1]**

ii) State one difference between the three types of wave. **[1]**

c The three types of electromagnetic wave can be dangerous. State one harmful effect that ultraviolet waves have on people. **[1]**

[Total marks: 4]

35 Here is a diagram of a 300 g mass hanging vertically on a spring. The mass is at rest.

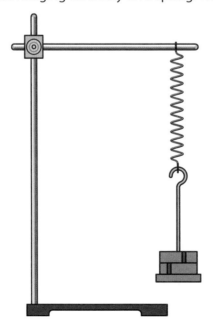

a   Calculate the force of gravity acting on the mass. [3]

b   State the value of the resultant force acting on the mass. [1]

c   A student pulls the mass down so that it stretches the spring further and then lets go. The mass oscillates up and down regularly.

     The student times how long it takes for the mass to oscillate up and down 10 times. The time interval is 7.2 s.

     Calculate the period of oscillation. [1]

d   Explain why this is a more accurate method than timing a single oscillation. [2]

[Total marks: 7]

36   State which one of these energy resources does not originally come from the Sun.

     A. biofuels

     B. nuclear

     C. solar

     D. water waves [1]

37   Lead-210 is a beta emitting radioactive source.

a   The stable isotope of lead is $^{206}_{82}$Pb. Explain why lead-210 is radioactive. Use ideas about the particles in the nucleus in your answer. [2]

b   Describe what happens to the particles in a lead-210 nucleus when it undergoes beta decay. [3]

c   State **two** differences between the path of alpha particles and beta particles when they move through a uniform magnetic field. [2]

[Total marks: 7]

38   Different materials can be classed as electrical conductors or insulators.

a   Describe an experiment to determine whether a material is an electrical conductor or an insulator. [3]

b   Give an example of a material that is

     i)   a conductor [1]

     ii)   an insulator. [1]

c   Explain why usually materials that are good **electrical** conductors are also good **thermal** conductors. [3]

[Total marks: 8]

39   Here is a diagram of particles of gas in a container.

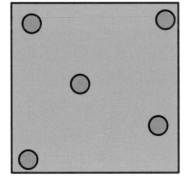

a Describe what happens to the motion of the particles when the temperature increases. [1]

b Explain how the motion of the particles results in the gas exerting a pressure on the container. [2]

c A student looks at the surface of milk through a microscope. They can see globules of fat suspended in the milk. The globules of fat jiggle around.

Explain how this is evidence for the particle model of matter. [3]

[**Total marks: 6**]

40 Here is an energy flow diagram for an athlete running at a constant speed up a hill.

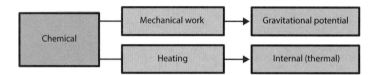

a Explain why there is no energy transfer to or from the kinetic energy store. [2]

b The athlete transferred 160 kJ out of their chemical store and 32 kJ into their gravitational potential store.

   i) Calculate how much energy was transferred to the internal (**thermal**) store. [1]

   ii) What scientific principle did you use to calculate the energy? [1]

S c Sketch a Sankey diagram to show the same energy transfers. [3]

[**Total marks: 7**]

S 41 A 5 kV power source is connected to a pair of parallel plates.

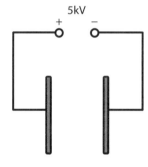

a Explain why no electric current flows out of the power source. [1]

b There is an electric field between the plates. On the diagram, draw electric field lines to show the shape and the direction of the field. [3]

c The power supply unit contains a 50 MΩ resistor, which limits the current that the supply can provide.

   i) Explain why the maximum current it can supply is 0.1 mA. [3]

Remember that the prefixes, k, M and m mean 1000, 1 000 000 and $\frac{1}{1000}$ respectively.

   ii) Suggest why the maximum current is limited in this power source. [2]

[**Total marks: 9**]

42 A loudspeaker is connected to a signal generator. This allows sound waves to be created at different frequencies.

a Describe how someone hearing the sound can tell if the frequency is increased. [1]

b As the frequency is increased, the sound becomes ultrasound.

   i) What is ultrasound?

   ii) What is the lowest frequency at which it can occur? [2]

S A sonar system was used by a submarine to calculate the distance, d, it was above the bottom of the ocean.

A pulse of ultrasound was aimed vertically downwards from the submarine. It took 0.16 s for the echo to return.

The speed of ultrasound in water = 1500 m/s

c Calculate the distance d. [3]

[**Total marks: 6**]

43 A researcher measures the half-life of a radioactive substance. Before they make any calculations, they have to correct the count rate for background radiation.

a **i)** Explain what is meant by the **background radiation**. [1]

   ii) State **two** sources of background radiation. [2]

S The researcher sets up a detector connected to a counter to measure the background count. The counter counts 260 counts over a time of 20 minutes.

b Explain why the researcher needs to measure the background count over a long period of time. [2]

The researcher then places the radioactive source in front of the detector and measures the counts/minute.

c The detector displays an initial count rate of 153 counts/minute. After 10 minutes, the detector displays a count rate of 48 counts/minute.

Calculate the half-life of the radioactive source. Assume the activity of the background radiation remains constant during the experiment. [4]

The detector displays the count rate before it has been corrected for the background radiation.

[**Total marks: 9**]

Practice Paper 1: Multiple Choice (Core)

Instructions

- There are 40 questions on this paper. Answer **all** questions.

- For each question choose **one** of the four possible answers, A, B, C and D.

- You may use a calculator.

- Take the weight of 1.0 kg to be 9.8 N (acceleration of free fall = 9.8 m / s^2).

- The total mark for the paper is 40. The time allowed is 45 minutes.

1 The diagram shows a magnified drawing of the end of a ruler. The ruler is used to measure the unstretched length of a spring.

What is the length of the spring?

A. 27 mm　　　　　**B.** 17 mm　　　　　**C.** 27 cm　　　　　**D.** 17 cm

.... [1]

2 A student wishes to carry out an experiment to measure the density of a small, irregularly shaped solid metal toy car.

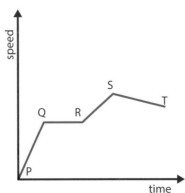

The following apparatus is available:

balance; ruler; measuring cylinder containing some water; Newton meter

Which apparatus is needed for this experiment?

A. the balance and the measuring cylinder

B. the balance and the ruler

C. the Newton meter and the ruler

D. the Newton meter only

.... [1]

3 The graph shows the motion of a motorbike.

In which section of the graph is the acceleration greatest?

A. P to Q   **C.** R to S

B. Q to R   **D.** S to T

.... [1]

4 The force of gravity on Earth is 9.8 N/kg. The force of gravity on the Moon is 1.6 N/kg.

Which statement about an astronaut standing on the Moon is correct?

A. Her mass on the Moon is more than her mass on Earth.

B. Her mass on the Moon is the same as her mass on Earth.

C. Her weight on the Moon is more than her weight on Earth.

D. Her weight on the Moon is the same as her weight on Earth.

.... [1]

5 An object is moving at a constant speed of 2.5 m/s.

What is the distance travelled by the object in 4 seconds?

A. 1.5 m   **B.** 1.6 m   **C.** 7.5 m   **D.** 10 m

.... [1]

6 An aluminium cube of dimensions 4.0 cm × 4.0 cm × 4.0 cm is placed on a balance.

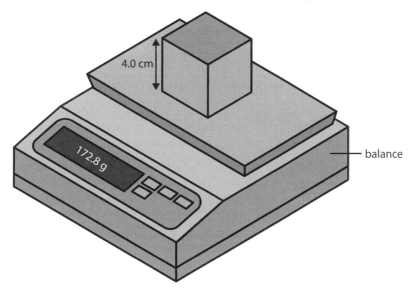

What is the density of aluminium?

A. 0.023 g/cm^3

B. 0.093 g/cm^3

C. 2.7 g/cm^3

D. 10.8 g/cm^3

.... [1]

7 The diagram shows the lengths of a spring with three different loads: 0 N, 3.0 N and 6.0 N.

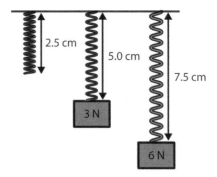

What is the **extension** of the spring with a load of 6.0 N on it?

A. 2.5 cm

B. 5.0 cm

C. 7.5 cm

D. 10.0 cm

.... [1]

8 The diagram shows a uniform rod pivoted at its centre.

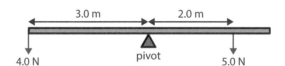

In which direction is the motion of the rod?

A. no motion – the rod is in balance

B. the rod rotates anticlockwise

C. the rod rotates clockwise

D. the rod slides to the right

.... [1]

9 Oil, wind and natural gas are common sources of energy.

Which row correctly describes the nature of each source?

	Coal	Wind	Natural gas
A.	non-renewable	renewable	non-renewable
B.	renewable	non-renewable	renewable
C.	non-renewable	non-renewable	renewable
D.	renewable	renewable	non-renewable

.... [1]

10 A shop assistant lifts 14 boxes of cereal, one at a time, from the floor up onto the highest shelf in a supermarket.

What extra information is needed to calculate the useful work done by the shop assistant in lifting the crate?

A. the time to lift all the cereal boxes and the height of the shelf

B. the time to lift all the cereal boxes and the volume of each box

C. the weight of each box and the time to lift all the cereal boxes

D. the weight of each box of cereal and the height of the shelf

.... [1]

11 A swimmer pushes a float on the water with a force of 5 N for a total distance of 60 m.

What is the total work done on the float by the swimmer?

A. 12 J

B. 55 J

C. 65 J

D. 300 J

.... [1]

12 A skier's boots have a combined area of 80 cm^2. Her skis have a combined area of 720 cm^2.

Why will the skier sink into the snow when she is wearing just her boots but she will not sink into the snow when she is wearing her skis?

A. the large area of her skis decreases the pressure on the snow

B. the large area of her skis decreases the weight on the snow

C. the large area of her skis increases the pressure on the snow

D. the large area of her skis increases the weight on the snow

.... [1]

13 The density of salt water is greater than the density of fresh water.

In which of the following situations is the water pressure on a scuba diver greatest?

	Type of water	Depth (m)
A.	fresh	1
B.	fresh	10
C.	salty	1
D.	salty	10

.... **[1]**

14 The diagram shows some carbon dioxide gas particles in the air space inside a sealed bottle of fizzy drink.

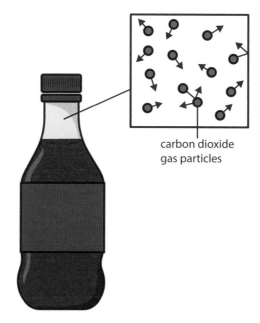

carbon dioxide
gas particles

The bottle is cooled in a refrigerator.

What happens to the particles of carbon dioxide gas?

A. They get further apart.

B. They hit the bottle walls with more force.

C. They increase in volume.

D. They move more slowly.

.... **[1]**

15 Brownian motion is seen when smoke particles are observed using a microscope.

What causes the smoke particles to move in random directions?

A. Air molecules hit the smoke particles.

B. Smoke particles rebound off the walls of the container.

C. The smoke particles are hot.

D. The smoke particles are moving at high speed.

.... [1]

16 Which of the following effects is **not** caused by thermal expansion on a very hot day?

A. a metal bridge bending

B. a railway track buckling

C. tarmac melting on a road surface

D. the wires between electricity pylons sagging

.... [1]

17 When matter changes state, energy is transferred. The diagram shows four lettered changes of state, P, Q, R and S.

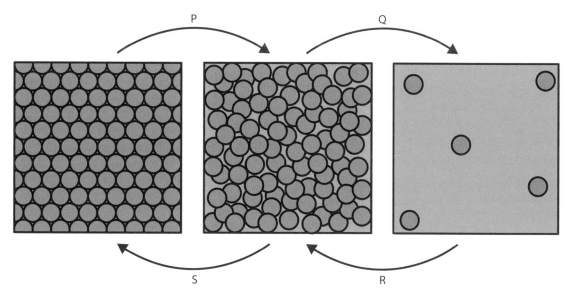

Which changes of state involve particles losing kinetic energy?

A. P and Q

B. P and S

C. Q and R

D. R and S

.... [1]

18 A room is heated by an open fire burning wood in a fireplace. The smoke produced leaves the room by flowing up a chimney.

Which thermal transfer processes are responsible for heating people in the room?

A. conduction and radiation

B. convection and radiation

C. conduction only

D. convection only

[1]

19 A solar water heater uses the Sun to heat water inside a container.

Which combination of colour and texture for the surface of the container will produce the greatest temperature rise of the water?

	Colour	Texture
A.	black	dull
B.	black	shiny
C.	white	dull
D.	white	shiny

[1]

20 A frying pan is made out of copper and it has a plastic handle.

Why are these materials used?

	Copper pan	Plastic handle
A.	Copper is a good thermal conductor.	Plastic is a good thermal insulator.
B.	Copper is a good thermal conductor.	Plastic is a poor thermal insulator.
C.	Copper is a poor thermal conductor.	Plastic is a good thermal insulator.
D.	Copper is a poor thermal conductor.	Plastic is a poor thermal insulator.

[1]

21 The diagram shows labelled parts of a wave.

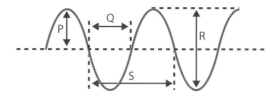

Which row describes the amplitude and the wavelength?

	Amplitude	Wavelength
A.	P	Q
B.	P	S
C.	R	Q
D.	R	S

.... [1]

22 Refraction of water waves occurs when the waves travel from deep water into shallow water.

Why does this happen?

A. The frequency of the water waves decreases.

B. The frequency of the water waves increases.

C. Water waves travel faster in deep water and slower in shallow water.

D. Water waves travel slower in deep water and faster in shallow water.

.... [1]

23 The diagram shows a ray of light from point O, incident on a mirror.

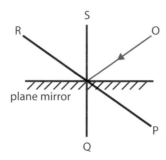

Which lines represent the path of the reflected ray and the normal line?

	Path of reflected ray	Normal line
A.	O to P	P to R
B.	O to P	Q to S
C.	O to R	P to R
D.	O to R	Q to S

.... [1]

24 A plane mirror forms an image of a student's face.

Which statement about the image is correct?

A. The image is real and bigger and closer to the mirror than the face.

B. The image is real and smaller than the face, but the same distance from the mirror.

C. The image is virtual and the same size and distance away from the mirror as the face.

D. The image is virtual and the same size as the face, but closer to the mirror.

.... [1]

25 The table shows the parts of the electromagnetic spectrum.

radio waves	microwaves	infrared waves	visible light	ultraviolet waves	X-rays	gamma rays

Which part is involved with the communication of mobile phones?

A. infrared waves

B. microwaves

C. radio waves

D. ultraviolet waves

.... [1]

26 A student stands 272 m away from the vertical, flat side of a tall building. They fire a starting pistol and the student hears the echo of the sound 1.6 seconds later.

What is the speed of sound?

A. 170 m/s   **C.** 340 m/s

B. 217.6 m/s   **D.** 435.2 m/s

.... [1]

27 Two permanent magnets are attracted to each other as shown in the diagram. End J is a South pole.

permanent magnet | J   K | L   M | permanent magnet

What are the polarities of ends K and L?

	End K	End L
A.	North	North
B.	North	South
D.	South	North
C.	South	South

.... [1]

28 A student charges a polythene rod with a cloth. They place the charged rod on a watch glass on a bench so that the rod can spin freely around.

They charge up a second polythene rod and bring it close to the charged end of the first rod sitting on the watch glass.

What happens to the polythene rod on the watch glass?

A. It does not move.

B. It is lifted off the watch glass.

C. It spins away from the second polythene rod.

D. It spins towards the second polythene rod.

.... [1]

29 The resistance of a piece of fuse wire, inside a fuse, can be measured using the circuit shown in the diagram. The variable resistor is altered until the meters read 1.5 A and 6.0 V.

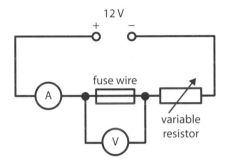

What is the resistance of the fuse wire?

A. 4 Ω   **B.** 4.5 Ω   **C.** 7.5 Ω   **D.** 9 Ω

.... [1]

30 An inductive cooker rated at 1020 W receives 120 V of potential difference. What is the magnitude of the current in the cooker?

A. 8.5 A   **B.** 107 A   **C.** 0.117 A   **D.** 1140 A

.... [1]

31 The circuit diagrams show four different lamp circuits. Each lamp has a resistance of 10 Ω. The electromotive force of the power supplies is 3 V each.

Which circuit has the lowest resistance?

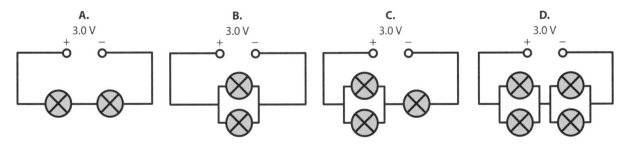

.... [1]

32 A string of LED lights has 50 lights, each connected in parallel, each drawing a current of 0.025 A.

Which is the best rating of fuse needed to protect this circuit?

A. 0.03 A

B. 0.13 A

C. 1.3 A

D. 13 A

[1]

33 A student moves a length of wire through the poles of a U-shaped magnet. The wire is connected at either end to a sensitive voltmeter. The student observes an electromotive force (**emf**) being induced.

Which statement about electromagnetic induction is correct?

A. An emf is only produced when the wire moves perpendicular to the magnetic field.

B. An emf is only produced when the wire is held stationary inside the magnetic field.

C. A stronger magnetic field would reduce any emf produced.

D. The emf is biggest when the wire moves closest to one pole of the magnet.

[1]

34 What is the name of the electrical component that changes mains 240 V a.c. to 5 V a.c. for use in a mobile phone charger?

A. generator

B. thermistor

C. transformer

D. variable resistor

[1]

35 A transformer has a primary input of 12 V at 6 A a.c. and a secondary output of 24 V at 3 A a.c.

What is this type of transformer called?

A. An isolator transformer

B. A relay transformer

C. A step-down transformer

D. A step-up transformer

[1]

36 The nuclide notation for the nucleus of an isotope of sodium is $^{23}_{11}$Na.

What is the number of neutrons in this nucleus?

A. 11   **B.** 12   **C.** 23   **D.** 34

[1]

37 Which row is correct about the nature of radiation emitted by an unstable nucleus?

	Alpha radiation	Beta radiation	Gamma radiation
A.	electromagnetic waves	helium nuclei	electrons
B.	electrons	electromagnetic waves	helium nuclei
C.	electrons	helium nuclei	electromagnetic waves
D.	helium nuclei	electrons	electromagnetic waves

.... [1]

38 A radioactive source has a measured count-rate of 800 counts/s and a half-life of 2 days.

What will be the count-rate after 6 days?

A. 400 counts/s

B. 200 counts/s

C. 100 counts/s

D. 50 counts/s

.... [1]

39 The Andromeda Galaxy is one of our nearby galaxies.

Which is the most likely distance to the Andromeda Galaxy?

A. 1 light-year

B. 2.6 light-years

C. 100 000 light-years

D. 2 600 000 light-years

.... [1]

40 Which statement correctly describes redshift?

A. the change in the observed brightness of light emitted from receding stars and galaxies

B. the change in the observed position of receding stars and galaxies

C. the change in the observed wavelength of light emitted from receding stars and galaxies

D. the change in the speed of light emitted from receding stars and galaxies

.... [1]

Practice Paper 2: Multiple Choice (Extended)

Instructions

- There are 40 questions on this paper. Answer **all** questions.

- For each question choose **one** of the four possible answers, A, B, C and D.

- You may use a calculator.

- Take the weight of 1.0 kg to be 9.8 N (acceleration of free fall = 9.8 m / s^2).

- The total mark for the paper is 40. The time allowed is 45 minutes.

1 Which of the following is a vector quantity?

   A. acceleration   **C.** mass

   B. energy   **D.** speed

                                                    [1]

2 Here is a velocity–time graph for an object. Which is the best description of its motion?

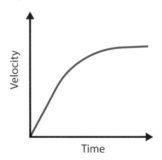

   A. decreasing acceleration   **C.** increasing acceleration

   B. decreasing deceleration   **D.** increasing deceleration

                                                    [1]

3 The gravitational field strength, *g*, on the surface of Mars is 3.7 N/kg. A rock with a mass of 5.0 kg on Earth was taken to Mars and then dropped to the ground. Which row of the table is correct for the rock?

	Mass on Mars (kg)	Acceleration downwards (m/s^2)
A.	5.0	3.7
B.	49	9.8
C.	18.5	3.7
D.	18.5	9.8

                                                    [1]

4 A spring has an unstretched length of 5.0 cm. When a 2.0 N force is applied the new length of the spring is 6.6 cm.

   What is the total length of the spring when a 4.0 N force is applied? Assume the limit of proportionality is not exceeded.

   A. 3.2 cm   **B.** 8.2 cm   **C.** 9.4 cm   **D.** 13.2 cm

                                                      [1]

5 Here is some data about the masses and volumes of some objects.

Object	Mass (g)	Volume (cm³)
1	20	300
2	60	100
3	100	1500
4	300	2000

Which **two** objects could be made from the same material?

A. Objects 1 and 2 C. Objects 1 and 3

B. Objects 3 and 4 D. Objects 2 and 4

.... [1]

6 If this object is pushed any further, it will topple over. Where is its centre of gravity?

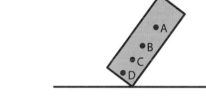

7

.... [1]

A ball has a mass of 0.30 kg. It is dropped to the floor and then it bounces upwards. The speed just before it hits the floor is 8 m/s. The speed just after it leaves the floor is 6 m/s.

When the ball is in contact with the floor, the average force on it is 5.0 N. For how long is the ball in contact with the floor?

A. 0.06 s C. 0.84 s

B. 0.12 s D. 2.80 s

.... [1]

8 A skydiver drops through the air at terminal velocity. Which energy changes occur?

A. gravitational potential energy → internal energy

B. gravitational potential energy → kinetic energy

C. kinetic energy → elastic energy

D. internal energy → kinetic energy

.... [1]

9 A ball has a mass of 0.50 kg and is dropped from a height of 2.0 m. As a result the ball has a kinetic energy of 45 J as it hits the ground. What is its speed as it hits the ground?

A. 13 m/s   **A.** 23 m/s   **B.** 90 m/s   **C.** 180 m/s

.... [1]

10 Which one of these does the most work?

A. a 2 kW drill operating for 10 s

B. a 500 MW laser operating for 2 μs

C. a crane holding a weight of 20 000 kg at rest in the air

D. a runner applying a force of 100 N over a distance of 22 km

.... [1]

11 A cyclist is pedalling hard and accelerating down a hill.

Which energy changes occur?

A. chemical energy + gravitational potential energy → kinetic energy + internal energy

B. chemical energy → kinetic energy + gravitational potential energy + internal energy

C. gravitational energy → chemical energy + kinetic energy + internal energy

D. kinetic energy → internal energy + gravitational potential energy

.... [1]

12 Water was poured to the **same height** into two different measuring cylinders as shown.

For measuring cylinder 1:

The weight of water = W

The pressure due to the water at the bottom = P

Which are the correct values for weight of water and pressure due to the water for measuring cylinder 2?

	Weight of water	Pressure due to the water at the bottom
A.	W	P
B.	W	2P
C.	2W	P
D.	2W	2P

[1]

13 Here are some properties of four different materials. Which **one** is a liquid?

Material	Can be compressed	Changes volume depending on its container	Changes shape depending on its container
A.	no	no	no
B.	no	no	yes
C.	yes	yes	yes
D.	yes	no	no

[1]

14 Here are some graphs showing how the average kinetic energy of gas particles depends on the temperature (in °C). Which graph is correct?

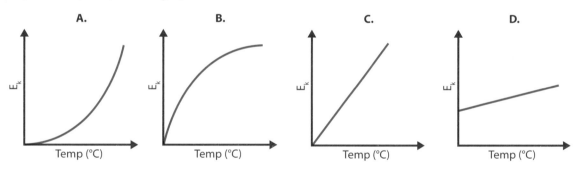

[1]

15 A gas stored in a cylindrical tank with a piston has a pressure of 100 kPa and a volume of 500 cm³. It is then compressed at a constant temperature to a volume of 200 cm³. What is its new pressure?

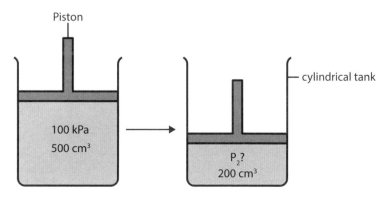

A. 500 kPa	**B.** 400 kPa	**C.** 250 kPa	**D.** 40 kPa

[1]

16 A thermometer calibrated to read temperature in the Kelvin scale reads 1000 K. What is the same temperature on another thermometer in °C?

A. 1273°C

B. 727°C

C. 273 000°C

D. 7270°C

.... [1]

17 A hot stone is placed into some water and the water heats up. The mass of the water is 2.0 kg. The temperature of the water rises from 20°C to 50°C. The specific heat capacity of water is 4200 J/(kg°C).

How much thermal energy transfers from the stone to the water?

A. 252 J   C. 126 000 J

B. 420 J   D. 252 000 J

.... [1]

18 The diagram shows a test tube of water. A cube of ice is held at the bottom with some gauze. A Bunsen burner heats the top of the water.

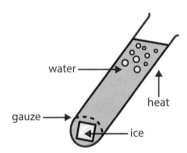

The top of the water boils but the ice at the bottom remains cold and solid.

This shows that:

A. water is a good conductor of thermal energy

B. water is a good convector of thermal energy

C. water is a poor conductor of thermal energy

D. water is a poor convector of thermal energy

.... [1]

19 Sometimes hot food is wrapped in shiny silver foil to keep it warm.

This is because:

A. the foil is a good absorber of thermal radiation

B. the foil is a good emitter of thermal radiation

C. the foil is a poor absorber of thermal radiation

D. the foil is a poor emitter of thermal radiation

.... [1]

20

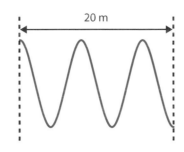

20 m

The wave in the diagram has a frequency of 32 Hz. What is its speed?

A. 256 m/s   **C.** 8 m/s

B. 128 m/s   **D.** 4 m/s

.... [1]

21 Which one of these words does **not** describe a wave effect?

A. diffraction   **C.** dispersion

B. diffusion   **D.** refraction

.... [1]

22 A ray of light is shone onto a mirror as shown in the diagram. The angle between the ray and the mirror is 20°.

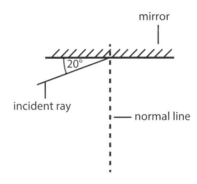

mirror

20°

incident ray

normal line

What is the angle of reflection?

A. 20°   **C.** 70°

B. 50°   **D.** 90°

.... [1]

23 The table shows the speed of light in glass and water. Calculate the critical angle for glass when it is under water.

Speed of light in glass	2.00×10^8 m/s
Speed of light in water	2.25×10^8 m/s

A. 64.0°   **C.** 48.6°

B. 62.7°   **D.** 41.8°

.... [1]

24 A converging lens is used as a magnifying glass. Which of these correctly describes the image?

    A. The image is real, inverted and larger than the object.

    B. The image is real, inverted and smaller than the object.

    C. The image is virtual, inverted and larger than the object.

    D. The image is virtual, not inverted and larger than the object.

.... **[1]**

25 The table shows the frequencies and types of two electromagnetic waves.

Frequency	Type of wave
1.0×10^{10} Hz	microwave
3.0×10^{17} Hz	ultraviolet

Which of these frequencies would be possible for a wave of infrared light?

    A. 5.7×10^{8} Hz

    B. 6.2×10^{12} Hz

    C. 3.1×10^{17} Hz

    D. 1.8×10^{18} Hz

.... **[1]**

26 Two people hear the same sound from a loudspeaker. The two individuals are at different distances from the loudspeaker. Person 1 is closer to the speaker than person 2.

person 1   person 2

loudspeaker

The sound wave at person 2 is different from the sound wave at person 1.

Here are some descriptions of how the sound wave is different when it reaches person 2. Which of these is correct?

    A. The frequency is larger and the wavelength is smaller.

    B. The frequency is smaller and the wavelength is smaller.

    C. The frequency is the same and the amplitude is smaller.

    D. The wavelength is larger and the frequency is the same.

.... **[1]**

27 Two balloons have become charged by friction. They are hung by pieces of insulating thread and they settle in position as shown in the diagram.

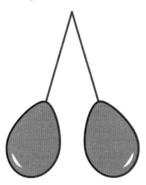

Which one of these descriptions could be correct?

A. Both balloons have gained electrons.

B. Both balloons have gained protons.

C. Electrons have moved from one balloon to the other balloon.

D. The balloons were charged by rubbing them together.

[1]

28 Which is the best description of e.m.f?

A. the force that a source exerts on a unit charge in a circuit

B. the frequency of the alternating current produced by a source

C. the work that a source does pushing a unit charge around a complete circuit

D. the work that a source does pushing a unit charge through a component

[1]

29 A 20 Ω and 40 Ω resistor are connected in a series circuit.

Which statement is correct?

A. The current through both resistors is the same.

B. The current through the 40 Ω resistor is twice the current through the 20 Ω resistor.

C. The p.d. across both resistors is the same.

D. The total resistance is less than 20 Ω.

[1]

30 A diode is connected in series with a resistor and an a.c. supply as shown in the diagram. A voltmeter measures the p.d across the resistor.

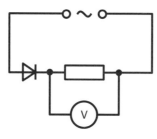

Which graph correctly shows how the p.d. across the resistor varies with time?

A

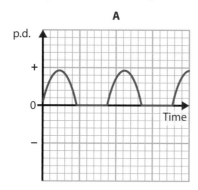

B

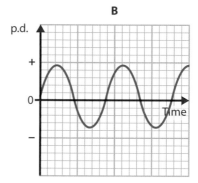

C

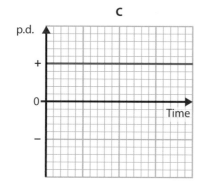

D

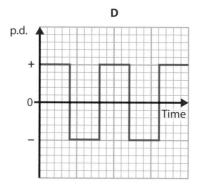

.... [1]

31 A bright light is shone onto the Light Dependent Resistor in the circuit shown in the diagram.

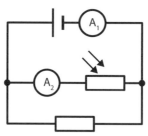

What happens to the ammeter readings?

	Ammeter A_1	Ammeter A_2
A.	stays the same	decreases
B.	increases	decreases
C.	increases	increases
D.	increases	stays the same

.... [1]

32 A small compass is held next to a wire as shown in the diagram. A large electric current passes through the wire. The compass points to the left.

⊗ —— Wire carrying a current into the page

⊕ —— Small compass

What change could be made to make the compass point to the right?

A. Move the compass down the page further from the wire.

B. Move the compass into the page parallel to the wire.

C. Move the compass slightly up the page, closer to the wire.

D. Move the compass up the page to the other side of the wire.

.... [1]

33 A metal conductor is held near a horseshoe magnet as shown in the diagram.

conductor   S   magnet
                   N

What action should be taken to demonstrate electromagnetic induction?

A. Connect the conductor to a power supply.

B. Move the conductor so it cuts through the magnetic field lines.

C. Place the conductor in a magnetic field and hold it still.

D. Rub the conductor with a cloth.

.... [1]

34 A nucleus of an isotope of thorium can be written as:

$$^{234}_{90}\text{Th}$$

How many protons are in this nucleus?

A. 90

B. 144

C. 234

D. 324

.... [1]

35 Which is the correct list for alpha, beta and gamma radiation in terms of **increasing ionising ability**?

    A. alpha, beta, gamma

    B. beta, gamma, alpha

    C. gamma, alpha, beta

    D. gamma, beta, alpha

[1]

36 The activity of a source decreases from 600 counts/s to 150 counts/s in 5.0 hours. What is the half-life of the source?

    A. 5.0 hours

    B. 3.75 hours

    C. 2.5 hours

    D. 0.83 hours

[1]

37 Radioactive tracers are materials that are injected into the human body. The radiation they produce passes out of the body and can be detected. This allows the path of the tracer through the body to be tracked.

Which one of these isotopes might be suitable to be used as a tracer?

	Type of emission	Half-life
A.	alpha	6 hours
B.	beta	12 years
C.	gamma	1.2 seconds
D.	gamma	8 hours

[1]

38 Which is the correct sequence for the evolution of a star like the Sun?

    A. protostar → stable star → red giant → neutron star

    B. protostar → stable star → red giant → white dwarf

    C. protostar → stable star → supergiant → white dwarf

    D. protostar → stable star → supernova → black hole

[1]

39 In 1959 it was estimated that Hubble's constant, $H_0 = 5.8 \times 10^{-18}\,s^{-1}$. What age of the universe would this value predict?

A. $1.0 \times 10^{17}\,s$

B. $1.7 \times 10^{17}\,s$

C. $5.0 \times 10^{17}\,s$

D. $5.8 \times 10^{18}\,s$

.... [1]

40 Here is some data for four different objects orbiting the Sun. At different parts along their orbit their kinetic energy changes as indicated in the table.

Object	Maximum kinetic energy (J)	Minimum kinetic energy (J)
A.	8.2×10^{33}	7.8×10^{33}
B.	2.2×10^{32}	2.0×10^{32}
C.	3.2×10^{23}	1.0×10^{20}
D.	6.7×10^{36}	6.3×10^{36}

Which of these objects is most likely to be a comet?

.... [1]

Practice Paper 3: Theory (Core)

Instructions

- There are 40 questions on this paper. Answer **all** questions.

- For each question choose **one** of the four possible answers, A, B, C and D.

- You may use a calculator.

- Take the weight of 1.0 kg to be 9.8 N (acceleration of free fall = 9.8 m / s^2).

- The total mark for the paper is 80. The time allowed is 1 hour 15 minutes.

1 A car races for a total of 10 seconds.

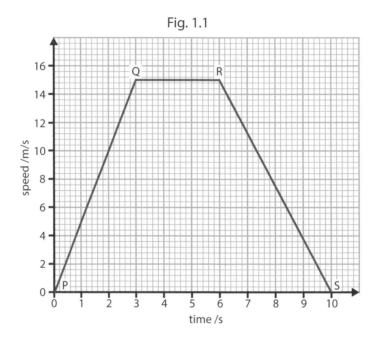

Fig. 1.1

a The diagram shows how the speed of a car varies over a 10-second period.

    i) State the section of the graph where the car is travelling at constant speed. [1]

    ii) Determine the total race distance travelled by the car. [4]

b Compare the motion of the car from P to Q to the motion of the car from R to S. [4]

[**Total marks 9**]

2 A student wishes to determine the identity of a metal alloy used to make a small solid statue of a rabbit.

They decide to measure the density of the metal alloy and then compare their value to the density of common metal alloys on the internet.

The following apparatus is available to the student:

electronic balance

ruler

beaker filled with water

measuring cylinder

a Describe an experiment to determine the density of the metal alloy used to make the statue. [5]

b The student makes the following measurements:

mass of statue = 236 g

volume of statue = 29.5 cm^3

Calculate the density of metal alloy used to make the statue and state a suitable unit for this value. [4]

c The student researches the following values from the internet:

Common statue metal alloys	Density (kg/m^3)
brass	8400–8730
bronze	7400–8000
steel	7750–7900
duralumin	2500–2800

State and explain the name of the alloy used to make the rabbit statue. [3]

[Total marks 12]

3 Two children, A and B, are sitting balanced on a see-saw, as shown.

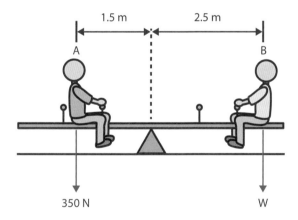

a What is the moment of the weight of Child A about the pivot? [4]

b Use your answer to **(a)** to calculate the weight, *W*, of Child B. [3]

c Use your answer to **(b)** to calculate the mass of Child B, in kg. [3]

[Total marks 10]

4 Electricity can be generated in a power station.

Hydroelectric power station

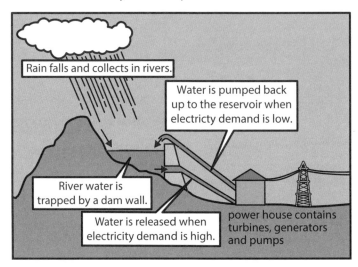

Coal fired power station

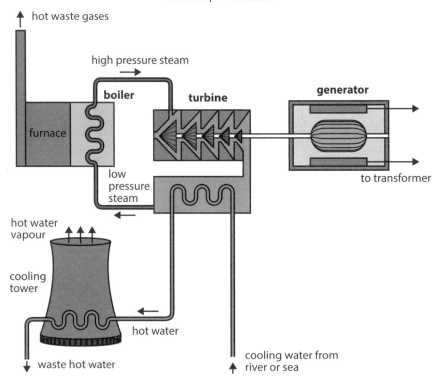

a Using information from this question only, state the electricity generation method that is renewable. [1]

b Suggest a reason why water in the hydroelectric power station is pumped back up into the reservoir at night. [1]

c State **one** advantage and **one** disadvantage of using hydroelectric power to generate electricity. [2]

d Energy may be stored as: kinetic; gravitational potential; elastic (**strain**); nuclear; chemical; electrostatic; and internal (**thermal**) energies.

Energy can transfer between stores by: mechanical work done; electrical work done; heating; or via waves.

The simple energy flow diagram shows the useful energy transfers through a coal-fired power station.

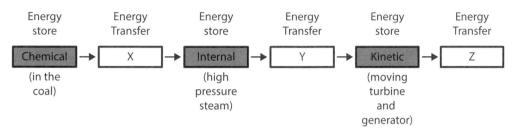

Identify the useful energy transfers, X, Y and Z. [3]

[Total marks 7]

5 The graph shows how the temperature of a sample of stearic acid (**soap**) varies with time as it cools in air.

Stearic acid is a pure substance with a boiling point of 360°C.

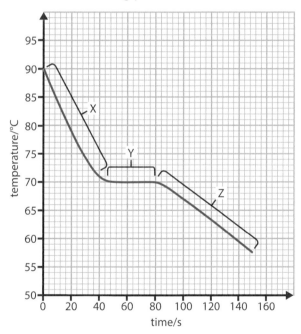

a Give the states of the particles of stearic acid in sections X and Z of the graph. [2]

b The graph shows a change in state.

   i) Give the name of the change of state shown in section Y. [1]

   ii) Explain, in terms of a particle model, how the arrangement, separation and motion of the particles changes in section Y, as the stearic acid changes state from X **to** Z. [3]

[Total marks 6]

6 > The diagram shows water waves being produced in a ripple tank.

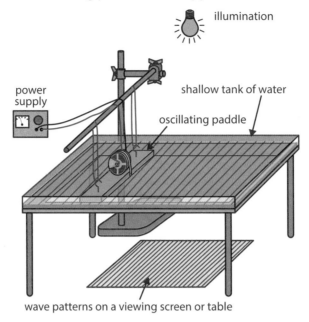

wave patterns on a viewing screen or table

The graph shows a **cross-sectional** diagram of part of the waves produced inside the ripple tank

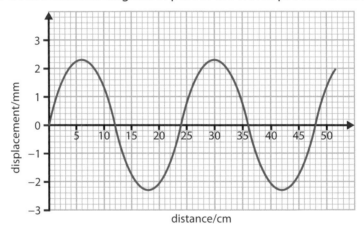

a   Explain how the ripple tank could be used to demonstrate the refraction of water waves.   [2]

b   Use the graph to determine

   i)   the wavelength of the waves, in cm   [1]

   ii)   the amplitude of the waves, in mm   [1]

c   The speed of the water waves shown in the graph is 18 cm/s.

   Calculate the frequency of the water waves in hertz (Hz).   [3]

[Total marks 7]

7 The resistors in Circuit diagram A and Circuit diagram B, all have the same value, R, equal to 20 Ω.

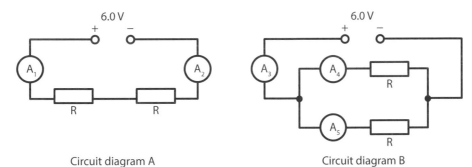

Circuit diagram A   Circuit diagram B

a Circuit diagram A is a series circuit.

    i) Calculate the total combined resistance of Circuit diagram A.   [1]

    ii) Calculate the current reading on ammeter A_1.   [2]

    iii) State the current reading on ammeter A_2.   [1]

b The combined total resistance of the resistors shown in the parallel Circuit diagram B is 10 Ω.

Calculate the readings on ammeters A_3, A_4 and A_5.   [4]

[Total marks 8]

8 The diagram shows an experiment to demonstrate electromagnetic induction.

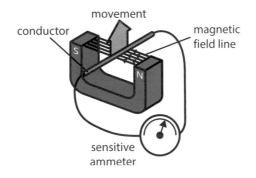

a Explain what is meant by electromagnetic induction.   [2]

b State **three** factors that could increase the magnitude of the reading on the sensitive ammeter.   [3]

[Total marks 5]

9 During the Stone Age, fishing hooks would be made from small pieces of animal bone, cut into a hook shape. When the animal was alive, its bone was absorbing carbon from the atmosphere, some of which is the isotope carbon-14.

Carbon-14 is unstable and undergoes radioactive decay.

a The equation for the radioactive decay of carbon-14 is

$$^{14}_{6}\text{C} \rightarrow ^{14}_{7}\text{N} + ^{A}_{Z}\text{X}$$

i) Determine the values A and Z. [2]

ii) State the type of radioactive decay and the nature of X. [2]

b The graph shows how the radioactive count-rate from a sample of bone fishing hook varies with time.

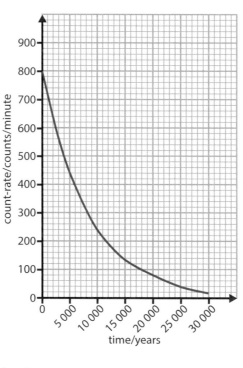

i) Determine the half-life of carbon-14, in years.

Show your working. [2]

ii) A sample of bone fishing hook, found at an archaeological site, had a count-rate of 40 counts/minute.

Use the graph to estimate the age of the bone fishing hook. Show your working. [2]

c Suggest and explain a reason why this method of dating samples is not very accurate for samples that are over about 35 000 years old. [2]

[Total marks 10]

10 **a** The force of attraction of the planets to the Sun is responsible for keeping the planets in orbit.

    i) Name the force responsible for this attraction. [1]

    ii) Describe how the strength of this force varies with the mass of the planet and its distance from the Sun. [2]

b In our Solar System, the inner planets are known to be small and rocky and the outer planets are large and gaseous.

Explain this difference in composition and structure between the planets in the inner and outer Solar System. [3]

[Total marks 6]

Practice Paper 4: Theory (Extended)

Instructions

- There are 40 questions on this paper. Answer **all** questions.

- Write your answer to each question in the space provided.

- You may use a calculator.

- Take the weight of 1.0 kg to be 9.8 N (acceleration of free fall = 9.8 m / s^2).

- The total mark for the paper is 80. The time allowed is 1 hour 15 minutes.

1 The diagram shows a velocity–time graph for a cyclist accelerating from rest on a horizontal road.

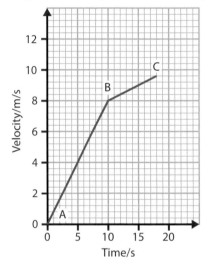

a Calculate the acceleration of the cyclist between points A and B.

....

....

acceleration = ... **[2]**

b How far did the cyclist travel between points B and C?

distance = ... **[3]**

c Between points A and B the resultant force on the bicycle is constant and equals 800 N.

i) Explain why the force driving the bicycle forwards needs to increase during this time.

....

....

....

[2]

ii) Calculate the resultant force on the bicycle between points B and C.

Resultant force = ... [3]

[Total marks 10]

2 ▶ Here is some data about an aeroplane that takes off from one country and lands in another.
- Mass of plane before take off = 80 000 kg
- Maximum height of the plane (above the runway) = 8.0 km
- Maximum speed = 200 m/s

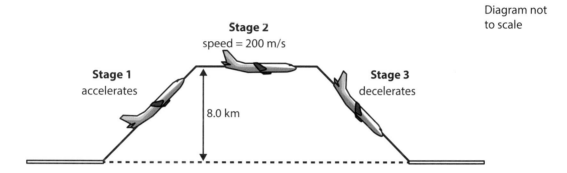

Diagram not to scale

Stage 2
speed = 200 m/s

Stage 1
accelerates

8.0 km

Stage 3
decelerates

There are three stages to the journey.

Stage 1: The plane takes off from rest and rises to its maximum height and accelerates to its maximum speed.

Stage 2: It then flies at its maximum height at its maximum speed.

Stage 3: Finally, it descends to ground level and slows down to rest as it lands.

a Explain why the mass of the plane is less at the end of its journey compared to the beginning.

.... [1]

b The mass of the plane decreases most during Stage 1 of the journey. Explain why. Use ideas about energy in your answer.

....

....

.... [3]

c At the end of Stage 2 the plane's mass is 60 000 kg.

Calculate the plane's gravitational potential energy at the end of Stage 2.

Gravitational potential energy = ... [3]

d The plane lands at the same height as it takes off. Calculate the total work done during Stage 3 of the journey.

Total work done = ... [4]

[**Total marks 11**]

3 The diagram shows a helium-filled balloon and a 1.00 m ruler balancing on a pivot. The ruler is horizontal. The balloon exerts an upwards force on the ruler.

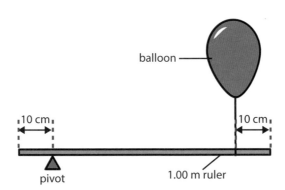

a State what is meant by the **centre of gravity**.

....

.... [1]

b The ruler is uniform in density and cross-sectional area. Add an arrow in the correct location on the diagram to show the gravitational force on the ruler. [2]

c The weight of the ruler is 3.0 N.

Calculate the upwards force the balloon exerts on the ruler.

Force = ... [3]

[**Total marks 6**]

4 The diagram shows bubble wrap used in packaging to protect the objects inside.

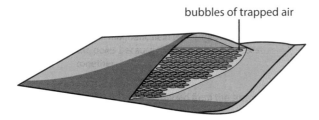

bubbles of trapped air

The bubble wrap is made from plastic with bubbles of trapped air.

a If the packaging is dropped on the floor, the bubbles increase the time it takes the objects to come to a stop. Explain how this protects the objects inside.

....

....

.... [2]

b The bubble wrap also acts as a good thermal insulator. Explain why.

....

....

.... [2]

c Explain, in terms of particles, how the pressure of the air inside the bubble wrap changes if the package is placed outdoors where the ambient temperature is higher.

....

....

.... [3]

d At a pressure of 100 kPa, the air in one of the bubbles has a volume of $1.25 \times 10^{-8}\,\mathrm{m^3}$ and a density of 1.3 kg/m³.

i) Calculate the mass of the bubble

[2]

ii) Calculate the new density of the air in the bubble when the pressure is increased to 250 kPa. Assume that the temperature remains constant.

[4]
[Total marks 13]

5 The diagram shows water waves in a ripple tank spreading out when they pass through a gap.

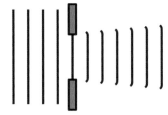

a State the name that describes this phenomenon.

.... [1]

b Describe what happens to the frequency, the wavelength and the speed of the wave when it passes though the gap.

....

.... [1]

c Suggest any change that can be made to the apparatus to make the waves spread out further.

.... [1]

The ripple tank is put on a small slope so one side of the water is deeper than the other.

A small stone is dropped onto the middle of the water to produce some ripples.

The diagram shows what the ripples look like.

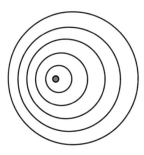

d Label the diagram to show which side of the ripple tank is deeper. [1]

[Total marks 4]

6 The diagram shows two rays from an object, which are incident on a plane mirror.

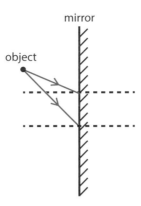

a Continue the path of the rays on the diagram and use this to show where the image is located. [3]

b State **two** properties of the image formed in a plane mirror.

1. ....

2. .... [2]

In 1969 astronauts installed reflectors on the Moon. A short pulse of laser light is shone from Earth to the Moon. It then reflects back to Earth.

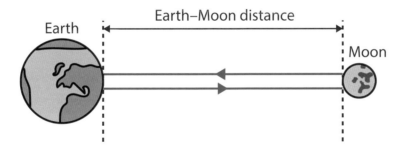

c If the time between sending and receiving the pulse on Earth is 2.6 s, calculate the distance between Earth and the Moon. Assume that the light always travels in a vacuum.

Distance = ... [3]

d The time between the pulses varies over the course of one month. What does this tell us about the shape of the Moon's orbit around Earth?

.... [1]

[Total marks 9]

189

7 Data can be transmitted using analogue or digital signals.

a Describe the difference between analogue and digital signals.

....

.... **[2]**

When signals are transmitted over long distances their amplitude is reduced and they can lose their shape because of interference.

b The diagram shows part of a digital signal after it has travelled a long distance.

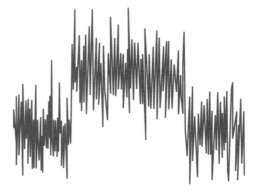

i) Describe how the data can be recovered perfectly from this digital signal.

....

.... **[2]**

ii) Explain why it is not possible to recover data perfectly for analogue signals.

....

.... **[2]**

[Total marks 6]

8 The diagram shows a circuit used to measure the resistance of a length of wire.

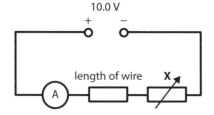

a State the name of component X.

.... [1]

b Add a voltmeter to the diagram to measure the p.d. across component X. [2]

c The ammeter reads 2.0 A and the p.d. across X = 6.0 V. Calculate the resistance of the length of wire. [3]

d Another length of wire is connected in parallel to the first one. The rest of the circuit is unaltered.

Explain how the p.d. across component X changes.

....

....

.... [3]

[Total marks 9]

9 The diagram shows a close-up of part of the surface of the Sun.

coronal loop

The coronal loop is formed from hydrogen and helium nuclei ejected at high speeds and then moving in the Sun's magnetic field.

a Explain whether hydrogen and helium nuclei have a positive or negative charge.

....

.... [2]

A hydrogen nucleus enters the Sun's magnetic field as shown in the diagram. The magnetic field is uniform at this location and it is directed into the page.

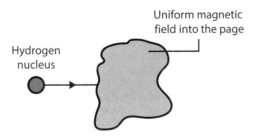

Uniform magnetic field into the page

Hydrogen nucleus

b **i)** On the diagram, draw the path the hydrogen nucleus continues to follow as it enters the magnetic field. [1]

    ii) Explain how you arrived at your answer to **(b) (i)**

.... [1]

The energy from the Sun comes from nuclear fusion reactions in its core.

One of these reactions is the fusion of two isotopes of hydrogen to form helium:

$$^{1}_{1}H + {}^{2}_{1}H \longrightarrow {}^{3}_{2}He$$

c Explain why the two hydrogen **(H)** nuclei are different isotopes of each other.

....

....

.... [2]

In another reaction in the Sun, two helium-3 nuclei fuse to form a helium-4 nucleus. Neutrons are also produced from this reaction.

d **i)** Fill in the in the bracket [ ] in the nuclear reaction to show how many neutrons are produced. [1]

$$^{3}_{2}He + {}^{3}_{2}He \longrightarrow {}^{4}_{2}He + [\ \ ]^{1}_{0}n$$

    ii) The fusion reaction releases energy. What happens to the total mass of the protons and neutrons involved in the reaction?

.... [1]

e Explain how the energy produced from the fusion reactions makes the Sun a stable star.

....

....

....

.... [2]

f Explain how massive stars in a distant galaxy can be used to determine how far the galaxy is from Earth.

....

....

.... [2]

[**Total marks 12**]

Practice Paper 6: Alternative to Practical

Instructions

- Answer **all** questions.
- You may use a calculator.
- You should show your working and use appropriate units.
- Take the weight of 1.0 kg to be 9.8 N (acceleration of free fall = 9.8 m / s^2).
- The total mark for the paper is 40. The time allowed is 1 hour.

1 A student is using filament lamps to light a model house she is building. She will use two lamps in series. She needs to determine the resistance of the lamps.

Fig. 1.1. shows the circuit she uses.

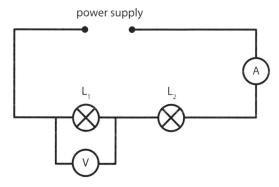

Fig. 1.1

a **i)** Read and record the current *I* in the circuit as shown in Fig. 1.2.

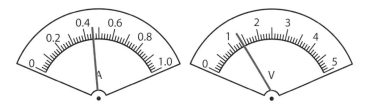

Fig. 1.2

I = ... A   [1]

ii) Read and record the voltage V_1 across lamp L$_1$ as shown in Fig. 1.3.

V_1 = ... V   [1]

iii) Calculate the resistance R_1 of lamp L$_1$. Use the equation $R_1 = \dfrac{V_1}{I}$. Include the unit.

R_1 = ...   [2]

b The student disconnects the voltmeter from the circuit. She then connects the voltmeter across lamp L_2.

The student measures the voltage V_2 across lamp L_2 and records her result.

$$V_2 = 1.5 \text{ V}$$

i) Explain why she does not need to remeasure the current in the circuit.

....

.... [1]

ii) Calculate the resistance R_2 of lamp L_2. Use the equation $R_2 = \dfrac{V_2}{I}$.

....

....

$R_2 =$ .... [1]

c Calculate the total resistance, R_T of the two lamps. Use the equation $R_T = R_1 + R_2$.

....

....

$R_T =$ .... [1]

d The student wants to make the lamps brighter. She increases the voltage of the power supply. She records the new voltage V_N.

$$V_N = 3.5 \text{ V}.$$

Calculate the new current I_N in the circuit at this voltage. Use the equation $I_N = \dfrac{V_N}{R_T}$.

....

....

$I_N =$ .... A [1]

e The student would like each lamp in the circuit to work even if one of them breaks.

She decides to put the lamps into a parallel circuit.

Draw a circuit diagram to show a circuit that the student could use.

....

....

....

....

....

.... [2]

f The student would also like to change the current in the circuit without changing the voltage of the power supply.

She could use a variable resistor to do this.

Draw the symbol for a variable resistor.

....

....

.... [1]

[Total marks 11]

2 A student investigates the cooling of water. He uses different thicknesses of insulating material to see how the cooling rate changes.

Fig. 2.1 shows some of the apparatus he uses.

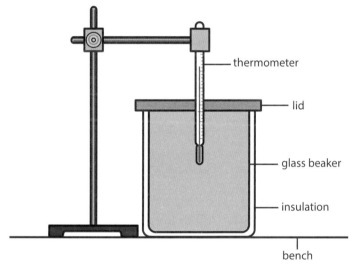

Fig. 2.1

a The thermometer in Fig. 2.2. shows the room temperature θ_R at the beginning of the experiment.

i) Record θ_R.

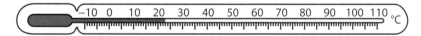

Fig. 2.2

$\theta_R =$ .... °C [1]

ii) State how you would make sure the temperature measurement is as accurate as possible.

....

.... [1]

b The student removes the lid from the beaker and pours 200 ml of hot water into the beaker.

He replaces the lid and puts the thermometer into the water.

He starts a stopwatch and records the temperature θ_0 of the water at time $t = 0$.

He measures the water temperature every 60 s. His readings are recorded in Table 2.1.

At the end of 5 minutes the student empties the beaker. He adds a second layer of insulation to the beaker and repeats the experiment.

i)   Complete the column headings in Table 2.1.

Complete the time t column in Table 2.1.

Table 2.1

$t/\ldots$	1 layer of insulation $\theta_0/\ldots$	2 layers of insulation $\theta_1/\ldots$
0	80	80
	76	78
	72	76
	69	72
	65	69
	63	67

[2]

ii) Look at the readings in Table 2.1.

Tick the appropriate box to show your conclusion from the readings.

	The beaker with 1 layer of insulation has a smaller rate of cooling than the beaker with 2 layers of insulation.
	The beaker with 1 layer of insulation has a greater rate of cooling than the beaker with 2 layers of insulation.
	The water cooled at about the same rate for all three insulation levels.

[1]

iii) Justify your conclusion by reference to the readings.

....

....

....

....

[2]

(c) State two variables that were controlled to make this experiment a fair test.

1. .... 2. .... [2]

(d) A student in another country wants to repeat the experiment. Suggest why they should try to have the classroom at the same room temperature during the experiment to obtain similar results. [1]

[Total marks 10]

3 A student investigates how a spring stretches when different loads are attached to it.

Fig. 3.1 shows the apparatus that she uses.

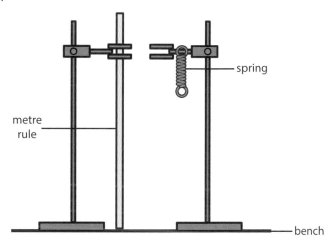

Fig. 3.1

(a) Fig. 3.2 shows the spring and a section of the half-metre rule. Take two readings from Fig. 3.2 and calculate the unstretched length, l_0, of the coil of the spring. Use an appropriate number of significant figures in your value for l_0.

Fig. 3.2

reading 1 .... cm

reading 2 .... cm

$l_0 =$ .... cm [4]

b The student adds a load L of 0.5 N to the bottom of the spring. She measures the new length of the spring. She calculates the extension, e, of the spring.

She repeats the measurement for 4 more loads.

Table 3.1 shows the values she obtains.

Table 3.1

L/N	l/cm	e/cm
0	....	0
0.5	4.1	......
1	6.3	4.3
1.5	8.4	6.4
2	10.5	8.5
2.5	12.3	10.3

Complete the missing values for length (l) and extension (e) in table 3.1   [2]

c Plot a graph of e/cm (y-axis) against l/N (x-axis).

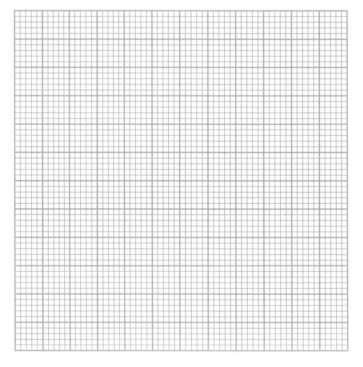

[4]

d Determine the gradient G of the graph. Show clearly how you obtained the information on the graph.   [2]

[Total marks 12]

4 Some students are investigating energy transfers between gravitational potential and kinetic stores using a very smooth inclined track and a ball bearing.

Fig. 4.1 shows the track the students use.

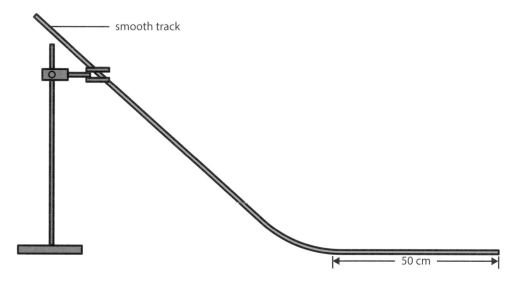

Fig. 4.1

Plan an experiment to investigate the relationship between the starting gravitational potential of a ball bearing and the kinetic energy of the ball bearing as it reaches the flat section of track.

Gravitational potential energy is calculated using the equation:

gravitational potential energy = mass × acceleration of free fall (g) × vertical height

Kinetic energy is calculated using the equation:

kinetic energy $= \frac{1}{2} \times$ mass $\times$ (velocity)^2

Gravitational potential energy and kinetic energy are both measured in joules.

Acceleration of freefall = 9.8 m/s^2

The following apparatus is available to the students:

- Metre rules

- A ball bearing that fits on the track

- An electronic balance

- A stopwatch

In your plan you should include:

- any additional apparatus needed

- a key variable to keep constant

- an explanation of how to carry out the investigation, including what is measured and how this is done

- a table, or tables, to show how to display the readings, including column headings

- a suggestion for a suitable graph to be drawn from the results.

You may add to Fig. 4.1 to help explain your plan.

[7]

[Total marks 7]

Pages 6-26: Section 1 Revise Questions

Page 7: Physical quantities and measurement techniques
1. average = (261 + 260 + 262 + 261 + 261) /5 = 261 mm
2. t = 1.1 s
3. **S** resultant velocity = 4 m/s − 1 m/s = 3 m/s

Page 9: Motion and speed–time graphs
1. 10 m/s
2. 5 m/s
3. 10 m/s
4. distance = area under the graph
   Calculate the area of the triangle.
   area = $\frac{1}{2} \times b \times h$ = $\frac{1}{2} \times 2 \times 10$
   distance = 10 m

Page 11: Acceleration and free fall
1. 9.8 m/s^2
2. **S** $a = \frac{1.5 \text{ m/s} - 0 \text{ m/s}}{0.75 \text{ s} - 0 \text{ m/s}}$ = 2 m/s^2.
3. **S** 0 m/s^2

Page 13: Mass, weight and density
1. 205.8 N
2. Volume of block = 8 cm^3; density = 8.9 g/cm^3
3. The ball will float because its density is less than the density of water.

Page 15: Effects of forces
1. Change the: shape; size; motion
2. There is a resultant upward force, so the plane will get higher (move upwards).
3. Drag friction
4. 140 N

Page 17: Turning effect of forces, centre of gravity and circular motion
1. Magnitude of the force and perpendicular distance of the force from the pivot
2. 4 Nm
3. Moments are in opposite directions and equal.
4. **S** Force decreases

Page 19: Springs and momentum
1. 5 cm
2. **S** 200 N/m
3. **S** 48 kg m/s

Page 21: Energy
1. Any three from: kinetic, gravitational potential, chemical, elastic (strain), nuclear, electrostatic, internal (thermal)
2. Energy can be neither created nor destroyed, but can be transferred between stores.
3.

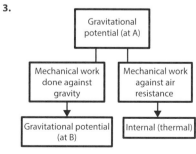

Page 23: Energy resources
1. Any three from: biofuels, wave, tidal, hydroelectric, geothermal, light/ electromagnetic radiation
2. Any one from: solar cells, solar panels

---

3. Release carbon dioxide; cause air pollution
4. **S** Nuclear fusion

Page 25: Calculating energy, work and power
1. 22.5 J
2. 5 W
3. **S** 0.4 J
4. **S** 29.4 J

Page 27: Pressure
1. 50000 Pa
2. 0.04 m^2
3. Depth and density of the liquid
4. 58 800 Pa

Pages 28-41: Section 1 Practise Questions

Page 28: Physical quantities and measurement techniques
1. C [1]
2. a) 2.3 s [1]
   h) 2.51 s [1]
   c) Each measurement includes reaction time [1]; for student 2 the reaction time is a smaller fraction of the measurement so affects the measurement less [1]
3. Readings are 1.8 cm^3 and 2.2 cm^3 [1]; Volume = 0.4 cm^3 [1]
4. **S** C [1]

Page 29: Motion and speed–time graphs
1. C [1]
2. **S** A: increasing speed [1]; B: constant speed [1]; C: stationary [1]
3. a) Area under graph between 0 and 5 s = 17.5 m [1]; area under graph between 5 s and 10 s = 35 m [1]; area under graph between 10 s and 20 s = 35 m [1]; total distance = 87.5 m [1]
   b) 7 m/s , 0 m/s [1]; slowing down [1]

Page 29: Acceleration and free fall
1. 9.8 m/s^2 [1]
2. **S** B [1]
3. **S** 2 m/s^2
4. a) 10 m/s [1]
   b) i) Decelerating (negative acceleration) [1]; ii) No acceleration [1]

Page 31: Mass, weight and density
1. C [1]
2. D [1]
3. a) 9000 N [1]; b) i) the same [1]; ii) 3330 N [2]
4. **S** i) vegetable oil above liquid soap and/ or water [1], liquid soap below water [1]
   ii) Liquids with a lower density will float on top of liquids with a higher density. Soap has the highest density so it will be at the bottom of the column [1], and vegetable oil has the lowest density so it will be at the top of the column [1].

Page 33: Effects of forces
1. B [1]
2. a) i) 5 N [1]; ii) change its shape/stretch it [1]
   b) i) 2 N [1]; ii) ball moves to the right/ towards B [1]
3. B [1]
4. **S** a) i) force to right = (10 + 20) N = 30 N [1]; resultant = 15 N [1]
   ii) to the right [1]
   b) $a = \frac{F}{m}$ [1]; $a = \frac{15 \text{ N}}{10 \text{ kg}}$ = 1.5 m/s^2 [1]

Page 34: Turning effect of forces
1. B [1]
2. Object is in equilibrium is when both turning effects [1] and resultant forces are zero [1]
3. Moment = force × perpendicular distance from the pivot [1]; 108 Nm [1]
4. **S** a) Sum of clockwise moments = sum of anticlockwise moments [1]
   b) clockwise moments = (3.0 N × 20 cm) + (X N × 40 cm) [1]; anticlockwise moments = (8.0 N × 40 cm) [1]; 60 N cm + 40X N cm = 320 N CM , 40 X N cm = (260 N cm) [1]; X = 6.5 N [1]

Page 35: Centre of gravity
5. Vase B [1]; centre of gravity is well within the base area of the vase [1]

Page 35: Circular motion
6. **S** a) Tension [1]; increase [1]

Page 35: Springs
1. D [1]
2. 5.2 N [1]
3. **S** 0.2 kg [1]; 1.96 N [1]; 0.8 cm [1]; 2.45 N/cm

Page 36: Momentum
4. **S** C [1]
5. **S** a) (0.1 × 1) − (0.1 × −0.8) [1]; 1.08 kg m/s [1]
   b) 1.08 N s [1]
   c) $\frac{1.08}{0.002}$; 540 N [1]
6. **S** a) (0.3 kg × 2 m/s) [1]; 0.6 kg m/s [1]
   b) combined mass = 0.4 kg [1]; 0.6 kg m/s = 0.4 × v [1]; 1.5 m/s [1]

Page 37: Energy
1. C
2.

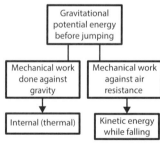

3. **S** a) Energy is neither created nor destroyed. It can be transferred between stores.
   b) Energy before = 2 000 000 J
   Energy after = 800 000 J + 125 000 J + internal energy [1]
   But energy before = energy after
   Energy before = gravitational potential energy + kinetic energy + internal energy [1]
   Internal energy = Energy before − (gravitational potential energy + kinetic energy)
   Internal energy = 2 000 000 J − (800 000 J + 125 000 J) [1]
   Internal energy = 1 075 000J [1]
4. **S** kinetic store = 1600 J [1]; internal (thermal) store = 400 J [1]

Page 39: Energy resources
1. A [1]
2. **S** C [1]

3. **a)** kinetic [1];
   b) any one from: quicker to install, no radioactive waste, can be built on a smaller scale [1];
   c) any one from: needs a larger space to put turbine/solar cells can be put on roof, wind turbines produce noise/visual pollution [1]

4. **S** $\frac{2}{5} \times 100\%$ [1]; 40% [1]

Page 39: Calculating energy, work and power

1. **S a)** $E_p = 0.05 \times 9.8 \times 1$ [1]; $E_p = 0.49$ J [1]
   b) $E_k = \frac{1}{2} \times 0.05 \times (3)^2$ [1]; $E_k = 0.225$ J [1]
   c) i) efficiency $= \frac{\text{useful energy out}}{\text{total energy in}} \times 100\%$ [1]; therefore efficiency $= \frac{E_k}{E_p} \times 100\%$ [1]; 46% [1]
   ii) Energy is transferred into internal (thermal) energy of the toy car and its surroundings by friction [1]

2. C [1]

3. 750 000 J (or 750 kJ) [1]

4. **a)** 5000 J [1]; **b)** power $= \frac{\text{energy transferred}}{\text{time}}$ [1]; 100 W [1]

Page 40: Pressure

1. C [1]
2. 50 Pa [1]
3. Pressure = 20 000 Pa [1]; force = pressure × area [1]; force = 25 MN (25 000 000 N) [1]
4. **a)** Weight = 16 000 N [1]; pressure = 400 000 Pa [1]
   b) Pressure exerted by tractor is less than the pressure that the bridge can withstand and it will not break. [1]
5. **S** $\Delta p = 1020 \times 9.8 \times 30$ [1]; 299 880 Pa [1]

Pages 42-53: Section 2 Revise Questions

Page 43: States of matter and the kinetic particle model of matter

1. Evaporation
2. Condensation
3. Speed increases (they get faster)
4. Particles are randomly arranged, closely packed together, and are able to move past each other.
5. Brownian motion – the random motion of microscopic particles suspended in a fluid.

Page 45: Gases and temperature

1. The pressure decreases
2. The pressure decreases
3. $60 + 273 = 333$ K
4. **S** $pV =$ constant
5. 337.5 cm^3

Page 47: Thermal expansion and specific heat capacity

1. As the temperature increases its particles move around more and take up more space.
2. A gas
3. mercury in thermometers expands as it increases in temperature and so rises up the scale to show a higher temperature.
4. The energy in joules required to increase the temperature of 1 kg of a substance by 1°C

Page 49: Melting, boiling and evaporation

1. It stays the same / doesn't change
2. 0 °C and 100 °C
3. **S** Evaporation can happen at any temperature and is when particles leave the surface of a liquid. Boiling can only happen at the boiling point and is when particles throughout the liquid have enough energy to leave it.
4. **S** Increase the temperature, increase the surface area, increase the air movement above it.

Page 51: Transfer of thermal energy: conduction, convection

1. Convection
2. **S** Metals have free (delocalised) electrons, which move quickly and transfer thermal energy by collisions with the metal ions.
3. **S** The particles in a gas are far apart and exert negligible forces on each other.

Page 53: Transfer of thermal energy: radiation

1. Radiation
2. Infrared
3. Because they are good thermal conductors and heat up quickly when in use
4. Because they are poor thermal conductors so do not become hot
5. Infrared and (mainly) convection

Pages 54-57: Section 2 Practise Questions

Page 54: States of matter and the kinetic particle model of matter

1. **a)** Melting is the process by which a solid turns into a liquid [1]
   b) Particles in a solid are arranged in a regular pattern but are randomly arranged in a liquid [1]; particles in a solid are closely packed together but are a little less closely packed in a liquid [1]

2. **a)** Evaporation [1]
   b) Molecules are randomly arranged [1], moving around very quickly [1], and are far apart from each other [1]
   c)

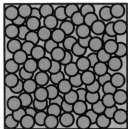

Particles touching [1]; random arrangement [1]

Page 55: Gases and the absolute scale of temperature

1. **a)** Pushing down the plunger decreases the volume of the air [1] so the particles collide more frequently with the walls of the syringe [1]
   b) $p_1 V_1 = p_2 V_2$ OR $pV =$ constant
   OR $1.0 \times 10^5 \times 10 = p_2 \times 4$
   OR $\frac{1 \times 10^5 \times 10}{4} = p_2$ [1]
   $p_2 = 0.25 \times 10^6$ pa [1]

2. Pressure decreases AND particles have a lower speed/velocity/kinetic energy (at lower temperature) [1]
   Particles collide less frequently/less often (with inside of football) [1]
   particles collide with a smaller force/smaller change of momentum/smaller impulse [1]

Page 55: Thermal expansion and specific heat capacity

1. D (rearrange $c = \frac{\Delta E}{m\Delta\vartheta}$ to get $\Delta\vartheta = \frac{\Delta E}{mc}$, put in numbers: $\Delta\vartheta = \frac{22500}{2.5 \times 900} = 10$) [1]

2. **a)** Molecules speed up or gain kinetic energy [1], so they move further apart [1]
   b) Forces between particles in a liquid are weaker than the particles in a solid [1], so can move further apart for the same increase in energy [1]

Page 56: Melting, boiling and evaporation

1. As sweat evaporates, faster moving/more energetic particles molecules escape/leave the surface of the sweat [1], so average kinetic energy of particles of sweat is reduced [1], so temperature of sweat is lowered [1] and energy is transferred from hotter body to cooler sweat, thus cooling down the body [1]

2. 70 °C [1]

Page 57: Transfer of thermal energy

1. White surfaces are poor absorbers of thermal radiation (so the houses do not get as warm) [1]

2. A [1]

3. The fleece material traps air, which is a poor conductor, reducing thermal energy transfer away from the student's body [1]; the shiny material reflects infrared radiation back towards the student's body [1]

Pages 58-67: Section 3 Revise Questions

Page 59: General properties of waves

1. A wave that travels parallel to the direction of vibrations, e.g. sound wave
2. A wave that travels at right angles to the direction of vibrations, e.g. electromagnetic wave
3. A change in the direction of a wave because of a change in its speed
4. Spreading out of a wave travelling through a gap or past an edge
5. **S** When the size of the gap is similar to the wavelength of the wave

Page 61: Light – reflection and refraction

1. Angle of incidence = angle of reflection
2. A line at right angles to another line or surface
3. The angle of incidence when the angle of refraction for a ray of light is 90°.
4. When no light is refracted at the boundary between two mediums, and all light is reflected back (inside the first medium)
5. **S** $n = \frac{\sin i}{\sin r}$

Page 63: Lenses and dispersion of light

1. Cause them to spread out (diverge)
2. AN image that cannot be projected onto a screen
3. Diverging lens
4. Dispersion
5. **S** Light of a single frequency (or wavelength)

Page 65: Electromagnetic spectrum

1. Low Earth Orbit (LEO) and geostationary
2. Ultraviolet, X-ray, gamma
3. Infrared
4. **S** They can pass through walls.
5. **S** Easier to process, and they transmit high rates of data over vast distances; easier to restore or regenerate so range of transmission can be increased

Page 67: Sound
1. Reflection of a sound wave
2. Amplitude
3. Sound of frequency above 20 000 Hz (20 kHz).
4. **S** Two from: medical scanning; industrial scanning; sonar
5. **S** It passes through living tissue without harming it.

Pages 68-73: Section 3 Practise Questions

Page 68: General properties of waves
1. A [1]
2.

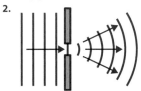

At least 3 curved lines after gap [1], equally spaced [1], spreading out (diverging) [1]
3. 0.6 m [3]

Page 69: Light – reflection and refraction
1. D [1]
2. Line drawn showing ray is reflected, with angle of incidence equal to angle of reflection [1]

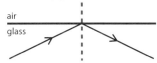

Page 70: Lenses and dispersion of light
1. Diverging [1]
2. **S** a) 5 cm
   b) Rays to lens drawn correctly [1]; rays extended back from lens drawn correctly [1]; upright arrow drawn from principal axis to where dashed lines intersect [1]

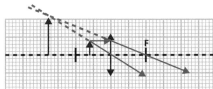

   c) Upright [1], magnified [1], virtual [1] (in any order)

Page 71: Electromagnetic spectrum
1. C [1]
2. D [1]
3. An analogue signal is continuous [1], but a digital signal can only take one of two values, on or off / high or low [1]

Page 72: Sound
1. C [1]
2. C [1]
3. distance = speed × time [1] = 1600 × (1.2 ÷ 2) [1] = 960 m [1]
   OR: distance = (speed × time) ÷2 = (1600 × 1.2) ÷ 2 [2] = 960 m [1]

Pages 74-95: Section 4 Revise Questions

Page 75: Magnetism
1. You can switch it on and off.
2. A temporary magnet is only magnetised when in a magnetic field. A permanent magnet is always magnetised.

3. The direction of a magnetic field is the direction of the force on a north pole. The head of the arrow of a compass is a north pole so it will point in the direction of the field.
4. **S** The magnetic field is strongest near to the poles because the field lines are closest together.

Page 77: Electric charge
1. Electrons have transferred from the surface of the cloth onto the polythene rod.
2. Metals have a sea of free electrons, which can move freely inside the metal.
3. **S** The field lines point towards the negative charge but away from the positive charge. The direction of the field is the direction of the force it would exert on a positive charge. The negative point charge would attract a positive charge, and a positive point charge would repel it.

Page 79: Current, potential difference and electromagnetic force
1. Free electrons drift through the wires.
2. In d.c. (direct current) the charge always moves the same way. In a.c. (alternating current) the charge keeps swapping the direction of its motion.
3. 4 V
4. **S** $t = 60$ s
   $Q = It = 2.5 \times 60 = 150$ C.
   $W = QV = 150 \times 2 = 300$ J

Page 81: Resistance, electrical energy and electrical power
1. $V = IT = 0.20 \times 50 = 10$ V
2. **S** Resistance is inversely proportional to area, so if the area is 4 times larger, the resistance will be $\frac{1}{4}$ as big. $\frac{20}{4} = 5\,\Omega$
3. The resistance of the lamp is not constant. If a larger current flows through it, the lamp becomes hot making it harder for the free electrons to move through it (because the ionic lattice vibrates more), thus increasing the resistance.
4. Power = $5 \times 100 = 500$ W. Power in kW $= \frac{500}{1000} = 0.5$ kW
   Energy in kW h = power in kW × time in hours $= 0.5 \times 16 = 8$ kW h
   Cost $= 25 \times 8 = 200$cents = $2.00

Page 83: Electrical symbols and series circuits
1. Thermistor

   LDR

   The resistance of a thermistor would be high if its temperature was very cold. The resistance of an LDR would be high if it was very dark.
2. **S** The light will flash on and off. Current is being pushed in opposite directions by the a.c. supply and the diode will only conduct when the current is pushed the correct way.
3. Maximum e.m.f. = 7 V, minimum e.m.f. = 3 V. When the a.c. supply pushes the current in the same direction as the d.c. supply, the overall e.m.f. will be $5 + 2 = 7$ V. When the a.c. supply pushes the current in the opposite direction, the overall e.m.f. will be $5 - 2 = 3$ V.

4. Overall resistance = 20 Ω + resistance of the lamp. So the lamp's resistance $= 100 - 20 = 80\,\Omega$.

Page 85: Parallel circuits
1. They can be turned on and off independently of each other.
2. Less than 1 Ω
3. **S** a) 48 Ω
   b) $80\,\Omega: I = \frac{V}{R} = \frac{12}{80} = 0.15$ A;
      $120\,\Omega: I = \frac{V}{R} = \frac{12}{120} = 0.1$ A
   c) 0.15 A + 0.1 A = 0.25 A

Page 87: Potential dividers and electrical safety
1. **S** 16V. Find p.d. across 1200 Ω resistor: $\frac{V_1}{1200} = \frac{4}{400}$ so $V_1 = 12$ V. Therefore total p.d. = 12 V + 4 V = 16 V
2. $I = \frac{P}{V} = \frac{1000}{110} = 9.1$A. So, the 13 A fuse is best.
3. Earth wire is connected to the metal case. If there is a fault and the case becomes live, a large current flows through the earth wire which blows the fuse.

Page 89: Electromagnetic induction and the a.c. generator
1. a) The magnetic field is changing (increasing).
   b) Move the magnet faster; use a stronger magnet
2. **S** To the left (thumb is the relative motion of the conductor)
3. **S** A side of the coil alternately moves up and down through the magnetic field and so the e.m.f. induced alternates its direction.
4. **S** The time for each complete rotation is less; the peaks would be more positive and the troughs more negative (since the magnitude of the induced e.m.f. is larger).

Page 91: Magnetic effect of a current
1. Circles going in the same direction, centred on the wire. The circles go round in the opposite direction.
2. Anticlockwise
3. Inside the solenoid, the field is stronger and it is uniform.
4. An electromagnetic switch. When a current flows through it the switch closes.
5. The cone will only move in one direction so it won't vibrate. Vibrations are needed to produce sound.

Page 93: Force on a current-carrying conductor and the d.c. motor
1. In electromagnetic induction, a motion generates an e.m.f. (and current). For demonstrating the magnetic force, a current from a power supply produces motion.
2. Faster: larger current, stronger magnets, more turns. Direction: connect the power supply the other way round, switch the direction of the magnetic field.
3. **S** Upwards
4. **S** The force on one side of the coil will always be the same way. The force needs to swap direction every time the side of the coil makes half a turn.

Page 95: Transformers

1. Step-up increases the voltage; step-down decreases it.
2. 5000 turns
3. Advantage: current is reduced so there is less power loss. Disadvantage: high voltages are dangerous.
4. **S** Voltage increases by a factor of 550. So current is $\frac{1}{550}$th of original value. $I^2 = \frac{1}{302\,500}$ so the power loss is reduced by a factor of 302 500.

Pages 96-105: Section 4 Practise Questions

Page 96: Magnetism

1. B [1]
2. Arrow points to the right → [1]
3. a) The iron nails become **temporary** magnets [1]; this means they are **attracted** to the electromagnet [1]
   b) The poles at the flat end of the nails will both be N poles [1]; like poles repel each other [1]
   c) The iron nails will behave the same [1]; the induced magnetic poles of the nails will be swapped around (to become S poles) but the flat ends will still repel each other (because like poles repel) [1]
4. a) The magnets are repelling [1]; field lines go from the N pole to the S pole so the two poles in the middle are S poles [1]; like poles repel [1]
   b) **S** The two regions are next to the poles on the left- and right-hand sides of the diagram (where the field lines are closest together) [2]
   c) **S** The two magnetic fields are interacting with each other [1], which produces a magnetic force [1]

Page 97: Electric charge

1. C [1]
2. D [1]
3. **S** Arrow points to the left [1]
4. a) Charges can move freely in conductors [1]; charges cannot move in insulators [1]
   b) When the polythene rod is near the conductors it repels their electrons [1]; therefore electrons move from sphere B to sphere A [1]
   When the spheres are separated, A is **negatively charged** (because it has extra electrons) [1] and B is **positively charged** (because it has lost some electrons) [1]

Page 98: Current, potential difference and electromagnetic force

1. a.c. means alternating current [1]; d.c. means direct current [1]. In a.c. the charge keeps changing direction; in d.c. the charge keeps moving in the same direction [1]
2. a) Analogue [1]
   b) 7.4 mA [1]
   c) The current is larger than the top value of the range [1]; the pointer would move off the scale to the right and get stuck (so the current could not be measured) [1]

3. a)

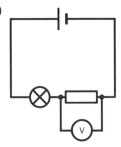

   Correct symbol for voltmeter [1]; voltmeter is connected across (in parallel with) the resistor [1]
   b) 1.5 V [1]
   c) 2 V [1]
   d) $2 - 1.5 = 0.5$ V [1]
4. **S** a) Coulomb(s) [1]
   b) $Q = It$ [1];
   $I = 100 \times \frac{1}{1000} = 0.1$ A [1]; $t = 10 \times 60 = 600$ s [1]; so $Q = 0.1 \times 600 = 60$ C [1]
   c) $E = QV$ [1]; $V = 2000$ V [1]. So $E = 60 \times 2000 = 120\,000$ J [1]

Page 99: Resistance, electrical energy and electrical power

1. A [1]
2. a) $R = \frac{V}{I}$ [1] $= \frac{0.90}{0.12} = 7.5\Omega$ [1]
   b) $P = IV$ [1] $= 0.12 \times 0.90 = 0.11$ W [1]
   c) $E = IVt$ [1] $= 0.90 \times 1.5 \times 20 = 27$ J [1]
3. a) The energy [1] transferred when a 1 kW device operates for 1 hour [1]
   b) 2500 W = 2.5 kW [1]; 210 minutes = 3.5 h [1]
   Number of kW h $= 2.5 \times 3.5 = 8.75$ [1]; cost $= \$0.60 \times 8.75 = \$5.25$ [1]
4. **S** a) A variable resistor can change the current through (or p.d. across) a component [1]. You need to obtain readings at different currents (or p.d.s) to plot a graph [1]
   b) Diode [1] because the component only conducts a current in one direction [1]
   c) When a larger current passes through the lamp, the filament gets hotter [1]; this makes it harder for the electrons to pass through the filament (since the rest of the metal – the ionic lattice – is vibrating more) [1] and so the resistance increases [1]

Page 100: Electrical symbols and series circuits

1. C [1]
2.

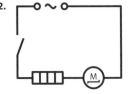

   Correct symbols used for a.c. supply [1], switch [1], heater [1] and motor [1]. Components are connected in a single loop using straight lines [1].
3. a) 120 Ω [1]
   b) $I = \frac{V}{R}$ [1] $= \frac{3.0}{80} = 0.0375$ A [1]
   c) Current through 40 Ω resistor is also 0.0375 A [1], $V = IR$ [1] $= 0.0375 \times 40 = 1.5$ V [1]

Page 101: Parallel circuits

1. a) The lamps can be switched on and off independently (or if one lamp blows the others remain on) [1]
   b) The student is not correct [1] because the combined resistance should be less than the smallest resistance in the circuit (so less than 40 Ω) [1]
2. a) 4.0 A [1]; the current leaving the (right-hand) junction = the sum of the currents entering it [1]
   b) A_1 stays the same [1]; A_2 stays the same [1]; A_3 increases [1]. The current in a branch depends on the p.d. across it and its resistance and these are unchanged for A_1 and A_2 [1] but the source needs to push a current that is the sum of the currents in all the branches, which needs to increase because there is a third branch [1]
3. a) The 40 Ω and 60 Ω resistors are in parallel. Let their combined resistance = R.
   $\frac{1}{R_T} = \frac{1}{R_1} + \frac{1}{R_2} = \frac{1}{40} + \frac{1}{60} = \frac{1}{24}$ [1]
   Therefore, $R = 24\Omega$ [1]
   R is in series with the 16Ω resistor. So, the total resistance = 16 + 24 = 40Ω [1]
   b) 40Ω and 60Ω [1]
   c) Current through the 16Ω resistor is the same as current from the source = e.m.f. / total resistance.
   $I = \frac{V}{R} = \frac{12}{40}$ [1] $= 0.3$ A [1]

Page 102: Potential dividers and electrical safety

1. The more devices you plug in, the higher the current in the wires (behind the plug socket) [1]; the larger the current the hotter the wires [1]; so there is an increased risk of fire [1]
2. a) A fuse consists of a thin metal wire [1], which gets hotter the higher the current [1]. At a certain current, the fuse wire melts and breaks the circuit [1] It breaks the circuit before a current becomes dangerously high [1]
   b) The normal operating current is much lower than 13 A
   ($I = \frac{P}{V} = \frac{20}{220} = 0.09$ A) [1] so the current can become much higher than is normal before the fuse breaks the circuit [1] Replace the 13 A fuse with one with a lower current rating [1]
   c) Live [1]; if a switch wasn't in the live wire, then some parts of the lamp would be live even when it was turned off [1]
   d) There are two layers of insulation between live parts of the lamp and the outside [1]; the outside of the lamp is an insulator (rather than a metal) [1] so there is no risk of an electric shock [1]
3. **S** $\frac{R_1}{R_2} = \frac{V_1}{V_2}$ [1]; $\frac{50}{50} = \frac{V_1}{V_2}$, so $V_1 = V_2$ [1]
   The total p.d. $= V_1 + V_2 = 12$ V [1]

   So, since the p.d.s are the same they must be 6 V each [1]
4. a) The resistance doubles (because resistance and length are proportional) [1]
   b) The wire is the same length above **A** as it is below [1]
   c) The resistance above **B**, R_1, is three

times greater than the resistance below **B**, R_2 **[1]**

$\frac{R_1}{R_2} = \frac{V_1}{V_2}$, so $\frac{V_1}{V_2} = 3$ **[1]**

V_1 needs to be $3 \times$ bigger than V_2 and they both need to add up to 12 V **[1]** If $V_1 = 9$ V and $V_2 = 3$ V, both these conditions are satisfied **[1]**

d) A quarter of the way down the wire **[1]**

Page 103: Electromagnetic induction and the a.c. generator

1. Move the wire **[1]**; change the magnetic field **[1]**

2. **S** a) An e.m.f. is generated in the coil (because the magnetic field is changing) **[1]**; the e.m.f. drives a current through the LED **[1]**

   b) N pole **[1]**; any electromagnetic effects produced by a generated e.m.f. act to oppose its production in the first place **[1]**; therefore, the electromagnetic effect of the coil would be to repel the magnet **[1]**

   c) The LED does not light **[1]**; an e.m.f. is generated in the opposite direction **[1]** and the LED only conducts in the direction of the original e.m.f. **[1]**

3.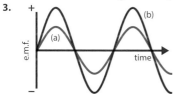

   a) e.m.f. alternates from positive to negative **[1]**; correct shape of graph **[1]**

   b) Peaks are higher and troughs are lower **[1]**; time for one complete cycle is the same **[1]**

Page 104: Magnetic effect of a current

1. C **[1]**

2. a) Set up a circuit that makes a (large) current pass through a straight wire **[1]**; make the wire pass through some paper and sprinkle iron filings on the paper **[1]**; tap the paper **[1]**

   b) Place a small compass in the field **[1]**; it will point in the direction of the field **[1]**

3. a)

   Series of circles centred on the wire **[1]**; circles go clockwise **[1]**; gaps between the circles get further apart the further they are from the centre **[1]**

   b) The circles would point the other way **[1]**; the circles would be closer together **[1]**

Page 104: Force on a current-carrying conductor and the d.c. motor

1. The conductor moves up as before **[1]**; reversing the cell and reversing the direction of the field both reverse the direction of the force on the wire – if you reverse something twice you end up going in the same direction **[1]**

2. D **[1]**

3. **S** a) The direction of the force depends on the direction of the **conventional** current (and the magnetic field) **[1]**; the conventional currents of the ions are in opposite directions **[1]**

   b) The negative ions **[1]**; use Fleming's left-hand rule **[1]** – if the first finger points into the page, the second finger needs to point left to make the thumb point downwards **[1]**; so, the conventional current must be in the opposite direction to the motion **[1]**

4. **S** To keep the coil spinning the same way **[1]**; if the current in one side of the coil goes in the same direction, once the coil spins half a turn it will feel a force pushing it back the other way – and the coil will not spin **[1]**

Page 105: Transformers

1. a) $\frac{V_P}{V_S} = \frac{N_P}{N_S}$ **[1]**; $\frac{220}{18} = \frac{990}{N_S}$ **[1]**; $N_s = 81$ **[1]**

   b) A (soft) iron core **[1]**

2. **S** a) $P = I^2 R$ **[1]**
   $= 100^2 \times 100 = 1\ 000\ 000$ W **[1]** $= 1$ MW **[1]**

   b) Input power $= 0.25$ MW $+ 1$ MW

   $= 1.25$ MW **[1]**; efficiency

   $= \frac{\text{useful power output}}{\text{total power input}}$ **[1]**;

   $= \frac{0.25}{1.25} = 0.2 = 20\%$ **[1]**

   c) New power loss is $10^2 \times 100 = 10\ 000$ W $= 0.01$ MW **[1]**; new input power $= 0.25 + 0.01 = 0.26$ MW ; so new efficiency $= 0.25/0.26 = 0.9615... = 96\%$ **[1]**

   d) To reduce the current you need to use a high voltage (to deliver the same power) **[1]**; high voltages are dangerous **[1]**.

Pages 106-113: Section 5 Revise Questions

Page 107: The nuclear model of the atom

1. $9 - 4 = 5$

2. $^{13}_{6}C$

3. $+2$

4. **S** Most of the α-particles travel straight through the atom.

Page 109: Radioactivity and nuclear emissions

1. The spontaneous and random change in an unstable nucleus that results in the emission of α– or β–particles and/or γ–radiation

2. α and β

3. **S** $^{241}_{95}\text{Am} \longrightarrow {}^{237}_{93}\text{Am} + {}^{4}_{2}\alpha$

Page 111: Detection of radioactivity and safety

1. The amount of radiation all around us due to natural processes in the environment.

2. Any three from: radon gas (in the air); rocks and buildings (e.g. from granite); food and drink (radiation absorbed from the environment); OR cosmic rays (coming from space)

3. Ionising radiation can: mutate cells; kill cells; OR cause cancers.

4. **S** corrected count-rate = measured count-rate – mean background count-rate

5. **S** Reducing the exposure time limits the total amount of radiation energy living tissue is exposed to as less radiation passes into the living tissue.

Page 113: Half-life

1. The time taken for half the number of nuclei to decay / the time taken for the count-rate to halve in value.

2. 75 counts/s

3. **S** Alpha particles would be completely absorbed by the paper, gamma rays would be completely unaffected by the paper, but the count-rate of a beta source would vary, depending on the thickness of the paper.

4. **S** After one half-life the count-rate will be 80 counts/s, and after two half-lives the count-rate will be 40 counts/s, so if two half-lives is 90 minutes, the half-life is $\frac{90}{2} = 45$ minutes

Pages 114-121: Section 5 Practise Questions

Page 114: The nuclear model of the atom

1. a) Isotopes (of an element) have the same number of protons but different numbers of neutrons. **[1]**

   b) 7 **[1]**

   c) **[1]** for each correct column – max **[3]**

Atom	Number of protons	Number of neutrons	Number of electrons
Nitrogen-14	7	7	7
Oxygen-16	8	8	8

   S d) 14 **[1]**; 15 **[1]**; 8 **[1]**

2. **S** C **[1]**

Page 115: Radioactivity and nuclear emissions

1. C **[1]**

2. a) Alpha particles are highly ionising **[1]**; but will not penetrate any further into the body than the skin **[1]**

   b) Gamma rays are the most penetrating and will pass through the soil to the surface to be detected. **[1]**

   c) Marking point 1: Apparatus needed: different absorbers and stopwatch (both needed for **[1]**)
   Marking point 2: Measure and record count from detector for stated time (e.g. 30 seconds). **[1]**
   Marking point 3: Insert paper between rock and detector and measure and record the count rate. **[1]**
   Marking point 4: Repeat for the other two absorbers. **[1]**
   Marking point 5: Key variable: One from: rock sample; distance between sample and detector; count time. **[1]**
   Marking point 6: Table with columns for type of absorber and count rate. Correct unit for count rate, e.g. cp30s, required. **[1]**
   Marking point 7: alpha emission absorbed by paper; beta emission absorbed by aluminium; gamma emission absorbed by lead. **[1]**

3. **S** One mark for each correct daughter nucleus nucleon number **[3]**; one mark for each correct daughter nucleus proton number **[3]**

   $^{212}_{82}\text{Pb}$

   $^{212}_{83}\text{Bi}$

   $^{208}_{81}\text{Tl}$

Page 117: Detection of radioactivity and safety

1. a) X = 7 [1]; Y = 15 [1]
   b) The radon level is very high and radon is a radioactive gas, emitting radiation, which could damage living tissue [1]; the radon sump prevents the radon gas from accumulating in the house and irradiating the occupants [1]
2. C [1]
3. a) i) $\frac{1811 + 1802 + 1787}{3} = 1800$ [1]
   ii) mean count rate $= \frac{1800}{6 \times 60} = 6$ counts/s [1]
   b) The source is stored in a lead-lined box to prevent irradiation of the body during storage and transport [1]; tongs are used to handle the source to prevent the hands being irradiated [1]; The source points away from the student to prevent direct exposure to radiation [1]
4. **S** a) mean background count
   rate $= \frac{27 + 30 + 32 + 24 + 27}{5}$
   $= 28$ counts/min [1]
   b)

Distance from source (cm)	1	3	5	7	9
Count-rate (counts/min)	1044	334	134	118	70
Corrected count-rate (counts/min)	1016	306	106	90	42

[1]

c) i)

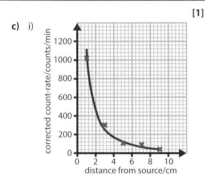

Correct labels and units on axes [1]; scale covering over half of plottable area of grid [1]; all points plotted accurately (tolerance $\pm\frac{1}{2}$small square) [2]; only one plotting mistake [1]
ii) Best-fit curve with decreasing gradient [1]
iii) As distance increases, so the count-rate decreases; [1] at a decreasing rate [1]

Page 119: Half-life

1. a) i) 15 minutes [1]; ii) 3 counts/minute [1]
   S b)

Time	Count rate (counts/minute)
0	6400
1 half-life	3200
2 half-lives	1600
3 half-lives	800
4 half-lives	400
5 half-lives	200

5 half-lives [1] = 5 × 138 days = 690 [1] days
2. **S** C [1]
3. **S** a) $^{24}_{11}\text{Na} \longrightarrow ^{24}_{12}\text{Mg} + ^{0}_{-1}\beta$ both for [1]

b) i) 8 counts/s [1]; ii) 320; 202; 127; 80; 50; 32; 20 [1];
iii)

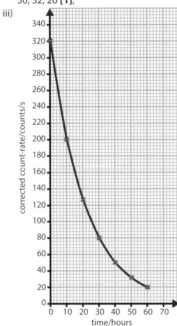

All 7 points plotted accurately ($\pm\frac{1}{2}$ small square) [2]; 6 points plotted accurately (one mistake) [1]
Accurate best-fit curved line [1]
iv) 15 hours [1]
c) Copper-66 – half-life too short, there would not be enough time for the water engineer to locate the leak [1]; Radon-211 – alpha emitter, so radiation will be absorbed by the ground and the water engineer will be unable to locate the leak [1]; Cobalt-60 – gamma emitter, so the pipe will not absorb the gamma rays and there will be no noticeable change in gamma ray emission along the length of the pipe, hence the leak will not be detectable [1]

Pages 122–129: Section 6 Revise Questions

Page 123: Earth and the Solar System

1. A year is the time taken for the Earth to orbit the Sun once. A day is the time taken for the Earth to fully rotate on its axis once.
2. The Moon orbits the Earth once every month (27 days). There are 12 months in a year, so we get 12 full moons per year.
3. A moon is a natural satellite of a planet. A comet is a natural satellite of the Sun, in a highly elliptical orbit.
4. Mercury, Venus, Earth, Mars. The force of the Sun's gravity is strongest closest to the Sun, allowing the material to clump closer together. The temperature is also much higher, causing most of the gas to be blown off into the outer Solar System.

Page 125: Orbits and using planetary data

1. The mass or density of the Earth
2. The Sun has a massive gravitational field because it has most of the mass of the Solar System.
3. **S** The kinetic energy of a planet increases as it gets closer to the Sun, and so the orbital speed increases.

4. **S** $v = \frac{2\pi r}{T} = \frac{2\pi \times 108.2 \times 10^6}{224.7 \times 24} =$
   $126064.5 \approx 126100$ km/h (4 s.f.)

Page 127: Stars

1. Infrared, visible light and ultraviolet
2. A large collection of stars, 'close' to each other in space
3. **S** The mass of the red supergiant
4. **S** distance (in km)
   $= \frac{4.2 \text{ ly} \times 9.5 \times 10^{15} \text{ m/ly}}{1000 \text{ m/km}} =$
   3.99×10^{13} km

Page 129: The Universe

1. The theory that the Universe came into being at a single point approximately 14 billion years ago and is expanding outwards.
2. Redshift provides evidence for the fact that the Universe is expanding.
3. **S** The microwave remnant of the redshifted gamma rays produced just after the Big Bang.
4. **S** $H_0 = \frac{v}{d} \Rightarrow v = H_0 d = 2.2 \times 10^{-18}$
   $\times 17.3 \times 10^6 = 3.9 \times 10^{-11}$ light-years/s

Pages 130–135: Section 6 Practise Questions

Page 130: Earth and the Solar System

1. C [1]
2. a) 365 days [1]
   b) i) The Sun appears to move from East to West across the sky because the Earth rotates on its axis once every 24 hours [1], whereas the relative positions of the Sun and the Earth hardly change [1]
   ii) On June 21st the tilt of the Earth's axis in the Northern Hemisphere is towards the Sun, so the Sun appears higher in the sky [1]; on December 21st, the tilt of the Earth's axis in the Northern Hemisphere is away from the Sun, so the Sun appears lower in the sky [1]
3. C [1]
4. a)

An accretion disc formed around the Sun.	3
An interstellar cloud of gas and dust started to rotate and collapse.	1
Material at the centre of the interstellar cloud collapsed to form the Sun.	2
Small rocky planets formed close to the Sun and large gaseous planets formed further away.	5
Material inside the accretion disc started to collapse and form planets.	4
The present day Solar System.	6

All 4 correct = 2 marks
2 or 3 correct = 1 mark
   b) Near to the Sun small rocky planets formed because the force of gravity is higher, so the heavier material in the accretion disc was attracted closer to the Sun [1]; further from the Sun large gaseous planets formed because the temperature was low enough for the light gases (hydrogen and helium) to stay bound to the planets [1]

Page 131: Orbits and using planetary data

1. A [1]

2. a) Gravity [1]
   b) The mass (or density) of Mars is less than the mass (or density) of the Earth [1]
   c) i) time taken $= \dfrac{\text{distance travelled}}{\text{speed}} =$
      $\dfrac{225 \times 10^6 \text{ km}}{300000 \text{ km/s}}$ [1] $= 750$ s [1]
      ii) The minimum time delay between a visual signal leaving Curiosity, getting to Earth, and then a response command being received by Curiosity is $(2 \times 750) = 1500$ s $= 25$ minutes. It is impossible to drive Curiosity in real time – the time delay is too big. [1]

3. S a) As the mean orbital distance from the Sun increases, the mean orbital speed decreases [1] at a decreasing rate [1]
   b) i) 18 [1] km/s [1]
      ii) $v = \dfrac{2\pi r}{T} \Rightarrow T = \dfrac{2\pi r}{v}$ [1] $=$
      $18 = 139626340$s [1] $=$
      $\dfrac{139626340}{86400} = 1616$ [1] days
   c) The density of Ceres is less than the densities of all the rocky inner terrestrial planets [1] but more than the densities of the outer gaseous Jovian planets [1] so Ceres must have some high density rock components and some lower density water ice components [1]

4. S A [1]

Page 132: Stars
1. A [1]
2. a) A large collection of stars, 'close' to each other in space. [1]
   b) i) The Milky Way [1]; ii) Distance from centre to the edge of the galaxy $=$ half the diameter of the galaxy $= 50\,000$ [1] light-years
      Distance from centre to the Sun
      $= \dfrac{X}{2} = \dfrac{50000}{2} = 25\,000$ [1] light-years
3. S A [1]
4. a) {nebula → protostar} [1] → {star → red supergiant} [1] → {supernova → black hole} [1]
   b) 1600 ly $\times 9.5 \times 10^{15}$ m/ly
      $= 1.5 \times 10^{19}$ m [1]
      $\dfrac{1.5 \times 10^{19} \text{ m}}{1000 \text{m/km}} = 1.5 \times 10^{16}$ km [1]
   c) i) 30 solar masses [1]; ii)
      $30 \times 2 \times 10^{30} = 60 \times 10^{30}$ kg [1]

Page 134: The Universe
1. D [1]
2. a) The Universe started from a single point [1]
   b) The Universe is expanding [1]
   c) The space of the Universe is expanding, stretching the wavelength of light emitted by distant galaxies [1]
3. S a) Any two of the following:
   The CMBR has a characteristic (microwave) frequency
   The CMBR has a characteristic (microwave) wavelength
   The CMBR was produced shortly after the Big Bang
   The wavelength of the CMBR has increased since the Big Bang
   The CMBR is the same in all directions
   [2 × 1 mark]

   b) The energy released at the time of the Big Bang was in the form of gamma rays [1]; these gamma rays have had their wavelength stretched [1]; as the space of the Universe expanded [1]; and their wavelength now corresponds to a microwave wavelength – the CMBR [1]

4. S a) $H_0 = \dfrac{v}{d}$ [1]
   $\Rightarrow d = \dfrac{v}{H_0}$ [1] $= \dfrac{7.04 \times 10^{-11}}{2.2 \times 10^{-18}}$ [1]
   light-years $= 32\,000\,000$ [1] light-years
   b) i) $H_0 = \dfrac{v}{d}$ [1] $= \dfrac{6.0 \times 10^6}{2.5 \times 10^{24}}$ [1] $=$
      2.4×10^{-18} [1] /s
      ii) age of the Universe (in seconds)
      $= \dfrac{1}{H_0}$ [1] $= \dfrac{1}{2.4 \times 10^{-18}}$ [1] $=$
      4.17×10^{17} [1] s

      age of the Universe (in years)
      $= \dfrac{\text{age of the Universe (in seconds)}}{\text{number of seconds in one year}}$ [1]
      $= 13.2 \times 10^9$ [1] years

Pages 136-151: Mixed Exam-Style Questions

1. a) C [1]
   b) Uranus [1] and Neptune [1]
   c) The planets closest to the Sun are rocky [1]; whereas the ones further away are gaseous [1]
   d) The Sun is much more massive than anything else [1]; so its force of gravity dominates the solar system [1]

2. $P = IV$ [1]; $I = \dfrac{P}{V} = 0.1$ A [1]; $V = IR$ [1];
   $R = \dfrac{V}{I} = 1100 \, \Omega$ [1]

3. a) Neutron: 0 [1]; Electron: -1 [1]
   b) $239 - 94 = 145$ [1]
   c) S $+94$ [1]
   d) S $^{239}_{93}\text{Np} \rightarrow ^{239}_{94}\text{Pu} + ^{0}_{-1}\beta$ [1 mark for identifying that it is a beta particle; 1 mark for the top numbers correct; 1 mark for the bottom numbers correct]

4. a) No resultant force [1]; no resultant moment [1]
   b) A is heavier [1]; the moments of A and B are the same [1]; A is closer to the pivot so exerts a larger force down to produce the same moment [1]

5. a) Object

   [Ray carries on in a straight line through the middle of the lens [1]; ray parallel to the principal axis bends and moves through f [1]; image drawn upside-down where the rays cross [1]]
   b) Real [1]; enlarged [1]; inverted [1]
   c) S The lens would have a shorter focal length [1]; so the object would be slightly further away from the focal length [1]; this would make the image larger [1]

6. S C [1]

7. a) e.g. they can all travel through a vacuum [1]; they all travel at the same speed in a vacuum [1]
   b) i) Ultraviolet light is not part of the visible spectrum [1]

      ii) Ultraviolet light is dangerous [1]; you need to be able to tell if the light bulb is switched on (to take necessary precautions) [1]
   c) e.g. detecting false banknotes [1]; special security marks glow (fluoresce) when UV light is shone on genuine banknotes [1]

8. a) e.g. They are both produced when a nucleus decays [1]; alpha is a strong ioniser, gamma is a weak ioniser [1]; alpha has a positive electric charge but gamma has no charge [1]; gamma has a greater penetrating ability than alpha [1]
   b) Put a source of americium within 1 cm of a detector [1]; place a piece of paper in the gap [1]; if the count rate falls significantly then the source produces alpha radiation [1]; keep the paper in place and add aluminium in the gap too [1]; if there is still a reading (above background) and the aluminium does not affect it, then the source also produces gamma radiation [1]

9. S a) An alternating current in the primary coil produces an alternating magnetic field [1]; the iron makes the field pass through the secondary coil [1]; the changing magnetic field through the secondary coil induces a voltage in the coil [1]
   b) i) The pointed ends have a smaller cross-sectional area [1]; resistance is inversely proportional to the area, so a smaller area means a higher resistance [1]
      ii) Because the resistance is greater, more power is dissipated because $P = I^2R$ [1]; more energy transfers by heating every second and so the pointed ends of the nails heat up quicker [1]
   c) It should have a large number of turns [1]; this means that the current in the secondary coil is large [1]; which means more power is available for heating the nails [1]

10. a) Distance $=$ area [1] $= \dfrac{1}{2} \times 2 \times 8$ [1] $= 8$ m [1]
    b) S Gravitational field strength $=$ acceleration of free fall $=$ gradient of the graph [1]; $= \dfrac{8}{2} = 4$ N/kg [1]
    c) S Line is a straight line through the origin [1]; with a gradient $= 9.8$ (so the speed is 19.6 m/s at a time of 2 s) [1]; distance $=$ area under line $= \dfrac{1}{2} \times 2 \times 19.6 = 19.6$ m [1]

11. a) As the radiation has been moving through the universe, the universe has been expanding [1]; this expansion has stretched the wavelength of the radiation [1]
    b) S i) They observe supernova of stars in the galaxy [1]; the apparent brightness of the supernova is measured [1] and by comparing this with the known brightness they can calculate the distance [1]
       ii) $8000000 \times 9.5 \times 10^{15} = 7.6 \times 10^{22}$ m [1]

iii) Use $H_0 = \frac{v}{d}$ [1]; $v = H_0 d = 2 \times 10^{-18}$ [1] $\times 7.6 \times 10^{22} = 152000$ m/s [1]

$c = 3.00 \times 10^8$ [1];

$Z = \frac{152000}{3 \times 10^8} = 5.1 \times 10^{-4}$ [1]

12. a) The microwaves aren't spreading out enough to reach receiver B [1]

b) The microwaves are now detected [1]; because the edge of the metal plate makes the waves diffract [1] (so they spread out and reach **b)**)

13. a)

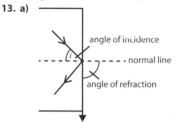

angle of incidence

normal line

angle of refraction

[3 – 1 mark for each correct label]

b) The angle of refraction is at 90° [1]; If the angle of incidence is increased then refraction is impossible so total internal reflection occurs [1]

c) [S] $n = \frac{1}{\sin c}$ [1]; so $c = \sin^{-1}\left(\frac{1}{1.5}\right)$ $= 41.8°$ [1]; for reflection, $i = r$, so the angle of reflection $= 41.8°$ [1]

14. a) [S] Vectors have a direction but scalars don't [1]

b) e.g. Scalar: time [1]; Vector: momentum [1]

c) resultant force

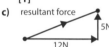

5N

12N

[1 mark for joining the original forces on the diagram correctly and 1 mark for indicating the resultant force correctly]; find the resultant force by using a scale diagram or by calculation: $F = \sqrt{12^2 + 5^2} = 13$ N [1]

15. a) The particles have a range of speeds / kinetic energies [1]; the fastest particles escape the surface [1]; this makes the average kinetic energy decrease, which reduces the temperature [1]

b) [S] If the surroundings are hot, the energies of the water particles on the outer surface are higher and this increases the likelihood of evaporation [1]; if the surroundings are dry then it is more likely that the particles of water leave the surface (cooling it down) than arrive at the surface from the air (warming it up) [1]

c) e.g. make air flow around the pots [1]

16. a) It is summer in the northern hemisphere [1]; it is winter in the southern hemisphere [1]

b) In summer the Earth is tilted towards the Sun [1]; this makes the hours of daylight (when the Earth gains energy) longer than the hours of darkness (when the Earth loses energy) [1]; so there is a net transfer of energy from the Sun to the Earth [1]

c) [S] $v = \frac{2\pi r}{T}$ [1]; $= \frac{2\pi \times 150000000}{3.15 \times 10^7}$ [1]; $= 29.9$ km/s [1]

17. a) i) There are two layers of electric insulation [1] between the live wire and the outside [1]

ii) There is no earth wire in the cable [1]; double insulated appliances don't need an earth wire [1]

b) $P = IV$ [1]; so $I = \frac{P}{V} = \frac{800}{220} = 3.6$ A [1]; a 3 A fuse would not be suitable [1]; because the normal operating current is higher than 3 A and would blow the fuse [1]

18. a) $W = mg$ [1]; $= 2.0 \times 9.8 = 19.6$ N [1]

b) Minimum area $= 0.10 \times 0.15 = 0.015$ m² [1] $P = \frac{F}{A}$ [1] $= \frac{19.6}{0.015} = 1300$ Pa (to 2 s.f.) [1]

19. [S] **a)** Momentum of A $= mv$ [1] $= 2000 \times 20 = 40\,000$ kg m/s [1]. Momentum of B $= 2500 \times -19.6 = -49\,000$ kg m/s [1] So total momentum $= 9000$ kg m/s [1] to the left [1]

b) Total mass of cars $= 4500$ kg [1]; so velocity $= \frac{9000}{4500} = 2$ m/s [1] to the left [1]

20. a) Vibrations for a transverse wave are perpendicular [1] and vibrations for a longitudinal wave are parallel to [1] the direction of propagation [1].

b) ii) both [1]

iii) both [1]

iv) transverse [1]

21. a) Energy is conserved [1]; so the energy transferred to gravitational potential energy $= 2.4 - 0.3 = 2.1$ J [1]

b) [S] Kinetic energy $= \frac{1}{2}mv^2$ [1]; $2.4 = 0.5 \times m \times 4.0^2$ [1]; $m = 0.30$ kg [1]

c) [S] Gravitational potential energy $= mgh$ [1]; $2.1 = 0.3 \times 9.8 \times h$ [1]; $h = 0.71$ m [1]

22. a) Mass of liquid $= 143.4 - 23.4 = 120$ g [1]; volume $= 75$ cm³ [1]; Density $= \frac{\text{mass}}{\text{volume}}$ [1] $= \frac{120}{75} = 1.6$ g/cm³ [1]

b) Density of ball in g/cm³ $= \frac{1180}{1000} = 1.18$ g/cm³ [1]; this is less dense than the liquid so the ball will float [1]

23. a) Draw a vertical line on the card in the direction of the thread [1]; hang the card from a different place [1]; draw a new vertical line and the centre of gravity is where the two lines meet [1]

b) The card remains balanced on the pin [1]; there is no resultant moment (from the gravitational force) about the pivot so the card does not topple [1]

24. a) The distance [1] that light travels (in a vacuum) in a year [1]

b) i) The Milky Way [1]

ii) 100 000 light years [1]

c) The galaxies are moving away from us [1] because the universe is expanding [1]

25. [S] **a)** Some energy is used to heat up the kettle/surroundings rather than the water [1]

b) Temperature change = 80 °C [1]; useful energy supplied $= mc\Delta\vartheta = 1.5 \times 4200 \times 80 = 504\,000$ J [1]; Time $= 4.0 \times 60 = 240$ s [1]; Useful power $= \frac{\text{energy}}{\text{time}} = \frac{504000}{240} = 2100$ W [1]

c) i) $0.8 \times P = 2100$ [1]; $P = \frac{2100}{0.8} = 2625$ W [1]

ii) Power = 2.625 kW [1], time $= \frac{4}{60} = 0.066\ldots$ hours [1]; energy $= 2.625 \times 0.067 = 0.175$ kW h [1]

26. C [1]

27. a) You would be unable to move forward [1] because there would be no friction to stop your feet from sliding backwards [1]

b) The arrow is horizontal and pointing to the right (forwards) [1]

c) [S] This increases the force of friction [1], which enables them to have a larger acceleration [1] from $F = ma$ [1]

28. a)

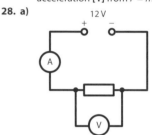

12 V

A

V

Correct symbols for ammeter and voltmeter [1]; ammeter connected in series [1]; voltmeter connected in parallel [1]

b) $R = \frac{V}{I}$ [1] $= \frac{12}{0.8} = 15\ \Omega$ [1]

c) The combined resistance of the parallel circuit must be less than the original resistance [1]

d) [S] $\frac{1}{R} = \frac{1}{15} + \frac{1}{7.5} = 0.2$ [1]; so $R = \frac{1}{0.2} = 5\ \Omega$ [1]

29. a)

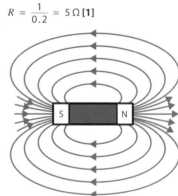

S N

Field lines loop from one pole to the other pole [1]; direction is N pole to S pole [1]; field lines don't touch [1]

b) The field lines would be closer together [1]

30. a) 50 s [3] [1 mark for using two points on the graph and finding the time between them; 1 mark for using one point that has half the count rate of the other point; 1 mark for calculating the half-life as 50 s]

b) [S] You need 3 half-lives [1]; so the time is $50 \times 3 = 150$ s [1]

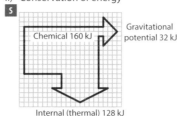

31. a) i) Microwaves **[1]**

ii) e.g. microwave cooking **[1]**; mobile phone communication **[1]**

b) The satellite is always vertically above the same point of the ground **[1]** so you don't need to keep repositioning your transmitter or receiver **[1]**.

c) Speed of electromagnetic waves is 3.0×10^8 m/s **[1]**; time $= \dfrac{\text{distance}}{\text{speed}}$ **[1]** $= \dfrac{75000000}{3.0 \times 10^8} = 0.25$ s **[1]**

32. B **[1]**

33. S **a)** A current through a wire produces a magnetic field **[1]**.

b) Place the thumb, first finger and second finger of your left hand at right angles to each other **[1]**; orientate your hand so your thumb points in the direction of the force **[1]** and your second finger points in the direction of the current **[1]**; your first finger will show the direction of the magnetic field **[1]**

c) The left-hand pole should be labelled "S" and the right-hand pole "N" **[1]**

34. a) Infrared **[1]**

b) i) e.g. they all travel the same speed in a vacuum **[1]**

ii) e.g. they have different wavelengths **[1]**

c) e.g. they can give people skin cancer **[1]**

35. a) $W = mg$ **[1]** $m = 0.300$ kg and $g = 9.8$ N/kg **[1]**; so $W = 0.3 \times 9.8 = 2.94$ N **[1]**

b) 0 N **[1]**

c) 0.72 s **[1]**

d) The inaccuracy of timing 10 oscillations is about the same as timing 1 oscillation **[1]**; so when you divide by 10, the inaccuracy is only a tenth as much as it would have been **[1]**

36. B **[1]**

37. S **a)** Lead-210 has an excess of neutrons in the nucleus **[1]**, which makes it unstable **[1]**

b) A neutron **[1]** turns into a proton **[1]** and an electron **[1]**

c) They curve in opposite directions **[1]**; the beta particles curve more sharply than the alpha particles do **[1]**

38. a) Set up a series circuit with a power source and the material **[1]**; include e.g. an ammeter that shows whether a current flows **[1]**; if the material is a conductor then a current flows, and no current flows if it is an insulator **[1]**

b) i) e.g. metal **[1]**

ii) e.g. plastic **[1]**

c) S They have free electrons inside **[1]**; the moving electrons can form a current in an electrical conductor **[1]**; and they can transfer kinetic energy quickly through collisions in a thermal conductor **[1]**

39. a) They move faster **[1]**

b) They collide **[1]** with the walls of the container **[1]**

c) The particles move rapidly **[1]** and randomly **[1]** and collisions with the globules of fat makes them jiggle **[1]**

40. a) The athlete is running at a constant speed **[1]**, so their kinetic energy remains the same **[1]**

b) i) 128 kJ **[1]**

ii) Conservation of energy

c) S

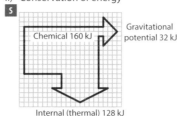

Chemical 160 kJ → Gravitational potential 32 kJ
↓
Internal (thermal) 128 kJ

[Correct shape **[1]**, gravitational potential energy arrow is $\frac{1}{5}$ the width of the original arrow **[1]**; internal (thermal) arrow is $\frac{4}{5}$ the width **[1]**]

41. S **a)** There is not a complete circuit **[1]**.

b) Field lines are horizontal **[1]**, equally spaced **[1]** and point from the left-hand (positive) plate to the right-hand plate **[1]**

c) i) 50 MΩ = 50 000 000 Ω **[1]**.

If this was the only resistance in the circuit, then the current $= \dfrac{V}{R} = \dfrac{5000}{50000000} = 0.0001$ $A = 0.1$ mA **[1]**; since you cannot make the resistance any less than 50 MΩ, 0.1 mA would be the maximum current **[1]**

ii) The 5 kV supply could drive a dangerous current through you if you touch it **[1]**; limiting the current makes it safer **[1]**

42. a) The pitch of the sound will increase **[1]**

b) i) Ultrasound consists of soundwaves with frequencies too high for the human ear to hear **[1]**

ii) 20 kHz **[1]**

c) S Distance the pulse travels = speed × time **[1]** $= 1500 \times 0.16 = 240$ m **[1]**; so $d = \dfrac{240}{2} = 120$ m **[1]**

43. a) i) Radioactive emissions from naturally occurring materials **[1]**

ii) e.g. cosmic rays **[1]**; food and drink **[1]**

b) The radiation is random **[1]** so you need a long time interval to get an average reading **[1]**

c) S Background count rate $= \dfrac{260}{20} = 13$ counts/minute **[1]**; corrected initial count rate = 153 − 13 = 140. Corrected final count rate = 48 − 13 = 35 **[1]**; therefore 2 half-lives have passed (since 140 ÷ 2 ÷ 2 = 35) **[1]**; half-life $= \dfrac{10}{2} = 5$ minutes **[1]**

Pages 152-163: Practice Paper 1 (1 mark each)

1. B	**11.** D	**21.** B	**31.** B
2. A	**12.** A	**22.** C	**32.** C
3. A	**13.** D	**23.** D	**33.** A
4. B	**14.** D	**24.** C	**34.** C
5. D	**15.** A	**25.** B	**35.** D
6. C	**16.** C	**26.** C	**36.** B
7. B	**17.** D	**27.** B	**37.** D
8. B	**18.** B	**28.** C	**38.** C
9. A	**19.** A	**29.** A	**39.** D
10. D	**20.** A	**30.** A	**40.** C

Pages 176-183: Practice Paper 2 (1 mark each)

1. A	**11.** A	**21.** B	**31.** C
2. A	**12.** C	**22.** C	**32.** D
3. A	**13.** B	**23.** B	**33.** B
4. B	**14.** D	**24.** D	**34.** A
5. C	**15.** C	**25.** B	**35.** D
6. C	**16.** B	**26.** C	**36.** C
7. C	**17.** D	**27.** A	**37.** D
8. A	**18.** C	**28.** C	**38.** B
9. A	**19.** D	**29.** A	**39.** B
10. D	**20.** A	**30.** A	**40.** C

Pages 164-175: Practice Paper 3

1. a) i) Q to R **[1]**

ii) Distance P to Q $= \frac{1}{2} \times 15 \times 3 = 22.5$ m **[1]**

Distance Q to R = $15 \times 3 = 45$ m **[1]**

Distance from R to S $= \frac{1}{2} \times 15 \times 4 = 30$ m **[1]**

Total distance $= 22.5 + 45 + 30 = 97.5$ m **[1]**

b) From P to Q the car is accelerating **[1]** at $\frac{15}{3} = 5$ m/s^2 **[1]**

From R to S the car is decelerating **[1]** at $-\frac{15}{4} = -3.75$ m/s^2 **[1]**

2. a) Measure the mass of the statue **[1]** using the electronic balance **[1]**; measure the volume of the statue **[1]** by putting the statue into the water and measuring the volume of water displaced using the measuring cylinder **[1]**

Calculate the density using: density $= \dfrac{\text{mass}}{\text{volume}}$ **[1]**

b) density $= \dfrac{\text{mass}}{\text{volume}}$ **[1]** $= \dfrac{236}{29.5}$ **[1]** $= 8$ **[1]** g/cm^3 **[1]**

c) Convert 8 g/cm^3 to kg/cm^3 **[1]**

8 g $= \dfrac{8}{1000} = 0.008$ kg

1 cm$^3 = \dfrac{1}{100 \times 100 \times 100} = 1 \times 10^{-6}$ m^3

8 g/cm$^3 = \dfrac{0.008}{1 \times 10^{-6}} = 8000$ kg/m^3 **[1]**

The alloy must be bronze **[1]**

3. a) moment = weight × distance from pivot **[1]**

moment $= 350 \times 1.5$ **[1]** $= 525$ **[1]** N m **[1]**

b) moment of A = moment of B **[1]**

$525 = 2.5 \times W$

$W = \dfrac{525}{2.5}$ **[1]** $= 210$ **[1]** N

c) weight = mass × gravitational field strength / $W = mg$ **[1]**

$m = \dfrac{W}{g} = \dfrac{210}{9.8}$ **[1]** $= 21.4$ **[1]** kg

ANSWERS

4. **a)** Hydroelectric power station [1]
   b) The electricity needed to run the pumps is cheaper at night [1]
   c) Advantage: renewable / reliable / low environmental impact / very short start-up time – any [1]
   Disadvantage: can only run for a short period of time (until all the water has run out of the reservoir) / only available in hilly locations – any [1]
   d) X is heating [1]; Y is mechanical work done [1]; Z is electrical work done [1]
5. **a)** X is liquid [1]; Z is solid [1]
   b) i) freezing / solidifying / melting [1]
      ii) Particles are: forming a regular structure [1]; becoming closely packed [1]; vibrating about a fixed point [1]
6. **a)** Place a thin, flat glass sheet into the water [1] to change the depth of the water (above the glass sheet) [1]
   b) i) wavelength = 24 cm [1]
      ii) amplitude = 2.3 mm [1]
   c) wave speed $v = f\lambda$ [1]; $f = \frac{v}{\lambda} = \frac{18}{24}$ [1] = 0.75 Hz [1]
7. **a)** i) 40 Ω [1]
      ii) $R = \frac{V}{I} = \frac{6.0}{40}$ [1] = 0.15 A [1]
      iii) 0.15 A [1]
   b) $R = \frac{V}{I} \Rightarrow I = \frac{V}{R}$ [1]; Reading A_3
      $= \frac{6.0}{10} = 0.6$ A [1]
      As resistors have the same resistance, R, reading $A_4 = \frac{0.6}{2} = 0.3$ A [1]
      Reading $A_5 = A_4 = 0.3$ A [1]
8. **a)** The production of an emf across (or current through) a conductor [1] when it moves across a magnetic field [1] (or when a changing magnetic field [1], links with a conductor producing an emf/current [1])
   b) Move the conductor faster [1]; coil the conductor [1]; increase the strength of the magnetic field [1]
9. **a)** i) A = 0 [1]; Z = −1 [1]
      ii) Beta decay [1]; X is a beta particle / electron [1]
   b) i) Half of 800 = 400 counts/minute [1]; Moving along the value of Count rate = 400 until it reaches the graph line and subtending down gives a value between 5500 and 5900 years [1]
      ii) Moving along the value of count rate = 40 until it reaches the graph line [1] and subtending down gives a value between 25 000 years [1]
   c) Over 35 000 years old the count rate will be very low [1], so it will be difficult to accurately decide where the horizontal line hits the graph line and so determine the age of the sample [1]
10. **a)** i) Gravity [1]
      ii) The force of gravity between the Sun and a planet:
      increases with the mass of the planet [1]
      decreases with the distance of the planet from the Sun [1]

   b) The planets formed from an accretion disc around the Sun [1]; the temperature of the Sun is higher closer to the Sun, so only elements with high melting points have remained solid close to the Sun and the gaseous elements concentrated in the outer Solar System [1]; there are fewer high melting point solid elements, so the inner planets are smaller [1]

Pages 184–192: Practice Paper 4

1. **a)** Gradient = $\frac{8}{10}$ [1] = 0.8 m/s² [1]
   b) Area = (8×8) [1] + $(0.5 \times 8 \times 1.6)$ [1] = 70.4 m [1]
   c) i) As the cyclist accelerates the frictional force from the air increases [1]; resultant force = forward force − frictional force, so the forward force must increase to keep the resultant force the same [1]
      ii) Acceleration between B and C $= \frac{1.6}{8} = 0.2$ m/s² [1]; this is $\frac{1}{4}$ the acceleration between A and B so the resultant force needs to be $\frac{1}{4}$ as large [1]; resultant force = $\frac{800}{4} = 200$ N [1]
2. **a)** It burns fuel [1]
   b) This is where it uses most fuel [1]; since energy has to transfer from the chemical store to the gravitational potential and kinetic energy stores [1]; for the other stages energy is only used for manoeuvring (powering the electric systems in the plane) and overcoming frictional forces [1]
   c) Vertical height = 8000 m [1]; Gravitational potential energy = mgh [1]; = 60 000 × 9.8 × 8000 = 4704 MJ [1]
   d) Work done = energy transferred = loss of gravitational potential energy + loss of kinetic energy [1]; Loss of kinetic energy = $\frac{1}{2}mv^2$ [1] = 0.5 × 60 000 × 200² = 1200 MJ [1]; so total work done = 4704 + 1200 = 5904 MJ [1]
3. **a)** It is the point where all of the object's weight appears to act [1]
   b) Tail of the arrow is half-way along the ruler [1]; arrow points vertically downwards below the ruler [1]
   c) The weight force is at a perpendicular distance of 40 cm (0.4 m) from the pivot and the force from the balloon is at a perpendicular distance of 80 cm (0.8 m) [1]; principle of moments: 3.0 × 40 = F × 80 (where F is the force from the balloon) [1]; F = 1.5 N [1]
4. **a)** Force is the change of momentum per unit time [1]; so if the time is increased, the force on the objects is less when they hit the floor [1]
   b) The air inside the bubble wrap is a gas [1]; gases are poor thermal conductors [1]
   c) The pressure increases [1]; because the air particles move faster [1]; which makes them collide with the walls of the bubble wrap harder and more frequently [1]

   d) i) $m = \rho V$ [1] = 1.3 × 1.25 × 10⁻⁸ = 1.625 × 10⁻⁸ kg [1]
      ii) pV = constant [1]; so 250 × new volume = 100 × 1.25 × 10⁻⁸ [1]; new volume = 5 × 10⁻⁹ m³ [1]; $\rho = \frac{m}{V} = \frac{1.625 \times 10^{-8}}{5 \times 10^{-9}} =$ 3.25 kg/m³ [1]
5. **a)** Diffraction [1]
   b) They all stay the same [1]
   c) Make the gap smaller / make the wavelength bigger [1]
   d) Ripple tank is deeper on the right side of the diagram (since the ripples are moving faster) [1]
6. **a)**

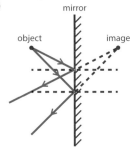

   Reflected rays drawn correctly [1]; lines extending from the reflected rays behind the mirror [1]; image labelled where the lines meet [1]
   b) Any two from: virtual; laterally inverted; same size as object; same distance behind mirror as object is in front [2]
   c) Speed of light = 3.0 × 10⁸ m/s [1]; distance for the light beam's round trip = speed × time = 3.0 × 10⁹ × 2.6 = 7.8 × 10⁸ m [1] Earth-Moon distance = $\frac{7.8 \times 10^8}{2}$ = 3.9 × 10⁸ m [1]
   d) It is not circular [1]
7. **a)** Analogue signals can have any value within a range [1]; whereas digital signals can only have two values [1]
   b) i) The original shape of the signal can be recreated [1]; because the signal obviously goes from low to high to low [1].
      ii) It is not possible to know what the original shape of the analogue signal looked like [1]; so it would be difficult to know which part of the signal is due to interference in order to remove it [1]
8. **a)** Variable resistor [1]
   b) Correct symbol for voltmeter (V in a circle) [1]; connected in parallel across component X [1]
   c) p.d. across length of wire = 10.0 − 6.0 = 4.0 V [1]; $R = \frac{V}{I}$ [1] = $\frac{4.0}{2.0}$ = 2.0 Ω [1]
   d) Resistance of the circuit decreases [1]; so current in circuit increases [1]; so p.d. across X increases [1]
9. **a)** They have a positive charge [1] because they have protons inside [1]
   b) i) The nucleus deflects upwards as it enters the field [1]
      ii) Fleming's left-hand rule [1]
   c) They have the same number of protons [1] but different numbers of neutrons [1]

d) i)   2 **[1]**
ii)   Their mass decreases **[1]**

e) The core of the Sun is raised to a high temperature **[1]**; the pressure produced by this temperature (expanding the Sun) balances out the gravitational forces (contracting the Sun) **[1]**

f) Some stars explode as a supernova (with a known brightness) **[1]**; the brightness of the supernova as it appears from Earth can be used to determine the distance (as the dimmer it appears, the further away it is) **[1]**

Pages 193-200: Practice Paper 6

1. **a)** i)   0.43 **[1]**
ii)   1.4 **[1]**
iii) 3.3 **[1]** Ω **[1]**

b) i)   The current in a series circuit is the same at all points in the circuit. **[1]**
ii)   3.5 Ω **[1]**

c) 6.8 Ω **[1]**

d) 0.5 A **[1]**

e) Two lamps in parallel, correct symbol **[1]**; other symbols and circuit correct **[1]**

f)   **[1]**

2. **a)** i)   23°C
ii)   perpendicular viewing of the thermometer **[1]**

b) i) t / s AND θ/°C **[1]**; 0, 60, 120, 180, 240, 300 **[1]**
ii)   Second box ticked **[1]**
iii) 1 layer cools more in the same amount of time **[1]**; pairs of readings quoted OR lower temperature quoted **[1]**

c) any two from: amount of water; use a lid; same starting temperature for 1 mark each **[2]**

d) room temperature will affect the cooling rate **[1]**

3. **a)** 6.2 cm **[1]**; 8.2 cm **[1]**; l_0 = 2.0 cm **[2]**

b) l = 2.0 cm **[1]**; e = 2.1 cm **[1]**

c) Axes correctly labelled with quantity and unit **[1]**; suitable scales **[1]**; all plots correct to $\frac{1}{2}$ small square **[1]**; good line of best fit using a single, continuous line **[1]**

d) Triangle method used and shown on graph **[1]**
G = 4.2 cm/N **[1]**

4. MP1 Additional apparatus: e.g. set square; piece of card to hold ball bearing at top of track before release.
MP2 control variable: name variable to be kept constant, e.g. shape of track/ball bearing/how the ball bearing is released at the top of the track.
MP3 method: Measure vertical height ball is dropped from AND measure time taken for ball to travel known distance along the flat section of the track.
MP4: repeat for different vertical height
MP5 additional points: repeat measurement five times for same vertical height/use set square to measure vertical height/method to release ball in same way, e.g. using card as a stop/measure mass of ball/calculate average value of velocity

MP6 table: table to show measured values – vertical height, time taken to travel a known distance, repeat measurements of each, average value for each AND table to show calculated values – gravitational potential energy, kinetic energy (may all be in a single table)
MP7 graph: GPE against KE

G

galaxy a large collection of stars, 'close' to each other in space   **127-129**

gas a state of matter where molecules or atoms are loosely bound to each other so as to allow for constant, chaotic motion, with atoms and molecules going every which way at different speeds   **42**

geostationary an earth-orbiting satellite that rotates in the same direction as the earth   **65**

gradient the slope of a curve   **8-10**

gravitational field the force field that exists in the space around every mass or group of masses   **12**

gravitational field strength (g) the force of gravity on a mass of one kilogram. The unit is the newton per kilogram, and it is different on different planets   **12**

gravitational potential the work done per unit mass that would have to be done by some externally applied force to bring a massive object to that point from some defined position of zero potential, usually infinity   **20**

gravitational potential energy a form of stored energy given by mass × g × height.   **24, 124**

H

half-life the time it takes for half of the radioactive nuclei in a sample to decay   **112**

Hubble constant H0, the constant in the relationship $H_0 = \frac{v}{d}$ **128, 129**

hydroelectric the harnessing of flowing water—using a dam or other type of diversion structure—to create energy that can be captured via a turbine to generate electricity   **22**

I

impulse the change of momentum of an object when the object is acted upon by a force for an interval of time   **19**

induced magnetism an object that becomes magnetic when placed in a magnetic field   **74**

infrared the part of the electromagnetic spectrum that has a slightly longer wavelength than the visible spectrum   **52, 64**

insulation the act of separating a body from others by non-conductors, so as to prevent the transfer of electricity or of heat   **86**

insulator a material in which electric current does not flow freely   **50, 77**

internal (thermal) the sum of the kinetic energies and the potential energies of its constituent particles   **20**

interstellar between stars   **123, 126**

ion an atom (or group of atoms) with a positive or negative charge, caused by losing or gaining electrons   **106**

ionising radiation charged particles or high-energy light rays that ionise the material they travel through   **108**

isotope atoms of the same element that contain different numbers of neutrons. Isotopes have the same atomic number but different mass numbers   **107**

J

junctions a point or area where (a) two or more conductors or (b) different semiconducting regions of differing electrical properties make physical contact   **84**

K

kelvin a unit of measurement for temperature   **45**

kilowatt-hour (kWh) a unit of energy equal to 3.6 megajoules   **81**

kinetic the study of the determinants of motion   **20**

kinetic energy the energy of moving objects, equal to $\frac{1}{2} \times$ mass × (speed)^2 **24**

L

law of reflection the angle of reflection equals the angle of incidence   **60**

length a measure of distance   **6, 80**

light dependent resistor (LDR) a resistor with a resistance that decreases when light is shone on it   **82**

light-emitting diode (LED) produce light (or infrared radiation) by the recombination of electrons and electron holes in a semiconductor, a process called "electroluminescence"   **82**

light-year the distance that light travels in one year through the vacuum of space   **127**

limit of proportionality the point up to which the extension of an elastic object is directly proportional to the applied force (once exceeded the relationship is no longer linear)   **19**

liquid a nearly incompressible fluid that conforms to the shape of its container but retains a nearly constant volume independent of pressure   **42**

longitudinal a wave in which the change of the medium is parallel to the direction of the wave   **58**

long-sightedness the inability to see close objects clearly while distant objects may be clear   **63**

M

magnetic field the region in which magnetic materials feel a force   **74**

magnetic field line the lines that show the path a free north-seeking pole would follow   **75**

magnetic material materials that are attracted to magnets and can be made into magnets   **74**

magnetised a material, or magnet is defined as magnetised when it exerts a magnetic field, either because of its interaction with an electromagnet or another permanent magnet   **74**

mass (m) the amount of material in an object, measured in kilograms   **12**

melting the change of state from a solid to a liquid   **42**

melting point the temperature (or more commonly temperature range) at which a substance undergoes a solid to liquid phase change (i.e., it melts) without an increase in temperature.   **48**

meniscus the curved upper surface of a liquid standing in a tube, from which measurements of volume are taken   **6**

microscopic objects and areas of objects that cannot be seen with the naked eye   **43**

minor planet a natural satellite of a star that is neither a planet nor a comet   **123**

molecules the smallest particle of a substance that has all of the physical and chemical properties of that substance   **43**

moment force × perpendicular distance from the pivot   **16**

momentum mass × velocity   **19**

monochromatic light that has the same wavelength so it is one colour   **63**

moon a natural satellite of a planet   **122, 123**

N

nebula an interstellar cloud of hydrogen and dust.   **126, 127**

negative charge (-) having more electrons than protons   **76**

neutron a particle in the nucleus of atoms that has mass but no charge   **106**

neutron star the extremely dense remnant of a massive supernova   **127**

non-magnetic material an air gap which is present between a magnet and an attracted object or between two magnets that are attracting each other   **74**

non-renewable an energy resource that will run out, such as oil or natural gas   **22**

normal at right-angles to / perpendicular to   **59**

north-seeking (N) pole the pole of a magnet that points toward the north when the magnet is suspended freely   **74**

nuclear fission the process where a large nucleus absorbs a neutron and then splits into two large fragments, releasing energy and further neutrons   **107**

nuclear fuel material used in nuclear power stations to produce heat to power turbines   **22**

nuclear fusion the process where the nuclei of small atoms such as hydrogen join together to form a larger nucleus, releasing energy   **22**

nucleon number the total number of protons and neutrons within a nucleus   **106-109**

nucleus, atomic the tiny centre of an atom, made up of protons and neutrons   **106**

O

ohms (Ω) a resistor in which the current is directlyproportional to the potential difference at a constant temperature   **80**

orbit the curved path followed by a planet, satellite, comet, etc. as it travels around a body that exerts a gravitational force upon it; also applies to the paths of electrons around a nucleus (which exerts an electrostatic force of attraction)   **126**

orbital speed how fast one object orbits another. It is calculated from orbital speed = (2 × π × orbital radius)/time.   **124**

transverse a wave in which the change of the medium is at 90 degrees to the direction of the wave. Light is an example. **58**

trip switch an electric switch arranged to interrupt a circuit suddenly and disconnect power from a running machine so that the machine is stopped **87**

U

ultrasound the vibration of sound with a frequency that is above the threshold of what humans can hear **66**

V

vacuum an underlying background energy that exists in space throughout the entire Universe **52**

variable resistor a component with a resistance that can be manually altered **80**

vector a variable quantity that has magnitude and direction **7**

velocity the speed and direction of an object. **7**

virtual image an image that cannot be projected onto a screen **62**

voltmeter a measuring meter that tells you how many volts are in a circuit **79**

volts (V) a unit of voltage. The energy carried by one coulomb of electric charge. **79**

volume the measure of the 3-dimensional space occupied by matter, or enclosed by a surface, measured in cubic units **6**

W

waves the repeating and periodic disturbance that travels through a medium (e.g. water) from one location to another location **22**

weight (W) the force of gravity on a mass, equal to mass × gravitational field strength. The unit of weight is the newton. **12**

white dwarf star the white, hot remnant of the collapse of a red giant star, emitting light due to its temperature **126**

wind the movement of air caused by the uneven heating of the Earth by the sun **22**

work done the energy transferred when a job is done, equal to force × distance moved in the direction of the force **24**

Published by Collins
An imprint of HarperCollins*Publishers*
The News Building, 1 London Bridge Street, London, SE1 9GF, UK

HarperCollins*Publishers*
Macken House, 39/40 Mayor Street Upper, Dublin 1, D01 C9W8, Ireland

Browse the complete Collins catalogue at
collins.co.uk

10 9 8 7 6 5 4 3 2 1

ISBN 978-0-00-867091-7

British Library Cataloguing-in-Publication Data
A catalogue record for this publication is available from the British Library.

Authors: **Carol Davenport, Mark Edwards, Jeremy Pollard, Alom Shaha**
Expert reviewers: **Frank Akrofi, Samuel Yeboah**
Publisher: **Elaine Higgleton**
Product manager: **Jennifer Hall**
Editors: **Susan Lyons, Tanya Solomons**
Proofreaders and answer checkers: **Clodagh Burke, Aidan Gill, Arlo Porter**
Cover designer: **Gordon MacGilp**
Cover artwork: **Maria Herbert-Liew**
Internal designer and illustrator: **PDQ Media**
Typesetter: **PDQ Media**
Production controllers: **Lyndsey Rogers**
Printed in India by Multivista Global Pvt. Ltd.

Acknowledgements
With thanks to the following teachers who provided feedback during the development stages: Frank Akrofi, The Roman Ridge School; Dr Raul Balbuena, Tama Rama Intercultural School; Shalini Reddy, Manthan International School; Dr Rahul Sharma, IRA Global School; Dániel Szücs, International School of Budapest; Samuel Yeboah, AVES International Academy.

Cambridge International Education material in this publication is reproduced under licence and remains the intellectual property of Cambridge University Press & Assessment.

This text has not been through the endorsement process for the Cambridge Pathway. Any references or materials related to answers, grades, papers or examinations are based on the opinion of the author(s). The Cambridge International Education syllabus or curriculum framework associated assessment guidance material and specimen papers should always be referred to for definitive guidance.

The publishers gratefully acknowledge the permission granted to reproduce the copyright material in this book. Every effort has been made to trace copyright holders and to obtain their permission for the use of copyright material. The publishers will gladly receive any information enabling them to rectify any error or omission at the first opportunity.

Photographs
P 139 Greg Schwimer/Shutterstock, p 176 Aki 2007/Shutterstock